TAX SHELTERS THAT WORK FOR EVERYONE

Also by Judith H. McQuown

INC. YOURSELF:
How to Profit by Setting Up
Your Own Corporation

TAX SHELTERS THAT WORK FOR EVERYONE

A Common Sense Guide to Keeping More of the Money You Earn

by
Judith H. McQuown

McGraw-Hill Book Company

NEW YORK   ST. LOUIS
SAN FRANCISCO   TORONTO
DÜSSELDORF   MEXICO

1 2 3 4 5 6 7 8 9 B P B P 7 8 3 2 1 0 9

LIBRARY OF CONGRESS CATALOGING IN PUBLICATION DATA
McQuown, Judith H
   Tax shelters that work for everyone.
   Includes index.
   1. Tax shelters—Law and legislation—United States.
I. Title.
KF6297.5.M3   343′.73′052   79-13675
ISBN 0-07-045713-1

Book design by Roberta Rezk

For my mother

Any one may so arrange his affairs [so] that
his taxes shall be as low as possible; he is
not bound to choose that pattern which will
best pay the Treasury; there is not even a
patriotic duty to increase one's taxes.

—Judge Learned Hand in *Helvering* v.
Gregory, 69 F. 2d 809, 810 (2d Cir.
1934), aff'd, 293 U.S. 465 (1935)

Contents

Acknowledgments   xi
Author's Note   xiii

Part One: INTRODUCTION TO TAX SHELTERS

Chapter   1 • Tax Shelters and How They Work   3
          2 • How to Choose a Tax Shelter   21
          3 • How to Examine and Analyze a Tax
              Shelter   35
          4 • Putting It All Together: Tax Savings   53

Part Two: CONSERVATIVE TAX SHELTERS

          5 • For Widows and Orphans:
              Tax-Exempt Securities   105
          6 • Life Insurance Tax Shelters   117
          7 • Clifford Trusts   125
          8 • Conservative Real Estate
              Tax Shelters   129
          9 • Charitable Gifts as Tax Shelters   135
         10 • Your Own Corporation as
              Tax Shelter   139

Part Three: HIGH-RISK TAX SHELTERS

11 • Municipal Bonds as Speculations   155
12 • High-Risk Real Estate Tax Shelters   159
13 • Oil, Gas, and Mineral Tax Shelters   169
14 • Be an Angel: Theatrical Investing   181
15 • Movie Tax Shelters   187
16 • Book, Record, and Cable Television
     Tax Shelters   193
17 • Equipment-Leasing Tax Shelters   197
18 • Do-It-Yourself: Urban Reclamation
     Tax Shelters   205
19 • Farming and Agricultural
     Tax Shelters   223

Appendix A • Internal Revenue Manual
             Supplement—
             Audit Procedures for Tax
             Shelters   229
Appendix B • State Requirements for General
             Business and Professional
             Corporations   241
Appendix C • Sample Minutes and Bylaws for
             a Small Corporation   264

Index   289

Acknowledgments

This book could not have been written without the help of many experts, for whose time, patience, and enthusiasm I am most grateful.

In particular I wish to thank James A. Bryans, President of James A. Bryans Books; Stanley Sanders, Haas Securities Corporation; John J. Ryan, Senior Staff Supervisor, Personal Insurance Consulting Service, Metropolitan Life Insurance Company; Paul J. Henry, Esq., Breed, Abbott & Morgan; Warren S. Shine, Esq., Tax Partner, Ernst & Ernst; Jesse Rubenstein and Gerald J. Roth, of Mann, Judd & Landau; Robert J. Bethony, National Director of Annuity Sales, E. F. Hutton; Stanley F. Witkowski, First Vice-President, Shearson Hayden Stone; Steven E. Scheinberg, Director of Retail Research, Municipal Bond Department, Shearson Hayden Stone; and George Cloos.

Special thanks go to Robert Willens, who suggested this project; to Martin O. Stelling, to Lawrence J. Winston, First Vice-President and National Director, Tax Sheltered Investment Programs, E. F. Hutton; to William Turchyn, Jr., Vice-President and Assistant National Director, Tax Sheltered Investment Programs, E. F. Hutton; to Martin Edelston, Publisher, *Boardroom Reports,* for his advice and for graciously consenting to limit my assignments while I wrote this book; and to Peter Haas and Miriam Hurewitz for reading the manuscript.

At McGraw-Hill I am grateful for the help and advice of Gladys Carr, my editor.

Most of all, my deepest thanks to Alfred Bester, for his patience in living through this book with me.

Author's Note

This book is meant to be a guide to tax shelters, not an "All You Ever Wanted to Know . . . But Were Afraid to Ask." There are a number of reasons for this.

First, I wanted to reach the average professional or business person—people successful in their own fields, but not accountants or tax lawyers. People successful enough to need some kind of protection against the Scylla of inflation and the Charybdis of taxation.

Second, the laws on tax shelters and, more important, the court cases whose decisions define and refine those laws, change so rapidly that only certain basic concepts can be discussed here. Otherwise this book would undergo so many revisions in preparation that it would never be ready for publication.

Third, this book must remain general because tax shelters—more than any other type of investment—must be tailored to the individual investor. Such factors as tax bracket, risk, timing of write-offs are critical and vary enormously from investor to investor. Both a well-provided-for widow with young children and the model of the year need tax shelters, but the shelters will—or should—be designed differently because the investors' tax brackets, acceptable risk, and investment objectives are different. The same is true of a retired executive, a farmer who sells his hundred-acre farm to a real estate developer, an athlete with a five-year contract, or a successful doctor. To avoid a thousand-page book full of examples followed immediately by all the exceptions, I have deliberately kept this book general, basic.

Obviously, then, this book is not designed to substitute for a lawyer, accountant, tax-shelter specialist, or financial planner. It is designed to serve as a guide and to help the reader make the most of their professional advice. Knowing what questions to ask can be as important as the answers to them.

Finally, a word about "sexist" language. There is no neuter pronoun for "person" in English. Repetition of the "he or she" or "him or her" constructions is awkward, wastes space, and ultimately gets on the reader's nerves, creating a dissonance which can only work against and interfere with the book's getting its message across. To simplify matters, I have used neuter terms like "investors/they" whenever possible, used "she/her" in addition to "he/him," and included sample tax returns of successful women as well as men.

Part ONE: INTRODUCTION TO TAX SHELTERS

1 Tax Shelters and How They Work

In a *Wall Street Journal* cartoon last January, a loudspeaker in an accountant's office blares: "This is a general tax alert! Everybody to the tax shelter."

Maybe it's so funny because it's so true. Nearly everyone can benefit from tax shelters. In fact, according to popular magazines, most people already have tax shelters. According to their definition, home ownership is a tax shelter; payments made for mortgage interest and real estate taxes are tax deductions. Most accountants, however, would disagree with this definition because interest and tax payments are made with *after-tax dollars*. Keogh Plans, IRAs, and corporate pension and profit-sharing plans are true tax shelters because contributions are made with *pretax dollars*.

The scope of this book, however, is, more properly, the *tax-sheltered investment*, which Arthur Andersen & Co., a major accounting firm, defines as "[an investment] that has an expectation of economic profit which is made even more attractive by the timing of the profit or the way it is taxed."

Tax-sheltered investments provide tax deductions which reduce taxable income and thus taxes. Tax shelters can offer

1. current deductions which offset or shelter current income (salaries, dividends, interest).
2. future deductions which shelter income from investments.
3. capital gain treatment of profits when the tax-sheltered investment is sold.

The very wealthy can hire professionals to manage their tax-sheltered investments. A typical tax-sheltered investment in real estate might be a $1,000,000 marina which the IRS says will depreciate (wear out) in 20 years—losing value of $50,000 per year. (This is the IRS valuation and has little bearing on whether the marina will really wear out in 20 years or will actually increase in value when and if it is sold, thus generating capital gains.) If the marina has a net income of $40,000, the owner offsets the income with the $50,000 depreciation and thereby not only creates $40,000 tax-sheltered income, but has $10,000 in depreciation to shelter income from another source—for example, salary, dividends, interest.

Tax Shelters for the Middle Class?

Tax shelters are also available to people who can afford only a fraction of a tax-sheltered investment. Through investment groups, people with as little as $5,000 or $10,000 to invest can participate in professionally managed tax-shelter programs which own such depreciable property as real estate, oil wells, computers, and aircraft. The amount of tax-shelter benefit is directly proportional to the size of the investment.

Who Needs a Tax Shelter?

Almost everybody. Today it's not very difficult to get inflated into the 50% bracket—especially for a two-income family. One accountant puts it even more strongly: "Two-income families can almost always benefit from tax shelters—if they can spare the $5,000 to $10,000 capital investment."

Federal income taxes aren't the only villain; most states

and many cities impose income taxes, too. (See Table 5.3.) A single New York City taxpayer reaches the 50% bracket (combining federal, state, and city income taxes) at approximately only $20,000 net taxable income. Married New York City taxpayers with only one income reach the 50% bracket at only $24,600 net taxable income. Married New York City taxpayers who both work (assuming that the net income is earned equally by both) hit the 50% bracket at approximately $30,000 net taxable income.

The 50% bracket is not sacred either, although it is a convenient yardstick. There can be substantial tax benefits obtained from tax shelters at the 35% or 40% level, although they will not be as great as at the 50% or 60% level. Table 5.1, "Tax-Equivalent Yields on Tax-Exempt Securities," illustrates that tax benefits are possible as low as the 33% and 40% levels.

Retirees with taxable pensions and interest and dividend income are a group who usually doesn't think of tax shelters. But some tax shelters are particularly appropriate for retirees, who are often in fairly high tax brackets, whose fixed income is especially vulnerable to inflation, and who can certainly benefit from tax-free and tax-sheltered income. (See Chapter Four for sample tax returns contrasting a retiree with and without a tax shelter.)

In fact, it is probably no exaggeration to say that if you are reading this book, you can benefit from some kind of tax shelter.

In order to understand how tax shelters work, it is necessary to explain some basic concepts:

- Depreciation
- Recapture
- Recourse versus nonrecourse/at risk
- Leverage
- Preference items
- Public offerings versus private placements
- General partners versus limited partners

Depreciation

Depreciation is the keystone of tax shelters. It refers to the loss in book value of an asset (piece of property) over time, even though the property may not actually lose market value. Depreciation is commonly called "writing off." The following paragraphs show the ways in which depreciation is calculated for tax-shelter purposes.

Three methods of depreciation are frequently used: straight-line, a form of accelerated depreciation called double declining balance, and sum-of-the-digits.

Assume that a company buys a lathe for $10,500. The lathe has a useful working life of 10 years, after which it can be sold as scrap for $500—its salvage value.

Using the straight-line method, the company subtracts the lathe's salvage value from its cost and then writes off the same amount of depreciation every year over the lathe's 10-year useful life:

$10,500	Cost of lathe
− 500	Salvage value
$10,000	Base

$10,000 ÷ 10 = $1,000 depreciation per year for 10 years.

Using the accelerated (double declining balance) method of depreciation, which can be used only if the life of the capital asset is at least 3 years, the *lathe's salvage value is not subtracted.* Instead of writing off 10% of the asset's value each year for 10 years, double the rate—or 20%—is subtracted each year from the recalculated base after write-offs:

$10,500	*Cost of lathe*
−2,100	20% depreciation—1st year
8,400	*Base for 2nd year*
−1,680	20% depreciation—2nd year

6,720	*Base for 3rd year*
−1,344	20% depreciation——3rd year
5,376	*Base for 4th year*
−1,075	20% depreciation——4th year
4,301	*Base for 5th year*
− 860	20% depreciation——5th year
3,441	*Base for 6th year*
− 688	20% depreciation——6th year
2,753	*Base for 7th year*
− 551	20% depreciation——7th year
2,202	*Base for 8th year*
− 440	20% depreciation——8th year
1,762	*Base for 9th year*
− 352	20% depreciation——9th year
1,410	*Base for 10th year*
− 282	20% depreciation——10th year
$ 1,128	
$ 9,372	*Total depreciation over 10 years*

Because the depreciation rate is calculated on a progressively smaller base, the total write-off is only $9,372—somewhat short of the $10,000 obtained in straight-line depreciation. (The greater the number of years of depreciation, the greater the difference between recovery of asset cost using the straight-line and accelerated methods. For example, if the lathe had been depreciated over only 5 years, the total write-off under accelerated depreciation would have been $9,683, or $311 more than the 10-year rate—and obtained in half the time; the straight-line method would have been $10,000 regardless of length of time.)

$10,500	*Cost of lathe*
−4,200	40% depreciation—1st year
6,300	*Base for 2nd year*
−2,520	40% depreciation—2nd year
3,780	*Base for 3rd year*
−1,512	40% depreciation—3rd year
2,268	*Base for 4th year*
− 907	40% depreciation—4th year
1,361	*Base for 5th year*
− 544	40% depreciation—5th year
$ 817	
$ 9,683	*Total depreciation over 5 years*

If the full cost of the asset can't be written off, why is accelerated depreciation still so popular? The answer is simple and is especially relevant during inflationary periods: it is much more desirable to take large write-offs now and smaller ones sometime in the future than to take a flat write-off each year.

Using the sum-of-the-digits method, the company subtracts the lathe's salvage value from its cost. Then the years of depreciation (the sum of the digits—in this case from 1 to 10 [55]—from which the method gets its name) are added to obtain a denominator, and the last year is taken as the first numerator, so that 10/55 is the multiplier for the first year of depreciation. The second year, the fraction is 9/55, and so on:

$10,500	Cost of lathe
− 500	Salvage value
$10,000	Base

$ 1,818	Depreciation	1st year	($10,000 ×	10/55)
1,636	''	2nd ''	(''	9/55)
1,455	''	3rd ''	(''	8/55)
1,273	''	4th ''	(''	7/55)
1,091	''	5th ''	(''	6/55)
909	''	6th ''	(''	5/55)
727	''	7th ''	(''	4/55)
545	''	8th ''	(''	3/55)
364	''	9th ''	(''	2/55)
182	''	10th ''	(''	1/55)
$10,000	Total depreciation		($10,000 ×	55/55)

Thus, like accelerated depreciation, the sum-of-the-digits method gets its biggest write-offs in the early years and is therefore a desirable method during inflationary periods.

Recapture

Recapture follows directly from depreciation. It is the difference at any point in time between accelerated depreciation and straight-line depreciation. It is important because this figure is taxed as ordinary income (subject to normal taxation). Let's return to the example of the lathe:

Year	Accelerated depreciation	Straight-line depreciation	Recapture
1	$2,100	$1,000	$1,100
2	1,680	1,000	680
3	1,344	1,000	344
4	1,075	1,000	75
5	860	1,000	0

The longer the asset is held, the smaller the amount of recapture—until at some point straight-line depreciation is greater than accelerated depreciation and there is no more recapture at ordinary-income rates.

Recourse versus Nonrecourse/At Risk

Recourse versus nonrecourse refers to the investor's liability for making future payments into a tax-sheltered investment. A recourse note is essentially an IOU that can be called at some point in the future; a nonrecourse note cannot be called. Before the Tax Reform Act of 1976, an investor could put up $5,000, sign a nonrecourse note for $20,000, and write off $25,000. Now, however, except for real estate, write-offs are *limited to the amount of money an investor actually has at risk*—that is, for which he has signed a recourse note.

The Tax Reform Act of 1976 and the Revenue Act of 1978 knocked out most of the year-end, multiple-write-off nonrecourse type of deals investors used to delight in. They'd wait until December 27, sell the 1,000 shares of Xerox they'd bought at 1½, and go out and get a 3-to-1 write-off deal that would shelter any capital-gains tax liability.

But that's all over now. The high-multiple 3-to-1 and 4-to-1 deals are still heard about at cocktail parties, but there's a joker: they're not really one-shot investments. Somewhere buried in the sheaf of papers the investor is signing so rapidly is a recourse note or a letter of credit; and somewhere along the road, at least 95% of the time, the investor will get a call to put up additional funds. In a way, it's like a margin call, or a deposit, with balance payable in 90 to 180 days. The investor who brags about a 4-to-1 write-off tax shelter with $100,000 worth of deductions for a $25,000 investment will most often find that a total-recourse note for $75,000 that he has unwittingly signed will be exercised within 6 months.

People are understandably confused when they hear about 3-to-1 deals, because they have heard that these deals have been banned by the 1978 Revenue Act. The problem is one of communication and definition and is often based on the fact that an investment in a tax shelter can be spread over 3 or 4 years. Very often a small payment is made in the first year, with an accompanying large write-off. However, the "fine print" may call for very large "balloon" payments in the second and subsequent years, with proportionately small write-offs. The real questions should be: How much is the *cumulative* investment, and how much is the *cumulative* write-off?

Still, one tax expert says that recourse loans or notes can be structured so that the investor won't be called for 10 years—and in that time, anything can happen. This is the way deals have been structured since the Tax Reform Act of 1976, which said: "No partnership can use nonrecourse financing except real estate." Prohibitions were specific against movies, farming, oil and gas, equipment leasing, and all other partnerships.

Now a tax-shelter promoter must speak out of both sides of his mouth to placate both the nervous investor and the IRS.

Assuming a $30,000 (3X) deal with a $10,000 payment and $20,000 (2X) in recourse notes, the promoter says to the nervous investor, "Don't worry—we'll never call on you for the remaining 2X of your 3X deal."

To the IRS, the promoter says, "Yes, there is a real recourse obligation."

Competent and responsible tax advisers will then say to the client, "Look, are you prepared to pony up $20,000 if you get a call?"

"Well," the client says, "the guy told me that I don't have to worry about it."

"But you signed a note. He can do it. What if you die? Your estate can be called for the note. What if Mr. Nice-Guy Syndicator dies and his estate and creditors say, 'We have assets. We have a note for $20,000'?" the adviser says.

Then the investor gets nervous. If he gets written guarantees that say, "We'll *never* call in the note," then it's nonrecourse, and the IRS will say, "You can't deduct this."

It's a Mexican standoff, and not recommended for people who like to sleep well at night.

Leverage

Leverage refers to the possibility of an investor's making a large gain on a relatively small investment through the use of borrowed funds. Its effects are most clearly seen in real estate tax shelters, where an investor's money may be matched by bank mortgages ranging anywhere from 3 to 7 times his investment. His $10,000 investment may have $40,000 to $80,000 in depreciable assets working for him. In equipment-leasing tax shelters, where an investor's money may be matched by bank loans up to 9 times his investment, his $10,000 investment will actually have $100,000 in depreciable assets working for him. Like the mechanical lever in physics, the concept of financial leverage involves a small input by the investor with the goal of receiving a large return.

The ultimate leveraged shelter strategy is to use 100% borrowed funds to purchase a depreciable asset whose real market value is actually increasing, and which generates enough income to pay off the loan. This is not an impossibility. In fact, it is accomplished fairly often with rental properties. Investors who prefer the do-it-yourself approach should investigate this area.

Preference Items

"Preference items" is a misnomer of sorts; they are treated *unfavorably* by the IRS and reduce benefits obtainable with tax shelters.

Preference items generate an *additional* tax which in most cases is equal to 15% of the taxpayer's preference items for the year, to the extent that they exceed the greater of either $10,000 or one-half the taxpayer's tax liability.

For example, if a taxpayer's share of intangible drilling costs is $18,000 and her tax liability is $12,000, her minimum tax on preference items is $1,200:

Tax preference income	$18,000
Minus the greater of $10,000 or half the tax liability (½ × $12,000 = $6,000)	10,000
Tax preference items subject to minimum tax	8,000
Minimum tax rate	× .15
Additional tax	$ 1,200

The position of the IRS seems to be: "If you're getting a tax benefit, you're going to pay for it." Still, the benefits are there, even though they may have been reduced substantially. Taxpayers can rejoice, however, that capital gains are no longer a preference item; the maximum tax on capital gains is only 28%.

The following are tax preference items: accelerated depreciation on real property, accelerated depreciation on leased personal property, depletion, amortization, stock options, adjusted itemized deductions, and intangible drilling costs. The items of tax preference of most concern to tax-shelter investors are accelerated depreciation on real property, depletion, and intangible drilling costs.

Public Offerings versus Private Placements

There are several major differences between public offerings and private placements of shares in tax-sheltered investments. Public offerings are regulated by the Securities and Exchange Commission (SEC) and often also by the various states in which the investment units are sold. Investments usually can be bought in $5,000 units and must be paid for in a lump sum.

In terms of total amount of money raised, public offerings are the tip of the iceberg, compared with private placements, which are unregulated by the SEC, are riskier, and are designed for wealthier investors. Investment units typically start at $25,000, and can be staged in 3 installments, 5 installments, etc. Because reporting requirements are much less stringent in the private sector, it's probably safe to say that private placements are more interesting and more highly leveraged than public offerings, which are safer. Because there has been a great deal of abuse in the private sector, investors must make sure that the disclosure satisfies them and their professional advisers. It's probably wisest for investors interested in private placements to stick with major New York Stock Exchange firms.

General Partners versus Limited Partners

Although some tax shelters are joint ventures, sole proprietorships, or Subchapter S corporations, most tax shelters are partnerships. The general partner may or may not put up any money, is responsible for running the business, and has unlimited liability. The limited partners are the investors who buy a fractional portion of the business. They share in the profits according to a predetermined arrangement; their liability is limited to the amount of their investment.

Now that the basic concepts have been reviewed, what actually happens when an investor buys a tax shelter? Essentially, buying a public-offering tax shelter is very much like buying stocks or bonds—except that the investor is buying a limited-partnership interest. The investor should receive periodic reports and, it is hoped, some checks. At the end of the year, the general partner files IRS Form 1065 (pp. 15–18) and sends the investor Schedule K-1 (pp. 19–20), which shows the investor's share of deductions for the year and tells him on what forms and schedules to insert these figures. After all the numbers are worked out, the investor should be able to write off a good chunk of income. And that's what tax shelters are all about.

(NOTE: To "keep the game honest," as it were, the IRS has laid down some very tough and intricate regulations for auditing tax shelters. These are shown in Appendix A, "Internal Revenue Manual Supplement—Audit Procedures for Tax Shelters.")

Form **1065**	Revised in Accordance with the Revenue Act of 1978 and the Energy Tax Act of 1978		
Department of the Treasury Internal Revenue Service	**U.S. Partnership Return of Income** For calendar year 1978, or other taxable year beginning ...., 1978, and ending ...., 19......		**1978**

A Principal business activity (See page 12 of instructions)	Use IRS label. Other-wise please print or type.	Name	D Employer Identification no.
B Principal product or service (See page 12 of instructions)		Number and street	E Date business started
C Business code no. (See page 12 of instructions)		City or town, State, and ZIP code	F Enter total assets from line 13, column (D), Schedule L $

IMPORTANT—Fill in all applicable lines and schedules. If more space is needed, see Instruction b. Enter any items specially allocated to the partners on Schedule K, line 16, instead of on the numbered lines on this page or in Schedules D through J.

G Is this a final return? ☐ Yes ☐ No

Income

1a	Gross receipts or sales $ .... 1b Less returns and allowances $ .... Balance ▶	**1c**
2	Cost of goods sold and/or operations (line 34, Schedule A)	**2**
3	Gross profit (subtract line 2 from line 1c)	**3**
4	Ordinary income or (loss) from other partnerships and fiduciaries (attach statement) . . .	**4**
5	Nonqualifying dividends	**5**
6	Interest	**6**
7	Income or (loss) from rents (Schedule H)	**7**
8	Royalties (attach schedule)	**8**
9	Net farm profit or (loss) (attach Schedule F (Form 1040))	**9**
10	Net gain or (loss) (Form 4797, line 11)	**10**
11	Other income (attach schedule)	**11**
12	**TOTAL** income (add lines 3 through 11)	**12**

Deductions

13a	Salaries and wages (other than to partners) $.................... 13b Less Jobs Credit $............. Balance ▶	**13c**
14	Guaranteed payments to partners (see line 14 instruction)	**14**
15	Rent	**15**
16	Interest	**16**
17	Taxes	**17**
18	Bad debts (see line 18 instruction)	**18**
19	Repairs	**19**
20	Depreciation (see Instructions for Schedule J)	**20**
21	Amortization (attach schedule)	**21**
22	Depletion (other than oil and gas—attach schedule—see line 22 instruction)	**22**
23a	Retirement plans, etc. (see line 23a instruction). (Enter number of plans ▶..............) . .	**23a**
23b	Employee benefit programs (see line 23b instruction)	**23b**
24	Other deductions (attach schedule)	**24**
25	**TOTAL** deductions (add lines 13c through 24)	**25**
26	Ordinary income (loss) (subtract line 25 from line 12) . . . . ▶.	**26**

Schedule A—COST OF GOODS SOLD AND/OR OPERATIONS (See line 2 instruction)

27	Inventory at beginning of year (if different from last year's closing inventory, attach explanation)	**27**
28a	Purchases $ .... 28b Less cost of items withdrawn for personal use $ .... Balance ▶	**28c**
29	Cost of labor	**29**
30	Material and supplies	**30**
31	Other costs (attach schedule)	**31**
32	Total of lines 27 through 31	**32**
33	Inventory at end of year	**33**
34	Cost of goods sold (subtract line 33 from line 32). Enter here and on line 2, above	**34**

35a Check valuation method(s) used for total closing inventory: ☐ Cost ☐ Lower of cost or market ☐ Other (attach explanation)

35b Check if Form 970 or other statement is attached for adoption of LIFO inventory method . . . . ☐

35c Are you engaged in manufacturing? ☐ Yes ☐ No. If "Yes," check if you valued your inventory in accordance with regulations section 1.471–11 . ☐

35d Was there any substantial change in determining quantities, cost, or valuations between opening and closing inventory? . . . . ☐ Yes ☐ No
   If "Yes," attach explanation.

Please Sign Here

Under penalties of perjury, I declare that I have examined this return, including accompanying schedules and statements, and to the best of my knowledge and belief, it is true, correct, and complete. Declaration of preparer (other than taxpayer) is based on all information of which preparer has any knowledge.

Signature of general partner	Date

Paid Preparer's Information	Preparer's signature ▶	Preparer's social security no.	Check if self-employed ▶ ☐
	Firm's name (or yours, if self-employed), address and ZIP code ▶	E.I. No. ▶	
		Date ▶	

15

Schedule D—CAPITAL GAINS AND LOSSES (See Instructions for Schedule D)

Part I   Short-term capital gains and losses—assets held one year or less

a. Kind of property and description (Example, 100 shares of "Z" Co.)	b. Date acquired (mo., day, yr.)	c. Date sold (mo., day, yr.)	d. Gross sales price less expense of sale	e. Cost or other basis	f. Gain or (loss) for the year (d less e)	g. Gain or (loss) after 10/31/78
1						

2 Partnership's share of net short-term gain or (loss), including specially allocated items, from other partnerships and from fiduciaries .　.　.　.　.　.　.　.　.　.　.　.　.　.

3 Net short-term gain or (loss) from lines 1 and 2. Enter here and on Schedule K (Form 1065), line 5 .　.　.　.

Part II   Long-term capital gains and losses—assets held more than one year

4						

5 Partnership's share of net long-term gain or (loss), including specially allocated items, from other partnerships and from fiduciaries .　.　.　.　.　.　.　.　.　.　.　.　.　.

6 Capital gain distributions .　.　.　.　.　.　.　.　.　.　.　.　.　.　.　.　.　.　.　.

7 Net long-term gain or (loss) from lines 4, 5, and 6. Enter here and on Schedule K (Form 1065), line 6 .　.　.　.

Schedule H—INCOME FROM RENTS (See line 7 instruction) If more space is needed, use Form 4831.

a. Kind and location of property	b. Amount of rent	c. Depreciation (explain in Schedule J)	d. Repairs (attach schedule)	e. Other expenses (attach schedule)

1 Totals .　.　.　.　.　.　.　.　.　.　.　.　.　.

2 Net income (loss) (subtract total of columns c, d, and e from column b). Enter here and on page 1, line 7 .　.　.

Schedule I—BAD DEBTS (See line 18 instruction)

a. Year	b. Trade notes and accounts receivable outstanding at end of year	c. Sales on account	Amount added to reserve		f. Amount charged against reserve	g. Reserve for bad debts at end of year
			d. Current year's provision	e. Recoveries		
1973.						
1974.						
1975.						
1976.						
1977.						
1978.						

Schedule J—DEPRECIATION (See Instructions for Schedule J) If more space is needed use Form 4562.

a. Description of property	b. Date acquired	c. Cost or other basis	d. Depreciation allowed or allowable in prior years	e. Method of computing depreciation	f. Life or rate	g. Depreciation for this year
1 Total additional first-year depreciation (NOT to exceed $2,000). (Do not include in items below, enter here and on Schedule K, line 2) ──▶						
2 Other depreciation:						
Buildings .　.　.　.　.　.						
Furniture and fixtures .　.　.						
Transportation equipment .　.						
Machinery and other equipment .　.						
Other (specify):						

3 Totals .　.　.　.　.　.　.　.　.

4 Amount of depreciation claimed in Schedules A and H .　.　.　.　.　.　.　.　.　.　.　.　.　.

5 Balance (subtract line 4 from line 3). Enter here and on page 1, line 20 .　.　.　.　.　.　.　.

Schedule K—PARTNERS' SHARES OF INCOME, CREDITS, DEDUCTIONS, ETC.

Enter the total distributive amount for each applicable item listed below. **Note:** Enter each partner's distributive share of partnership items on Schedule K–1.	Enter the number of partners in the partnership ▶	Are any partners in this partnership also partnerships? ☐ Yes ☐ No

Partnership's distributive share items	Total
1 a Guaranteed payments to partners:	
(1) Deductible by the partnership (page 1, line 14)	
(2) Capitalized by the partnership (see General Instruction d)	
b Ordinary income (loss) (page 1, line 26)	
2 Additional first-year depreciation (Schedule J, line 1)	
3 Gross farming or fishing income	
4 Dividends qualifying for exclusion (attach list) . . . . ◀. ▶	
5 Net short-term capital gain or (loss) (Schedule D, line 3): After 10/31/78 ▶............; Total for year ▶	
6 Net long-term capital gain or (loss) (Schedule D, line 7): After 10/31/78 ▶............; Total for year ▶	
7 Net section 1231 gain or (loss) from involuntary conversions due to casualty and theft (Form 4797, line 3): After 10/31/78 ▶............; . . . . Total for year ▶	
8 Net gain or (loss) from sale or exchange of property used in trade or business and certain involuntary conversion under section 1231 (Form 4797, line 6): After 10/31/78 ▶............; Total for year ▶	
9 Net earnings or (loss) from self-employment (Schedule N, line 10)	
10 a Charitable contributions (attach list): 50%............, 30%............, 20%............	
b Other itemized deductions (attach list)	
11 Expense account allowance	
12 New jobs credit or combined new jobs and targeted jobs credits	
13 Taxes paid by regulated investment companies on undistributed capital gains (attach schedule) . . .	
14 a Payments for partners to a Keogh Plan. (Enter type of plan ▶............) . .	
b Payments for partners to an Individual Retirement Arrangement	
15 a Other income, deductions, etc. (attach schedule)	
b Oil and gas depletion. Enter amount (not for partner's use) ▶............	/////////
16 Specially allocated items (attach schedule):	
a Short-term capital gain or (loss)	
b Long-term capital gain or (loss)	
c Ordinary gain or (loss)	
d Other	
17 Tax preference items (see instructions for Schedules K and K–1, line 17):	
a Accelerated depreciation on real property:	
(1) Low-income rental housing (section 167(k))	
(2) Other real property	
b Accelerated depreciation on personal property subject to a lease	
Amortization: **c** ...., **d** ...., **e** ...., **f**	
g Reserves for losses on bad debts of financial institutions	
h Depletion (other than oil and gas)	
i **(1)** Excess intangible drilling costs from oil, gas or geothermal wells under section 57(a)(11) . . .	
(2) Net income from oil, gas or geothermal wells	
18 Interest on Investment Indebtedness:	
a Investment interest expense:	
(1) Indebtedness incurred before December 17, 1969	
(2) Indebtedness incurred before September 11, 1975, but after December 16, 1969	
(3) Indebtedness incurred after September 10, 1975	
b Net investment income or (loss)	
c Excess expenses from "net lease property"	
d Excess of net long-term capital gain over net short-term capital loss from investment property . .	

19 Investment in property that qualifies for investment credit:		
Basis of new investment property	**a** 3 or more but less than 5 years	
	b 5 or more but less than 7 years	
	c 7 or more years	
Qualified progress expenditures	**d** 7 or more years　1974, 1975, 1976, and 1977	
	e 7 or more years　1978	
Cost of used investment property	**f** 3 or more but less than 5 years	
	g 5 or more but less than 7 years	
	h 7 or more years	

17

Schedule L—BALANCE SHEETS (See General Information)

ASSETS	Beginning of taxable year		End of taxable year	
	(A) Amount	(B) Total	(C) Amount	(D) Total
1 Cash				
2 Trade notes and accounts receivable				
a Less allowance for bad debts				
3 Inventories				
4 Gov't obligations: a U.S. and instrumentalities				
b State, subdivisions thereof, etc.				
5 Other current assets (attach schedule)				
6 Mortgage and real estate loans				
7 Other investments (attach schedule)				
8 Buildings and other fixed depreciable assets . .				
a Less accumulated depreciation				
9 Depletable assets				
a Less accumulated depletion				
10 Land (net of any amortization)				
11 Intangible assets (amortizable only)				
a Less accumulated amortization				
12 Other assets (attach schedule)				
13 Total assets				
LIABILITIES AND CAPITAL				
14 Accounts payable				
15 Mortgages, notes, and bonds payable in less than 1 year .				
16 Other current liabilities (attach schedule) . . .				
17 All nonrecourse loans (attach schedule) . . .				
18 Mortgages, notes, and bonds payable in 1 year or more . .				
19 Other liabilities (attach schedule)				
20 Partners' capital accounts				
21 Total liabilities and capital				

Schedule M—RECONCILIATION OF PARTNERS' CAPITAL ACCOUNTS (See Instruction for Schedule M)
(Show reconciliation of each partner's capital account on Schedule K–1, block L)

a. Capital account at beginning of year	b. Capital contributed during year	c. Ordinary income (loss) from line 26, page 1	d. Income not included in column c, plus nontaxable income	e. Losses not included in column c, plus unallowable deductions	f. Withdrawals and distributions	g. Capital account at end of year

Schedule N—COMPUTATION OF NET EARNINGS FROM SELF-EMPLOYMENT (See Instruction for Schedule N)

1 Ordinary income (loss) (page 1, line 26)		
2 Add: Guaranteed payments to partners included on Schedule K, lines 1a(1) and 1a(2) .		
3 Net rental loss from real estate (see instruction for Schedule N)		
4 Net loss from Form 4797 (page 1, Form 1065, line 10)		
5 Total		
6 Less: Nonqualifying dividends (page 1, line 5)		
7 Interest (see instruction for Schedule N)		
8 Net rental income from real estate (see instruction for Schedule N)		
9 Net gain from Form 4797 (page 1, Form 1065, line 10)		
10 Net earnings or (loss) from self-employment. Enter on Schedule K, line 9		

Note: *Any additional first-year depreciation taken by the individual partners will reduce their net earnings from self-employment. (See Schedule J Instructions.)*

	Yes	No
H Is the partnership a limited partnership (see General Instruction c)?		
I Is this partnership a partner in another partnership?		
J Has any material regarding the offering of a partnership interest or other security ever been registered or filed with a Federal or State agency or authority? . . . . If "Yes," attach a statement giving the name and address of the agency(s).		
K Did the partnership, at any time during the taxable year, have any interest in or signature or other authority over a bank, securities, or other financial account in a foreign country (except in a U.S. military banking facility operated by a U.S. financial institution)? See General Information		
L Was the partnership the grantor of, or transferor to, a foreign trust during any taxable year, which foreign trust was in existence during the current taxable year whether or not the partnership or any partner has any beneficial interest in the trust? If "Yes," you may be required to file Forms 3520, 3520–A, or 926. See General Information		

☆U.S. Government Printing Office: 1978—0-263-343　23-0916750

SCHEDULE K-1
(Form 1065)
Department of the Treasury
Internal Revenue Service

Partner's Share of Income, Credits, Deductions, etc.—1978

For Calendar year 1978 or fiscal year
beginning ...., 1978, ending ...., 19......
(Complete for each partner—See instructions on back of Copy C)

Copy A
(File with Form 1065)

Partner's identifying number ▶

Partnership's identifying number ▶

Partner's name, address, and ZIP code

Partnership's name, address, and ZIP code

		Yes	No
A Date(s) partner acquired any partnership interest during the year ▶			
B Is partner a nonresident alien?			
C Is partner a limited partner (see General Instruction c.3)? . .			
D (i) Did partner ever contribute property other than money to the partnership (if "Yes," complete line 21)?			
(ii) Did partner ever receive a distribution other than money from the partnership (if "Yes," complete line 22)? . .			
(iii) Was any part of the partner's interest ever acquired from another partner?			
E (i) Did partnership interest terminate during the year? . .			
(ii) Did partnership interest decrease during the year? . .			

F Enter Partner's percentage of:

	(i) Before decrease or termination	(ii) End of year
Profit sharing	.................%	.................%
Loss sharing	.................%	.................%
Ownership of capital	.................%	.................%
Time devoted to business		.................%

G IRS Center where partnership return filed ▶ ....

H What type of entity is this partner? ▶ ....

I Partner's share of liabilities (see instructions):

	(i) Incurred before 1/1/77	(ii) Incurred after 12/31/76
Nonrecourse . .	$..................	$..................
Other . . .	$..................	$..................

J Enter total amount of liabilities other than nonrecourse for which the partner is protected against loss through guarantees, stop loss agreements, or similar arrangements of which the partnership has knowledge:

Incurred before 1/1/77 . . . . . . $..................

Incurred after 12/31/76 . . . . . . $..................

K Partner's share of any pre-1976 loss(es) from a section 465 activity for which there existed a corresponding amount of nonrecourse liability at the end of the year in which loss(es) occurred . . . . $..................

L Reconciliation of partner's capital account:

a. Capital account at beginning of year	b. Capital contributed during year	c. Ordinary income (loss) from line 1b	d. Income not included in column c, plus non-taxable income	e. Losses not included in column c, plus unallowable deductions	f. Withdrawals and distributions	g. Capital account at end of year

a. Distributive share item	b. Amount	c. 1040 filers enter col. b amount as shown.
1 a Guaranteed payments to partner: (1) Deductible by the partnership . .		Sch. E, Part III
(2) Capitalized by the partnership .		Sch. E, Part III
b Ordinary income or (loss)		Sch. E, Part III
2 Additional first-year depreciation		Sch. E, Part III
3 Gross farming or fishing income		Sch. E, Part III
4 Dividends qualifying for exclusion		Sch. B, Part II, line 3
5 Short-term capital gain or (loss): **a** Total for the year . . . . . ▶		Sch. D, line 2, col. f
b After 10/31/78		Sch. D, line 2, col. g
6 Long-term capital gain or (loss): **a** Total for the year . . . . . . ▶		Sch. D, line 9, col. f
b After 10/31/78		Sch. D, line 9, col. g
7 Involuntary conversions gain or (loss)—casualty and theft: **a** Total . . ▶		Form 4797, line 1
b After 10/31/78		See Form 4797 instr.
8 Other gain or (loss)—from property under section 1231: **a** Total . . ▶		Form 4797, line 4
b After 10/31/78		See Form 4797 instr.
9 Net earnings or (loss) from self-employment		Sch. SE, Part I or Part II
10 a Charitable contributions: 50% ...., 30% ...., 20%		Sch. A, line 21 or 22
b Other itemized deductions (attach list)		See Sch. A
11 Expense account allowance		
12 New jobs credit or combined new jobs and targeted jobs credits		Form 5884, or Form 5884-FY
13 Taxes paid by regulated investment company		Line 61, add words "from 1065"
14 a Payments for partner to a Keogh Plan (Type ▶ ....). .		Line 25
b Payments for partner to an Individual Retirement Arrangement		Line 24
15 a Other income, deductions, etc. (attach schedule)		(Enter on applicable lines of your return)
b Oil and gas depletion. Enter amount (not for partner's use) ▶		
16 Specially allocated items: **a** Short-term capital gain or (loss)		Sch. D, line 2
(See attached schedule.) **b** Long-term capital gain or (loss)		Sch. D, line 9
c Ordinary gain or (loss)		Form 4797, line 10
d Other		Sch. E, Part III

19

17 a Accelerated depreciation on real property: **(1)** Low-income rental housing .	....	Form 4625, line 1(b)(1)
(2) Other real property . . .	....	Form 4625, line 1(b)(2)
b Accelerated depreciation on personal property subject to a lease	....	Form 4625, line 1(c)
Amortization: **c**................., **d**..................., **e**..................., **f**..................	....	Form 4625, line 1(d) thru (g)
g Reserves for losses on bad debts of financial institutions	....	Form 4625, line 1(h)
h Depletion (other than oil and gas)	....	Form 4625, line 1(j)
i (1) Excess intangible drilling costs from oil, gas or geothermal wells . .	....	See Form 4625 instr.
(2) Net income from oil, gas or geothermal wells	....	
18 Interest on Investment Indebtedness: **a** Investment interest expense—		
(1) Indebtedness incurred before 12/17/69	....	Form 4952, line 1
(2) Indebtedness incurred before 9/11/75, but after 12/16/69	....	Form 4952, line 15
(3) Indebtedness incurred after 9/10/75	....	Form 4952, line 5
b Net investment income or (loss)	....	Form 4952, line 2 or line 10(a)
c Excess expenses from "net lease property"	....	Form 4952, lines 11 and 19
d Excess of net long-term capital gain over net short-term capital loss from investment property	....	Form 4952, line 20

19 Property Qualified for Investment Credit:			
Basis of new investment property	**a** 3 or more but less than 5 years		Form 3468, line 1(a)
	b 5 or more but less than 7 years		Form 3468, line 1(b)
	c 7 or more years		Form 3468, line 1(c)
Qualified progress expenditures	**d** 7 or more years 1974, 1975, 1976 and 1977		Form 3468, line 1(d)
	e 7 or more years 1978		Form 3468, line 1(e)
Cost of used investment property	**f** 3 or more but less than 5 years		Form 3468, line 1(f)
	g 5 or more but less than 7 years		Form 3468, line 1(g)
	h 7 or more years		Form 3468, line 1(h)

20 Property Used in Recomputing a Prior Year Investment Credit (enter in corresponding column of Form 4255):

(1) Description of property (also state whether new or used)	(2) Date placed in service	(3) Cost or basis	(4) Estimated useful life	(5) Applicable percentage	(6) Original qualified investment (column 3 x column 5)	(8) Date item ceased to be investment credit property	(9) Period actually used	(10) Applicable percentage	(11) Qualified Investment (column 3 x column 10)
A									
B									

21 a Basis to partner of contributed property (other than money) at time(s) of contribution to partnership . . .	....	
b Value of contributed property in line 21a as reflected in the partner's capital account		
22 a Basis to partnership of distributed property (other than money) at time(s) of distribution to the partner . .	....	
b Value of distributed property in line 22a as reflected in the partner's capital account		

23 Partnership information regarding international boycotting. For partner's reporting requirements see Form 5713.

	Yes	No
a Did partnership have operations in a boycotting country?		
b Did partnership participate in or cooperate with an international boycott?		
c Did partnership file Form 5713?		

20

2 How to Choose a Tax Shelter

The Question of Risk

Because tax shelters cover a spectrum of risk ranging from very conservative to very aggressive to the borderline of virtually unacceptable risk, there are two key questions investors should ask themselves:

1. How much risk can I afford and feel comfortable with—do I want high risk, aggressive growth, or a much more conservative tax shelter designed primarily for tax-free income?
2. What is my tax bracket, and do I need a tax shelter to shelter one year's unusually high income or a tax shelter to provide substantial write-offs over a number of years?

Because all these variables impact so heavily on an investor's tax situation and because the suitability of a tax shelter is far more crucial than choosing one common stock from a list of a dozen recommendations, investors should beware of the broker who recommends a particular tax shelter in the first five minutes of conversation. Most reliable brokers will sit down with the investor and fill out a tax evaluation form like the one on page 23 to determine the impact of various shelters on the investor's income taxes.

For example, some tax shelters are too aggressive for an investor in the 30% bracket. A $10,000 drilling program with 100% write-offs in the first year would net him only a 30% deduction on his investment. He'd be accepting too much risk for a possible profitable investment, paying, in effect, $7,000 of his own money (and $3,000 that he'd otherwise be paying to the IRS). But an investor in the 60% bracket would have only about $4,000 of his own money in the deal, since the other $6,000 would otherwise have gone for taxes. This is a far more effective use of the deductions. If a broker gives the first investor that drilling deal, it's an unsuitable investment because the investor is taking on more risk than he should, and deriving less tax benefit.

Liquidity is another major problem for tax-shelter investors. Many investors assume that because they're buying a tax shelter from a stockbroker, they can turn around and sell it as easily as stocks or bonds. Unfortunately, it doesn't work that way. Most tax shelters are not liquid; if the investor needs his money back before the project matures, he may have to accept as little as 10 cents on the dollar. Therefore, most experts recommend that investors not commit any funds they might conceivably need in the next three to five years.

Actually, there are five different kinds of risks the investor is exposed to:

1. Risk as function of tax bracket—how much expense the government picks up versus the investor's real exposure
2. Psychological risk—how much risk the investor is comfortable in assuming
3. Business/investment risk—if there were no risk to the investment, Congress wouldn't make tax shelters attractive by offering investors a tax incentive
4. Tax risk—overly aggressive depreciation may alert the IRS to audit the tax return
5. Inflation risk—will the tax shelter keep pace with inflation

Tax Evaluation Service — TES (Please Print)

Client Name _____ Number of Dependents _____ Filing Status: ☐ Single ☐ Joint ☐ Head of Household Your Broker _____

Year of Birth _____ State of Residence _____ Branch Office _____

TES — Client Information

ITEM	CODE	Estimated 1978 (A)	Proposed 1978 Tax Shelter Variations B	C	D	COMMENTS
Tax Shelter Investment						
Write Off	K1					Total amount to be invested
Tax Preferences	G46					Tax loss for year. Do not include preferences on % Long Term Capital Gain or excess itemized deductions as these will be done automatically
Estimated Gross Income						
Employee Compensation	C6					Includes salary, bonus, employee pensions, directors fees, etc.
Interest from Federal Obligations	E9					Treasury notes and bills, etc.
Interest from State & Municipal Obligations	Y17					Issued by Cities, Counties, Towns, School Districts, etc.
All Other Interest	E1					Interest from Banks, Corporate Bonds, etc.
Dividends	D5					Total qualified and non-qualified Corporate Dists.
Partnership Sub-S & Trust Profit (or loss)	H1					Net flow-thru ordinary income
Earned Portion of Partnership Income	G22					Amount of ordinary income attributable to personal services
Rental Income	L2					Net income after expenses and depreciation
Sole Proprietor & Farm Profit (or loss)	M1					Indicate in parenthesis the percentage of net income attributable to personal services
Short Term Capital Gain (or loss)	P1					Include flow-thru items and loss carryovers
Long Term Capital Gain (or loss)	P4					Include flow-thru items and loss carryovers
Miscellaneous Income	K2					Unearned miscellaneous income, annuities, etc.
Estimated Deductions						
Keogh and/or IRA Deductions	F54					Amount to be contributed
Alimony Paid	W13					Periodic alimony—not child care support
Adjustments to Business Expenses	C55					Moving, overnight travel, local transportation, outside Salesmen's expenses, etc.
Medical Deductions	R8					Gross amount before limitation
State Income Tax Paid	T13					Prepayments this year—include estimates and withheld amounts
Real Estate Tax	T1					Primarily taxes paid on all personal residences
Other Taxes	T16					Except Sales Tax which will be computed by the computer
Non-Investment Interest Expense	V1					Interest on home mortgage & other personal items
Investment Interest Expense	V7					Interest on loans used for investment purposes
Charitable Contributions	S1					Both cash and fair market value of donations
Miscellaneous Deductions	W1					Professional fees, subscriptions & other deductions
Credit to Taxes						
Foreign Tax Credit	T35					Income Taxes paid to foreign countries
Investment Credit	M165					10% of 1978 Equipment Purchase
Net Taxable Income from Prior Years						
1977	B2					Line 34 Page 2 of 1977 Income Tax Return
1976	B4					Line 47 Page 2 of 1976 Income Tax Return
1975	B6					Line 47 Page 2 of 1975 Income Tax Return
1974	B8					Line 48 Page 2 of 1974 Income Tax Return

3459 11/78

23

Investors' preoccupation with paying minimum taxes rather than with the soundness of their investments has led one major accounting firm to send its clients who are considering tax-shelter investments the following cautionary letter which outlines some of the risks inherent in tax shelters:

Dear_____

You have indicated an interest in investing in tax shelters with the goal of reducing the impact of taxes on your present and future income. You should make a detailed study of the economics of the investment first. Too many decisions today are being made on the tax aspects first and the economics second. We will be pleased to furnish you tax advice to assist you in your decision.

While there are sizable returns to be derived from good investments that also produce tax deductions, we suggest that you consider the following prior to investing in any tax shelter.

- The business economics of the project must be sound and your investment decision should be based primarily on this consideration and tax savings secondarily.
- The risks and the fact that the promoter usually is being compensated for putting the deal together and has no sizable investment risk.
- The lack of liquidity and marketability (usually other investments will have to be looked to for quick cash).
- The low initial cash flow in most instances (some tax shelters produce their major cash flow upon ultimate sale).
- The information furnished us for projections is that of the promoter, builder, developer, etc., and we do not audit or verify in any manner the basic data.
- The investor will usually be depending on others to value and to manage the properties and/or operations. This introduces the possibility of the failure of people in addition to the other economic risks.

- The tax rules relied upon today might be changed in the future or our interpretation of the tax laws might be upset by revenue agents or the courts.
- The fact that many tax shelters (particularly apartment projects) are encouraged by the tax laws is an indication that Congress believes that investors need additional incentives. This in itself should warn us that without tax incentives a particular investment has not attracted sufficient capital.
- The artificial encouragement of investment due to tax incentives could produce an oversupply of a particular tax shelter.
- The most important element to protect the investor is good people managing the property. The promoter-operator should be honest and competent. Much of the initial investigating time should be devoted to checking out his background.

If after considering all of the above you wish to proceed on a program of investing in shelters, we will be pleased to analyze your personal tax position to enable you to make a decision as to which types of shelters could produce the most favorable tax results.

We are enthusiastic about plans that save you taxes; however, our advice is limited to accounting and income tax matters. The final investment decision must be made by you and your financial advisers. We will be pleased to meet with you and discuss these opportunities.

Very truly yours,

The Broker's Role

Before a reliable brokerage house agrees to sell a tax shelter, the proposal undergoes many levels of examination and investigation. As an example, here is how E. F. Hutton, the largest brokerage house involved in tax shelters, reviews oil and gas tax-shelter proposals:

Submissions come to the national director of the tax-sheltered investment programs and are passed on to a marketing research team, which makes the preliminary review. At this point, 95% of the proposals are rejected and filed so that time isn't wasted on reviewing them again if they're resubmitted in the future.

Most programs are rejected at this point because they are structured and built by promoters who are not in the oil and gas business. Instead, they are set up by management companies that are raising investment capital and they, in effect, are farming it out to drilling companies. Because these brokers and promoters take their slice of the action, the investor in the programs pays them a layer of what should be *his* profit. The ideal people to do business with are those in the oil and gas business who expect to earn money on oil and gas discoveries, not on commissions from selling oil and gas programs.

After this quick review, the surviving proposals go into a second level of review which involves checking with outside consultants in the oil and gas industry, running security checks—possibly through an investigative agency.

If the proposal still looks promising, it undergoes a third level of review, involving Hutton's underwriting-commitment committee, which is not controlled by the marketing department, and which acts as devil's advocate. The committee is composed of ten officers of the firm: the vice-chairman, four senior vice-presidents, one first vice-president, and four vice-presidents. During this adversary proceeding, the proposal's sponsor on the marketing research team makes his presentation and must answer questions, much like a doctoral candidate defending his dissertation.

If the proposal passes this level of review, outside experts in law, accounting, engineering, and petroleum economics are called in. Oil and gas programs are ideal to investigate. Not only can the promoter's track record be checked, which is also possible in real estate and other areas, but investigators can also carefully examine potential prospects to see if they're similar to areas where the promoter has had prior success. One red flag in particular: A promoter who has been drilling in Canada and suddenly wants to drill in southeast Louisiana. According to one expert, "That's like moving from Jupiter to Mars—a completely different world. He's got no business doing that."

If the outside experts are satisfied, Hutton's own engineers and accountants review the proposal. The engineers review prospects and determine not only possible reserves but also the risk involved in recovering them.

As a result of this stringent investigation, of the 85 publicly registered oil and gas programs, E. F. Hutton sells only 6 and has sold each of these from 2½ to 8 years.

And reviews do not stop when the program is sold. Reports to investors are tracked, and, since most drilling companies return to the marketplace with new programs every year, before Hutton sells the new program, it reviews the old programs as well as the new one. If any discrepancies are detected, the new program is not sold until the company corrects any practices in the old programs that are felt not to be in the investors' best interest. For the investors' benefit, performance records of past programs are available for examination before a new investment commitment is made.

The Professional Advisers' Role

Investors should have both their lawyers and their accountants examine tax-shelter prospectuses before any investment commitment is made. The lawyer is responsible for examining the investors' liability and right of recourse if there are later problems. These areas depend on how the prospectus and limited-partnership agreements are worded. The accountant is responsible for examining the financial statements and projections. The accountant's opinion is strictly a question of looking at numbers: "Assuming A, B, and C are true, D is a reasonable expectation. And, according to current tax law, the IRS will accept D."

Because accountants and lawyers may limit their analysis, investors should ask specific questions. The credentials and background of lawyers and accountants involved in putting together the offering should be checked thoroughly. Who are their other clients? What kind of companies or industries do they work for? Have they been involved in any litigation?

Similarly, the credentials of consultants connected with the offer should also be investigated. They should be able to provide names of companies and individuals they've worked for. It's always a good idea for investors to ask themselves: "How solid is this deal? Would I go into business with these people?" Because that's what a tax shelter really is—a business venture in an industry that the government thinks needs extra help and therefore has offered investors tax savings as a sweetener.

Some caveats are in order here:

- Good tax shelters don't use direct-mail solicitation and don't promise to double or triple the investment within a few months. Investors should beware of those that do as much as they'd avoid companies that offered to sell them diamonds or oil wells by mail.
- The smaller the minimum unit of investment, the worse it may be. It's true that it's easy to raise $100,000 to $250,000 per investor for good tax shelters, and that many plums go to the big investors who can hire experts to locate and review deals. Still, in the past few years, major brokerage houses have come to realize the potential market for $5,000 to $10,000 tax shelters for middle-income investors earning from $30,000 to $50,000. Thus, at this point, it's fair to say that management fees, finder's fees, and compensation to general partners are much higher in small-unit ($5,000 to $10,000) offerings, so that much less of the investor's money actually goes to work for him.
- Tax shelters far away from home are often suspect. If a California or Texas oil and gas deal is being promoted in New York, there may be good reason for its being marketed 3,000 miles away, rather than nearer its source. Why won't the Californians or Texans touch it?
- The higher the write-offs, the worse the deal. This is a

corollary of the textbook risk/reward ratio. Here there are several risks. First, very large write-offs indicate the riskiness of the venture. A shopping center in a prime location won't offer a 5-to-1 write-off, but high-risk government-subsidized rehabilitated housing may. Second, the IRS is more likely to examine high-multiple write-off tax shelters and to disallow certain write-offs or to reduce the high multiple. An additional risk: Deductions taken in excess of cash contributions will come back to haunt the taxpayer or his heirs—often at the most inopportune time. Taxes on the excess deduction may wipe out a good part of the advantage of the tax shelter—especially for investors whose sole source of income is salary, which is now taxed at a maximum of only 50%.

Many investors consider a tax shelter suitable only if they're totally sheltered. If they're in the 50% bracket, they insist on a 2-to-1 write-off so that, in effect, they haven't invested any of their own money in the deal. They've merely invested money that would otherwise have been paid as taxes.

But most tax-shelter professionals regard this attitude as shortsighted. They are more concerned about the soundness of the tax-shelter investment and its potential to provide capital gains as well as deductions, especially now that the Revenue Act of 1978 has reduced the maximum capital gains tax to 28%.

A Tax Adviser Comments on Oil and Gas Shelters

Middle management (those earning $50,000 to $100,000) and "sophisticated wealth" have traditionally been targets for gimmicky tax shelters. These investors pay far too little attention to the investment vehicle. All they've wanted to know is "What's my write-off?" and they have consistently gotten stung because they didn't realize that there's no such thing as a free lunch. People used to invest $25,000 in such gimmicky tax shelters as movies, records, books, coal mines, medical equipment, and be told they were going to get

$100,000 in write-offs. And this is where their thinking stopped. They didn't care and wouldn't listen when their advisers pointed out that the $75,000 difference between the $25,000 investment and the $100,000 write-offs would come back as ordinary income at the 70% bracket to shelter earned income whose maximum tax bracket was only 50%. This meant they'd actually be in the hole $2,500: $100,000 in write-offs in the 50% bracket equals $50,000, but $75,000 in the 70% bracket equals $52,500!

The Revenue Act of 1978 includes accelerated depreciation on real estate, equipment-leasing deals, IDCs (intangible drilling costs) to the extent that there's no income from other oil deals, and depletion as preference items. This means that when a tax adviser is reviewing a deal for a client who has solely earned income, taxed at 50%, the adviser cannot merely rest on the projections given to him by the syndicators. He must make a further analysis of what it does to his client's income tax.

Take a developmental oil program, for example. Many investors feel comfortable about these programs because they're dealing in areas euphemistically called "semi-proven." But the simple fact is that if they have a very high rate of "successful" wells that are not very productive, 90% of that write-off may be deemed a tax-preference item by the IRS.

The significance: If an executive has $200,000 in salary, it will be taxed at 50%. If he invests $20,000 in an oil and gas well that's almost all developmental and he gets an 80% write-off, that's $16,000. However, of that deduction, approximately 90%, or $14,000, may be a tax-preference item. That $14,000 takes $14,000 of what would have been 50% bracket income and raises it to 70%—a difference of approximately $2,800 in federal income taxes. It takes some of the edge off—he's not getting the benefit of a 50% write-off—it may come down to around 45%. If the deal makes money for him, then it's been successful. But he's not getting the full face-value benefit of the write-off.

A Tax Adviser Comments on Real Estate Tax Shelters

There's no free ride on losses in excess of investment. Eventually there's a day of reckoning, and that day is either when the partnership folds, or when the partnership sells the property, or when the investor sells the partnership unit, or when the property is foreclosed or abandoned. Then the difference between the losses and the *net investment* (investment less cash payouts) is a taxable gain—even though it's a negative number! In real estate, if the property has been held long enough, it's mostly capital gain, but there may be some recapture as ordinary income. The longer an investor holds the property, the better off he usually is.

An investor can make money just by deducting losses at ordinary-income rates and postponing capital gains, although appreciation will increase his gains even more.

The first months of 1979 have seen a huge number of hyped-up real estate deals which offer big write-offs over a relatively short period of time. These are not orthodox subsidized or insured projects; they're deals with very high markups. The syndicating group buys property, puts a wraparound mortgage on or otherwise inflates the price tremendously and thus gives investors a "shelter" because the new price is so high that the syndicate requires very little cash from the investor. It's all gravy: If the syndicate pays $1 million for property and turns around and sells it for $3 million, and the investors put up $300,000 and sign a note for $2.7 million, the interest deductions and depreciation on that $3 million deal are enormous.

The only problem is that the investors are not buying real estate, they're buying a tax shelter; and the IRS has the same ability as the promoter to know that the real estate is worth only $1 million. The IRS will simply say that since the real estate is worth only $1 million, all write-offs based on $3 million will be ignored.

There are some legitimate 5-to-1 and 6-to-1 real estate

tax shelters involving government-subsidized property that is in such distress that very little new cash is required—just enough to buy out the old investors. The property is tagged with such huge federal, state, and city loans that it's a walking tax shelter. And it's a perfectly legitimate one. The theory is relatively little cash, relatively little hope of a long-term investment. There's not very much hope that it can even survive because it's carrying such a tremendous mortgage load. It's really a shelter, not an investment as such. Possibly, 20, 30, or 40 years from now, it may have some residual value. But if it doesn't, and if it goes under at any time, then the amount written off in excess of the investment comes back to the investor as a capital gain.

Now that capital gains rates are 28% maximum, this alone can be a very attractive use of money: putting in $10,000 and writing off $40,000 or $50,000 over an extended period, then taking back a capital gain, ultimately, of $30,000 or $40,000. This shifts the $30,000 or $40,000 from the 50% bracket to the 28% bracket, for a savings of $6,600 or $8,800, respectively.

Choosing a Tax Shelter by Function

Although most prospectuses discuss investment suitability only in terms of investors' income, tax bracket, and net worth, many investment advisers believe that the function of a tax shelter should take priority. One adviser divides tax shelters into four categories by function: deferrals, equity builders, deep tax shelters, and "not really" tax shelters.

Deferrals are designed to postpone taxable income and are most suitable for people facing retirement whose taxable income will drop sharply in anywhere from 2 to 6 years. Typically, first-year write-offs will range from 50 to 200% of the investment (as high as 200% because they will be real estate tax shelters or there will be recourse notes). In subsequent years, depending on the type of tax shelter chosen, the investor starts receiving and/or reporting income. This technique is often called "throwing income down the road."

Typical deferral tax shelters are cattle breeding and feeding, where income is reportable in the second or third year, depending on the program, and equipment leasing, where write-offs are usually taken in the first through fifth years, and income is reported in subsequent years, depending on the type of equipment and the terms of the lease. Other kinds of deferral tax shelters are book publishing, movies, and records, although they are usually not as good as cattle and equipment-leasing tax shelters.

Equity builders are designed to increase an investor's net worth, rather than to provide immediate sizable write-offs. Depending on the type of tax shelter chosen, an investor will be able to write off anywhere from 30 to 100% of the investment in anywhere from the first year to the first 3 or 4 years. Typical equity-builder tax shelters are oil and gas ventures, conventional real estate, cattle breeding, and agriculture, where it is hoped that the land will appreciate substantially in value.

Deep tax shelters provide a series of very large, predictable tax losses which usually total 300 to 400% of the investment in stages over approximately 14 to 20 years. As such, they are perfect for investors who can offset high, predictable long-term incomes. There may be some cash flow, but it is usually minimal and should not be counted on; investors who buy deep tax shelters are really buying losses, although they may begin seeing a return on their investment in 16 to 20 years. Government-subsidized housing and net-lease tax-oriented real estate are deep tax shelters.

"Not really a tax shelter" is an odd term, but it fits here. This category covers investments that provide tax-free or tax-sheltered income, but that must be purchased with after-tax dollars because they do not generate any tax deductions. As opposed to a tax shelter which provides write-offs, for investments in this category, investors must first earn the investment money, then pay taxes on it, and finally make the investment. This is an important difference: an investor in the 50% bracket must earn $20,000 pretax in

order to purchase $10,000 of municipal bonds. Other investment vehicles in this category which are included in Part Two of this book because they provide tax-free or tax-sheltered income are annuities and income-oriented real estate.

3 How to Examine and Analyze a Tax Shelter

At some point, investors who are interested in tax shelters are confronted with piles of prospectuses on their desks. These intimidating documents often run more than one hundred pages, plus an additional forty and fifty pages of miscellaneous notes and exhibits.

While it is true that the SEC regulates public offerings, regulation has nothing to do with approval. In fact, most tax-shelter prospectuses say directly on the cover in bold-face type:

THESE SECURITIES HAVE NOT BEEN APPROVED OR DISAPPROVED BY THE SECURITIES AND EXCHANGE COMMISSION NOR HAS THE COMMISSION PASSED UPON THE ACCURACY OR ADEQUACY OF THIS PROSPECTUS. . . .

NEITHER THE ATTORNEY GENERAL OF THE STATE OF NEW YORK NOR THE ATTORNEY GENERAL OF THE STATE OF NEW JERSEY NOR THE BUREAU OF SECURITIES OF THE STATE OF NEW JERSEY HAS PASSED ON OR ENDORSED THE MERITS OF THIS OFFERING. . . .

In order to help educate and inform prospective tax-shelter investors, I have taken key items from a number of real estate and oil and gas prospectuses and briefly discussed their significance. *In no way should this be construed as meaning that even a moderately sophisticated investor analyze a tax-shelter prospectus completely on his own and make an investment decision solely on that basis.* The purpose of these paragraphs is to alert investors to where in the one hundred and fifty pages or so of prospectus the most important information lies so that they can most easily obtain answers and clarification from their professional advisers.

REAL ESTATE VENTURES

Part of the Prospectus	What the Investor Should Look For
Suitability standards	Does the prospectus indicate to what type of investor it is geared? Watch out for "blanket standards" which really say nothing. What is the size of the offering and how does it relate to suitability? (Are the promoters raising more money than they need?) Is the investor "morally" or "emotionally" expected to provide future needs of financing requested by the partnership?
Summary of the partnership and the offering	Do the general terms of the prospectus give the potential investor a feel for the partnership's activity and the general partner's objectives?
Summary of use of proceeds	Are the costs of the offering and the allocation of funds clear and concise? Is the total commission sub-

Part of the Prospectus	What the Investor Should Look For
	stantial? (REMEMBER: All costs are paid prior to cash distributions to the investors.)
Compensation and fees of general partners	Are there tremendous professional fees involved, or will most of the work be done by the general partners?
	Are there any industry statistics on the ratio of commissions and operating expenses to income? How does this venture compare to them?
Summary of relationships and conflicts of interest	Is any of the work, such as construction, financing, management operation, being done by related parties of the general partner? Are these contracts binding? How restrictive are these agreements? Will all costs be subcontracted?
Fiduciary responsibilities of the general partner	How broad are they? Do they extend further than the "intent" reflected in the prospectus?
	Does each investor have some say in the operations or types of investment selected?
Risk factors	Have the investments been preselected—at least, as to type? What risks are involved in these choices?
	Does the prospectus indicate to whom the property is to be rented or leased, or to what use it will be adapted? Is such an

38

Part of the Prospectus	What the Investor Should Look For
	item a "limited-use" piece of property? What risks are involved in these choices?
Prior performance of general partners	What is their track record? What is their Dun & Bradstreet rating? Has the group gained experience in only one geographic location? If this location is different, can they adapt?
Capitalization	How many general partners are there? What are the minimum and maximum investments by any one investor? Does the prospectus indicate how the general partners' investment was financed? Was it cash? Loan? Why was a loan necessary?
Investment objectives and policies	Are the types of properties to be invested in clearly defined? Commercial or residential? Old or new? Rent, sell, or lease? How is the project to be financed?
Government-assistance programs	What is the investor's liability? Is there any bad publicity relating to the property? Can the property be sold easily?
Federal taxes	Has a private ruling been requested to determine whether

Part of the Prospectus

What the Investor Should Look For

the project is a partnership or a corporation? What is the opinion of counsel?

Are there sub limited partnerships (which may be viewed as subsidiaries of partnerships), and what is their tax status:

1. How will gains and losses be allocated?

2. Can the investment be transferred easily without unfavorable tax impact?

3. How do the promoters deal with the "at-risk" requirements for tax-shelter treatment—specifically if they have subpartners? Do they offer strong legal opinions or are they hedging?

4. Will proceeds be used to pay off loans, or will they be distributed?

5. Will the interest expensed for partnership liabilities affect the investors' investment interest limits (net of $10,000, after deducting investment income)?

6. How will expenses during construction, interest and taxes, commitment fees, et cetera—be handled?

7. What type(s) of depreciation will be used? Do pro-

Part of the Prospectus	*What the Investor Should Look For*
	moters state they will use straight-line or accelerated depreciation? Will investments be specifically low-income subsidized government housing? (This is high-risk.) If partnership doesn't state what type of real estate it plans to invest in, can investor project what may happen, what write-offs will be?
State and local taxes	Is partnership subjecting the limited partners to various states' taxation?
Tax information	Will it be sent in time for investors' filing deadlines?
Management	What is the background of the individuals involved?
Use of proceeds	What is the intent, if any? How clearly or vaguely is it stated?
Summary of partnership agreement	Should be read along with the partnership agreement and the prospectus. Do they coincide, or are there differences? What are the limits of liability for the general partners? The limited partners? Who will provide liability coverage?
Reports	What type of reports will be available? Will they be audited?

Part of the Prospectus	What the Investor Should Look For
	How often will the partnership report?
Sales literature	Is it impressive? Vague? Clear? Misleading?
Legal matters and experts	To what extent have professional groups passed on the allegations of the project's originators?
Additional information	Is the prospectus subject to SEC rules?
	Does the prospectus have to be filed with governmental authorities? (This will guarantee additional reviews.)
Glossary	Must be read in detail. Are all terms defined? Are there any terms used which are "taken for granted" and not defined?
Financial statements	Who audited them? Are they complete?
Partnership agreement and subscription agreements	Are they attached to the prospectus? *They must be read very carefully because they usually give the general partners more authority than that defined in the prospectus.*

OIL AND GAS VENTURES

Part of the Prospectus	What the Investor Should Look For
Definitions	Are terms defined? Is there a glossary?

Part of the Prospectus	*What the Investor Should Look For*
	Do the definitions cross-reference accurately to each other?
	The investor should test his understanding of the terms by substituting their definitions in the text of the prospectus. Is he comfortable with them? Do they make sense?
Terms of the offering	Are the terms general or specific?
	Does the potential investor get a feel for the partnership's activity and the general partner's objectives?
• The offering	Does it set forth the total amount offered?
	What is the investor's minimum investment? Can the investor buy increments?
	Are there any hidden future assessments, or are they spelled out?
	What is the investor's percent share of the investment?
• Suitability standards	Does the prospectus talk about whi)ch categories of people should consider the investment?
	Does the prospectus make reference to certain tax brackets, which could indicate the level at which such an investment is beneficial to the investor from a tax standpoint?

Part of the Prospectus	What the Investor Should Look For
Transfer of units	Is the investment easy to transfer and market? (If so, it may lose its partnership status.)
	Can the investor get out? How? How much might he lose?
Limited right of presentment (right to present investment units for redemption)	What financial information relating to presentment will be disclosed periodically?
	Can the investment be presented for redemption? Under what circumstances? How often? How many units at one time?
Additional assessments	Under what conditions will they be made? Are assessments limited to certain conditions?
	Are additional assessments normal for the industry?
	Does the partnership have alternative sources of financing? To what extent is the investor bound by the general partner's decision on additional assessments?
• Development costs	Are they defined and limited?
• Notice and payment of assessments	Will assessments relate to deductions or to capital items?
	Will he receive an explanation? Can he refuse? If he refuses, what happens to his equity?
• Assessments in previous programs	Does the prospectus show what happened in previous programs, if any?

44

Part of the Prospectus	What the Investor Should Look For
	Are there any assurances given in the prospectus? Can they be relied on?
Plan of distribution	How will the promoters market the offering?
	What cost (commission) are they willing to pay for financing?
	If the offering is undersubscribed and the program is terminated, what start-up costs must the investor bear?
Proposed activities	Is the prospectus explicit?
• General	Does the prospectus clearly define its intent?
• Area of operations	Is the area limited? Does the limited partner incur a tax liability in another state since the partnership may be doing business in another state?
• Nature of operations	Who is responsible for limiting the areas involved?
	What risks are involved?
• Method of operations	How much say will the investor have in the daily or complete operations of the partnership?
	Is management's compensation based on work actually performed?
• Selection of prospects	Is the exploratory drilling being done on behalf of the general partner? (If so, there is a built-in market for the product, but this has its advantages and disadvantages, depending

Part of the Prospectus	*What the Investor Should Look For*
	on current supply and demand, price structure, etc.)
	Has the prospect been specifically defined prior to commencement of the operation?
• Title to properties	Is the title or the right to drill transferred to the partnership? (If title is in the name of the general partner, it is subject to his creditors.)
• Conditions of operation	Who has control? To what extent are the decisions to buy, sell, and control in the hands of the general partner?
Application of proceeds	How are the proceeds to be spent? Will the funds go directly to the driller, or to an investment group which will find a driller (and take a commission for doing so)? Will the funds be applied to drilling costs, which offer benefits of large tax write-offs, or to leasehold acquisition costs, which may not be currently deductible?
Participation in costs and revenues	How will the investor and general partners share in the costs and revenues? Is the division beneficial to the investor?
Compensation	How will the general partners or their designated manager share in the compensation?

Part of the Prospectus	What the Investor Should Look For
	How will reimbursement of expenses be controlled?
Management	What is the background of the individuals involved?
	What is their Dun & Bradstreet rating?
	Do they have a history?
	What is their track record?
	How will they be compensated?
	Can they be controlled? By whom? Under what circumstances?
• Interest of management and others in certain transactions	What is management's affiliation with other parties directly or indirectly involved with the prospectus?
Conflicts of interest	Are they defined?
	Can such involvement affect the partnership treatment if the project appears to be a sole proprietorship with financing? (If general partner retains total control, the IRS may hold the project to be a sole proprietorship, with the limited partners considered creditors, rather than limited partners in a partnership. Their investments would be regarded as loans, and write-offs would be disallowed.)
Prior activities—results of prior programs	A schedule or summary of past projects and their success

Part of the Prospectus	What the Investor Should Look For

should be included in the prospectus.

Tax aspects
• General

Who has reviewed these?

How strong are the statements and opinions made by attorneys and accounting firms in connection with the tax aspects? (Does it say: "We have reviewed and are satisfied ..." or just "We have reviewed and tender no opinion on the tax aspects"?)

Is there any statement made about indemnifying the investors if the IRS disagrees about the tax aspects?

• Partnership classification and partnership taxation

Will a ruling be requested to determine that the venture be identified as a partnership in order that the tax benefits go to the investor? Such benefits can be realized only if they can be used by the investor.

• Limitations on deductions

Will there be at-risk borrowings?

Will the losses deductible be limited due to the investment? The allocation of income and expenses? The method of allocation deductions for depletion?

• Special allocations

Do special allocations have a sustained economic effect, and has it been reviewed by com-

Part of the Prospectus	What the Investor Should Look For
	petent counsel and other necessary professionals?
• Intangible drilling and development costs	Will prepayments be authorized?
	Will the partnership elect to expense IDCs currently?
• Equipment	Will equipment be capitalized?
	What method of depreciation will be used?
	How will the investment credits be calculated?
• Leaseholds	How will the costs of abandonment be calculated and allocated?
	If the costs are disallowed by the IRS, who will pay and indemnify the limited partners for the resulting problems?
• Organizational expenses, syndication fees, and management fees	How are these fees deducted?
	Who will bear the brunt of the costs resulting from disallowances of deductions?
• Depletion	Will there be any proven wells? (Depletion is not allowed on these.)
• Gains and losses	Is the partnership's investment objective a quick turnover or full exploitation of the property?
	How do the promoters project the gain or loss on disposition of the property? Will it be taxed as ordinary income or capital gains? To what extent

Part of the Prospectus	*What the Investor Should Look For*
	do they comment on the tax treatment? What is their lawyer's or accountant's comment, if any?
• Minimum tax	To what extent will the limited partners be subject to a percentage depletion and intangible drilling costs? (These are subject to a minimum tax; they are tax-preference items.)
• Maximum tax for individuals	What is the effect of preference items on prospective investor's maximum tax? Is it heavy or light? Is it so heavy that it becomes a serious disadvantage?
• State and local taxes	Will the partnership subject limited partners to a state tax where the partnership is doing business?
• Other tax matters	Will the partnership be run on a calendar-year basis?
	How will deductions be made and assigned?
Competition, markets, and regulation • Competition • Marketing • Regulation • Oil-price regulation • Gas pricing	In this area, potential investors should get information from the brokerage house research department. What effect will economics, current events, and so forth have on the profitability of the venture? Specifically, why is this particular program better than any other being offered at this time? Is the brokerage house guaran-

Part of the Prospectus	*What the Investor Should Look For*
	teeing future marketability of investment unit?
Partnership agreement	Does it confirm the statements made in the prospectus?
Legal opinions and experts	To what extent do they assume liability for statements made in the prospectus and in the partnership agreement?
Financial statements	Are financial statements audited and fully disclosed? (Pay special attention to footnotes.) Are there financial statements on both the general partner and the promoting group?

Probably an entire book should be devoted to analyzing tax-shelter prospectuses; so little is stated plainly, for fear of SEC prosecution if the projects turn sour. As an example, one recent real estate prospectus did not state what type of real estate the partnership planned to invest in—even whether it would be commercial or residential—or what type of depreciation would be used. This was to be left completely to the promoters—after the fact. They were asking investors for money without making any disclosure—just on the basis of going into a "tax shelter." True, the promoters mention what the investors might possibly receive by way of write-offs and return on investment, but they gave no indication of the types of investments providing them.

Investors must understand that promoters can be totally vague in a prospectus, can state that no plans have been made for the proceeds of the underwriting, and can make similar uninformative comments. So long as there is no misrepresentation, the promoters are home free with the SEC. Theoretically, the promoters could say, "Our cocker spaniel will select the properties with the help of a Ouija board," and if this statement is accurate, the SEC has no basis for future prosecution on these grounds.

The problem of inadequate disclosure illustrated by these examples is the reason why the questions raised in this chapter are so crucial and must be asked before any investment is made. One accountant urges his clients to ask their lawyers exactly what is promised in the prospectus. He puts it wryly: "Basically, it's a matter of how many questions you can ask before they close the door on you." *Caveat emptor* was never more valuable advice.

4 Putting It All Together: Tax Savings

Since the primary purpose of tax shelters is tax savings, it is useful to run a comparison of tax returns which demonstrates how much money can be saved by taxpayers at varying income levels with different types of tax shelters. To simplify matters and save space, Schedule K-1 and Form 1065 shown in Chapter One will not be repeated here—only the Schedule E to which the numbers would be transferred—and the taxpayers will take the standard deduction.

Henry and Greta Hassel live and work in New York City and are thus subject to federal, state, and city income taxes on their joint salary of $43,000 and interest and dividends of $2,000. Even with exemptions for their two children, without a tax shelter, they would pay federal income tax of $11,330, state income tax of $2,776, and city income tax of $961, for a total of $15,067.

But with a $10,000 real estate tax shelter (which sometimes can be bought in installments), the Hassels pay only a federal income tax of $7,144, state income tax of $1,708.50, and city income tax of $637.50, for a total tax of $9,490. This represents a tax saving of $5,577, or 37.0%, for just one year. Their tax returns are shown on pages 56–67.

Maria Beaumont is a widow whose sole annual income

of $50,000 is unearned: its source is dividends and interest. Because her income is unearned, it cannot benefit from the maximum tax of 50% on earned income; part of it is taxed at 55%, and part of it is taxed at 60%. Her federal income tax is $18,180. If she switched to a portfolio 100% invested in municipal bonds, she would not have to pay any income tax at all. However, even if she were to switch to a portfolio only 50% invested in municipal bonds, providing $25,000 tax-free income, she would still enjoy substantial tax savings. Her taxes would then be $5,791, a saving of $12,389, or 68.1%. See pages 68–75 for her tax returns.

Ben Reich is a corporation executive and earns $100,000. His wife, Barbara, does not work, but receives $5,000 a year from a trust. Last year they sold some stock at a $20,000 long-term capital gain. Without a tax shelter, they would pay federal income tax of $47,478. Although Reich's earned income is taxed on a maximum of 50%, his wife's trust income and a portion of his capital gain are taxed at the 70% maximum.

However, if Reich offsets his capital gain by buying $25,000 worth of units in 3 exploratory oil and gas programs early in the year, so that all his drilling expenses, amounting to 90% of his investment, are taken during the calendar

Name	No. of exemptions	Earned income	Unearned income*	Total	Income taxes without shelter
Henry and Greta Hassel	4	$ 43,000	$ 1,800	$44,800	$15,067†
Maria Beaumont	1	0	$49,900	$49,900	$18,180
Ben and Barbara Reich	2	$100,000	$25,000	$125,000	$47,478
Olivia Presteign	1	$40,000	0	$40,000	$12,635
Odysseus Gaul	1	0	$17,500	$17,500	$2,965

* After dividend exclusion.
† Federal, New York State, and New York City income taxes.

year, the Reichs' federal income tax shrinks to $36,438. This is a saving of $11,040, or 23.3%. Their tax returns are shown on pages 76–89.

Olivia Presteign is an executive who earns $40,000. Without a tax shelter, she pays $12,635 in federal income tax. With a $10,000 conventional real estate (to-be-constructed) tax shelter, with a first-year write-off of $5,000, she pays only $10,135, a saving of $2,500, or 19.8%. See pages 90–96 for her tax returns.

Odysseus Gaul was chosen to illustrate that people needn't have enormous incomes, like Maria Beaumont, to benefit from tax-free income. Odysseus Gaul is retired and receives a pension of $15,000 and $2,500 income from savings-bank interest. Because his pension is fully taxable, his federal income tax is fairly heavy—$2,965. If he closes his bank accounts and invests the proceeds in municipal bonds, his federal income tax is reduced to $2,254, a saving of $711, or 24.0%. Thus, even at relatively modest income levels, taxpayers can save a substantial portion of their taxes through investment vehicles that provide tax-sheltered or tax-free income. Gaul's tax returns are shown on pages 97–101.

Following is a summary of the tax savings shown on the sample returns:

Type of shelter	Amount of shelter	Amount of write-off	Income taxes with shelter	Amount saved	Percent saved
Real estate	$10,000	$10,000	$9,490†	$5,577	37.0%
Municipal bonds	$25,000 income	$25,000	$5,791	$12,389	68.1%
Oil and gas	$25,000	$22,500	$36,438	$11,040	23.3%
Conventional real estate (to be constructed	$10,000	$5,000	$10,135	$2,500	19.8%
Municipal bonds	$2,500 income	$2,500	$2,254	$711	24.0%

† Federal, New York State, and New York City income taxes.

Form **1040**

Department of the Treasury—Internal Revenue Service
U.S. Individual Income Tax Return **1978**

For Privacy Act Notice, see page 3 of Instructions | For the year January 1–December 31, 1978, or other tax year beginning ____ , 1978, ending ____ , 19 ___ .

Use IRS label. Other-wise, please print or type.	Your first name and initial (if joint return, also give spouse's name and initial) HENRY + GRETA	Last name HASSEL	Your social security number 000 00 0000
	Present home address (Number and street, including apartment number, or rural route)		Spouse's social security no. 000 00 0000
	City, town or post office, State and ZIP code		Your occupation PROFESSOR
			Spouse's occupation ARTIST

Do you want $1 to go to the Presidential Election Campaign Fund? **Yes** ☐ **No** ☐
If joint return, does your spouse want $1 to go to this fund? . . **Yes** ☐ **No** ☐
Note: Checking Yes will not increase your tax or reduce your refund.

Filing Status
Check only one box.

1 ☐ Single
2 ☑ Married filing joint return (even if only one had income)
3 ☐ Married filing separate return. If spouse is also filing, give spouse's social security number in the space above and enter full name here ▶
4 ☐ Unmarried head of household. Enter qualifying name ▶ _____ . See page 6 of Instructions.
5 ☐ Qualifying widow(er) with dependent child (Year spouse died ▶ 19 ____). See page 6 of Instructions.

Exemptions
Always check the box labeled Yourself. Check other boxes if they apply.

6a ☑ Yourself   ☐ 65 or over   ☐ Blind   } Enter number of boxes checked on 6a and b ▶ **2**
b ☑ Spouse   ☐ 65 or over   ☐ Blind
c First names of your dependent children who lived with you ▶ EDGAR, EMMA   Enter number of children listed ▶ **2**

d Other dependents: (1) Name	(2) Relationship	(3) Number of months lived in your home	(4) Did dependent have income of $750 or more?	(5) Did you provide more than one-half of dependent's support?	Enter number of other dependents ▶

Add numbers entered in boxes above ▶ **4**

7 Total number of exemptions claimed . . . .

Income

Please attach Copy B of your Forms W–2 here.

If you do not have a W–2, see page 5 of Instructions.

8	Wages, salaries, tips, and other employee compensation	8	43,000 —
9	Interest income (If over $400, attach Schedule B)	9	1,000 —
10a	Dividends (If over $400, attach Schedule B) . . 1,000 ___ , 10b Exclusion . 200 ___		
10c	Subtract line 10b from line 10a	10c	800 —
11	State and local income tax refunds (does not apply unless refund is for year you itemized deductions)	11	0
12	Alimony received	12	0
13	Business income or (loss) (attach Schedule C)	13	0
14	Capital gain or (loss) (attach Schedule D)	14	0
15	Taxable part of capital gain distributions not reported on Schedule D (see page 9 of Instructions) . .	15	0
16	Net gain or (loss) from Supplemental Schedule of Gains and Losses (attach Form 4797)	16	0
17	Fully taxable pensions and annuities not reported on Schedule E	17	0
18	Pensions, annuities, rents, royalties, partnerships, estates or trusts, etc. (attach Schedule E)	18	0
19	Farm income or (loss) (attach Schedule F)	19	0
20	Other income (state nature and source—see page 10 of Instructions) ▶ _____	20	0
21	**Total income. Add lines 8, 9, and 10c through 20** . . . . ▶	21	44,800 —

Adjustments to Income

22	Moving expense (attach Form 3903)	22		
23	Employee business expenses (attach Form 2106) . .	23		
24	Payments to an IRA (see page 10 of Instructions)	24		
25	Payments to a Keogh (H.R. 10) retirement plan . . .	25		
26	Interest penalty due to early withdrawal of savings	26		
27	Alimony paid (see page 10 of Instructions)	27		
28	Total adjustments. Add lines 22 through 27 . . . . ▶		28	0

Adjusted Gross Income

Please attach check or money order here.

29	Subtract line 28 from line 21	29	44,800 —
30	Disability income exclusion (attach Form 2440)	30	0
31	Adjusted gross income. Subtract line 30 from line 29. If this line is less than $8,000, see page 2 of Instructions. If you want IRS to figure your tax, see page 4 of Instructions . . . . ▶	31	44,800 —

☆ U.S. GOVERNMENT PRINTING OFFICE: 1978—O-263-303 13-2687299

Form **1040** (1978)

Name(s) as shown on Form 1040 (Do not enter name and social security number if shown on other side) | Your social security number

HENRY + GRETA HASSEL   000 00 0000

| **Part I** Interest Income | **Part II** Dividend Income |

1 If you **received more than $400 in interest, Complete Part I.** Please see page 8 of the instructions to find out what interest to report. Then answer the questions in Part III, below. If you received interest as a nominee for another, or you received or paid accrued interest on securities transferred between interest payment dates, please see page 18 of the instructions.

3 If you received more than $400 in gross dividends (including capital gain distributions) and other distributions on stock, complete Part II. Please see page 9 of the instructions. Write (H), (W), (J), for stock held by husband, wife, or jointly. Then answer the questions in Part III, below. If you received dividends as a nominee for another, please see page 18 of the instructions.

Name of payer	Amount	Name of payer	Amount
FRIENDLY SAVINGS + LOAN	1,000 —	KIDDSTUFF, INC.	500 —
		BOARDROOM ENTERPRISES	500 —

2 Total interest income. Enter here and on Form 1040, line 9 . . . . **1,000** —

| **Part III** Foreign Accounts and Foreign Trusts |

If you are required to list interest in Part I or dividends in Part II, OR if you had a foreign account or were a grantor of, or a transferor to a foreign trust, you must answer both questions in Part III. Please see page 18 of the instructions.

	Yes	No
A Did you, at any time during the taxable year, have an interest in or signature or other authority over a bank, securities, or other financial account in a foreign country (see page 18 of instructions)? . . .		
B Were you the grantor of, or transferor to, a foreign trust during any taxable year, which foreign trust was in being during the current taxable year, whether or not you have any beneficial interest in such trust? . If "Yes," you may be required to file Forms 3520, 3520–A, or 926.		

4 Total of line 3 . . . .   **1,000** —

5 Capital gain distributions. Enter here and on Schedule D, line 7. See Note below . . .   0

6 Nontaxable distributions   0

7 Total (add lines 5 and 6)   0

8 Dividends before exclusion (subtract line 7 from line 4). Enter here and on Form 1040, line 10a . . . .   **1,000** —

B

Note: If you received capital gain distributions and do not need Schedule D to report any other gains or losses or to compute the alternative tax, do not file that schedule. Instead, enter the taxable part of capital gain distributions on Form 1040, line 15.

☆ U.S. Government Printing Office: 1978–O–263-309–E.I. # 52-0237640

57

SCHEDULE TC
(Form 1040)
Department of the Treasury
Internal Revenue Service

Tax Computation Schedule

▶ Attach to Form 1040.

1978

Name(s) as shown on Form 1040	Your social security number
HENRY + GRETA HASSEL	000 00 0000

Part I   Computation of Tax for Taxpayers Who Cannot Use the Tax Tables

Use this part to figure your tax if:

• Your income on Form 1040, line 34, is more than $20,000 and you checked Filing Status Box 1, 3, or 4 on Form 1040.

• Your income on Form 1040, line 34, is more than $40,000 and you checked Filing Status Box 2 or 5 on Form 1040.

• You had more exemptions than were covered in the Tax Table for your filing status.

• You figure your tax using the alternative tax computation on Schedule D (Capital Gains and Losses), Schedule G (Income Averaging), or Form 4726 (Maximum Tax on Personal Service Income).

1	Enter the amount from Form 1040, line 34	1	44,800 —
2	Multiply $750 by the total number of exemptions claimed on Form 1040, line 7	2	3,000 —
3	Taxable Income. Subtract line 2 from line 1. (Figure your tax on this amount by using the Tax Rate Schedules or one of the other methods listed on line 4.)	3	41,800 —
4	Income Tax. Enter tax and check if from: ☑ Tax Rate Schedule X, Y, or Z, ☐ Schedule D, ☐ Schedule G, or ☐ Form 4726	4	11,510 —

General Tax Credit

5	Multiply $35 by the total number of exemptions claimed on Form 1040, line 7. (If you are married filing a separate return, skip lines 6 through 9 and enter the amount from line 5 on line 10.)	5	140 —
6	Enter the amount from line 3, above	6	41,800 —
7	Enter { $3,200 if you are married filing a joint return or a qualifying widow(er) / $2,200 if you are single or an unmarried head of household . . . }	7	3,200 —
8	Subtract line 7 from line 6	8	38,600 —
9	Enter 2% of line 8 (but do not enter more than $180)	9	180 —
10	General tax credit. Enter the amount from line 5 or line 9, whichever is larger	10	180 —
11	Tax. Subtract line 10 from line 4. (If $0 or less, enter $0.) Enter this amount on Form 1040, line 35 . . . . ▶	11	11,330 —

TC

Part II   Computation for Certain Taxpayers Who Must Itemize Deductions

If you are included in one of the groups below, you MUST itemize. If you must itemize and the amount on Schedule A (Form 1040), line 40, is more than your itemized deductions on Schedule A, line 39, you must complete Part II before figuring your tax.

You MUST itemize your deductions if:

A. You can be claimed as a dependent on your parent's return and had interest, dividends, or other unearned income of $750 or more and less than $2,200 of earned income if single (less than $1,600 if married filing a separate return).

Note: If your earned income is more than your itemized deductions on Schedule A, line 39, enter your earned income in Part II, line 3, of this schedule, unless you are married filing a separate return and your spouse itemizes deductions. Generally, your earned income is the total of any amounts on Form 1040, lines 8,

13, and 19. See page 11 of the Instructions for Form 1040 for more details.

B. You are married filing a separate return and your spouse itemizes deductions. (There is an exception to this rule. You don't have to itemize if your spouse must itemize only because he or she is described in A and enters earned income instead of itemized deductions on Part II, line 3, of this schedule. If this is the case, don't complete Part II. Go back to Form 1040, line 33, and enter $0. Then go to Form 1040, line 34.)

C. You file Form 4563 to exclude income from sources in U.S. possessions. (Please see Form 4563, and Publication 570, Tax Guide for U.S. Citizens Employed in U.S. Possessions, for more details.)

D. You had dual status as a nonresident alien for part of 1978, and during the rest of the year you were either a resident alien or a U.S. citizen. However, you don't have to itemize if at the end of 1978, you were married to a U.S. resident or citizen and file a joint return reporting your combined worldwide income.

1	Enter the amount from Form 1040, line 31		1	
2	Enter the amount from Schedule A, line 40	2		
3	Enter the amount from Schedule A, line 39	3		
	Caution: If you can be claimed as a dependent on your parent's return, see the **Note** above. Be sure you check the box below line 33 of Form 1040.			
4	Subtract line 3 from line 2		4	
5	Add lines 1 and 4. Enter here and on Form 1040, line 34. (Leave Form 1040, line 33 blank. Disregard the instruction to subtract line 33 from line 32. Follow the rest of the instructions for Form 1040, line 34.) . . . . ▶		5	

Form 1040 (1978) Page **2**

Tax Computation	32 Amount from line 31	32	44,800 —
	33 If you do not itemize deductions, enter zero . . . . If you itemize, complete Schedule A (Form 1040) and enter the amount from Schedule A, line 41 . . . . }	33	0
	Caution: If you have unearned income and can be claimed as a dependent on your parent's return, check here ▶ ☐ and see page 11 of the Instructions. Also see page 11 of the Instructions if: • You are married filing a separate return and your spouse itemizes deductions, OR • You file Form 4563, OR • You are a dual-status alien.		
	34 Subtract line 33 from line 32. Use the amount on line 34 to find your tax from the Tax Tables, or to figure your tax on Schedule TC, Part I . . . . Use Schedule TC, Part I, and the Tax Rate Schedules ONLY if: • The amount on line 34 is more than $20,000 ($40,000 if you checked Filing Status Box 2 or 5), OR • You have more exemptions than those covered in the Tax Table for your filing status, OR • You use any of these forms to figure your tax: Schedule D, Schedule G, or Form 4726. Otherwise, you MUST use the Tax Tables to find your tax.	34	44,800 —
	35 Tax. Enter tax here and check if from ☐ Tax Tables or ☑ Schedule TC	35	11,330 —
	36 Additional taxes. (See page 11 of Instructions.) Enter total and check if from ☐ Form 4970, ☐ Form 4972, ☐ Form 5544, or ☐ Form 5405, or ☐ Section 72(m)(5) penalty tax . . . }	36	0
	37 **Total.** Add lines 35 and 36 . . . . ▶	37	11,330 —
Credits	38 Credit for contributions to candidates for public office . .	38	
	39 Credit for the elderly (attach Schedules R&RP)	39	
	40 Credit for child and dependent care expenses (attach Form 2441) .	40	
	41 Investment credit (attach Form 3468)	41	
	42 Foreign tax credit (attach Form 1116)	42	
	43 Work Incentive (WIN) Credit (attach Form 4874)	43	
	44 New jobs credit (attach Form 5884)	44	
	45 Residential energy credits (see page 12 of Instructions, attach Form 5695) . . .	45	
	46 **Total credits.** Add lines 38 through 45	46	0
	47 **Balance.** Subtract line 46 from line 37 and enter difference (but not less than zero) . ▶	47	11,330 —
Other Taxes	48 Self-employment tax (attach Schedule SE)	48	
	49 Minimum tax. Check here ▶ ☐ and attach Form 4625	49	
	50 Tax from recomputing prior-year investment credit (attach Form 4255)	50	
	51 Social security (FICA) tax on tip income not reported to employer (attach Form 4137) . .	51	
	52 Uncollected employee FICA and RRTA tax on tips (from Form W–2)	52	
	53 Tax on an IRA (attach Form 5329)	53	
	54 **Total tax.** Add lines 47 through 53 . . . . ▶	54	11,330 —
Payments Attach Forms W–2, W–2G, and W–2P to front.	55 Total Federal income tax withheld	55	
	56 1978 estimated tax payments and credit from 1977 return .	56	
	57 Earned income credit. If line 31 is under $8,000, see page 2 of Instructions. If eligible, enter child's name ▶	57	
	58 Amount paid with Form 4868	58	
	59 Excess FICA and RRTA tax withheld (two or more employers)	59	
	60 Credit for Federal tax on special fuels and oils (attach Form 4136) .	60	
	61 Regulated Investment Company credit (attach Form 2439)	61	
	62 **Total.** Add lines 55 through 61 . . . . ▶	62	
Refund or Due	63 If line 62 is larger than line 54, enter amount **OVERPAID** . . . . ▶	63	
	64 Amount of line 63 to be **REFUNDED TO YOU** . . . . ▶	64	
	65 Amount of line 63 to be credited on 1979 estimated tax . ▶	65	
	66 If line 54 is larger than line 62, enter **BALANCE DUE.** Attach check or money order for full amount payable to "Internal Revenue Service." Write your social security number on check or money order . . ▶ (Check ▶ ☐ if Form 2210 (2210F) is attached. See page 14 of instructions.) ▶ $	66	

Please Sign Here

Under penalties of perjury, I declare that I have examined this return, including accompanying schedules and statements, and to the best of my knowledge and belief, it is true, correct, and complete. Declaration of preparer (other than taxpayer) is based on all information of which preparer has any knowledge.

▶ Your signature	Date	▶ Spouse's signature (if filing jointly, BOTH must sign even if only one had income)

Paid Preparer's Information	Preparer's signature ▶	Preparer's social security no.	Check if self-employed ▶ ☐
	Firm's name (or yours, if self-employed), address and ZIP code ▶	E.I. No. ▶	
		Date ▶	

59

IT-201/208 New York State Income Tax **1978**
Resident Return

New York State Department of Taxation and Finance

With City of New York Personal Income Tax & Nonresident Earnings Tax

R

Or Fiscal Year Ended 1979

Page 1

PRINT OR TYPE

First name and initial (if joint or combined return, enter both) Last name	Your social security number	Occupation(s)
HENRY + GRETA HASSEL	000 00 0000	PROFESSOR, ARTIST
Home address (number and street or rural route) Apt. No.	Spouse's social security number	School district name
	000 00 0000	
City, village, post office and state ZIP code	County of residence	School district code

A) Change of State Residence—If you were a New York State resident for only part of the year, enter the number of months of residence in the box and attach Schedule CR-60.1 (see instructions page 18)

number of months

B) Filing Status — Check Only **One** Box — (1) ☐ Single (2) ☐ Unmarried Head of Household or Qualifying Widow(er) with dependent child
(3) ☐ Married filing joint Return (4) ☑ Married filing separately on **one** Return (5) ☐ Married filing separate Returns (on separate Forms)

If filing status (4) is checked, use Col. A and B. All others use Col. A.		Federal Amount		Column A		Column B	
1 Total Income (from page 2, Schedule A, line 16)	1	44,800	—	25,000	—	19,800	—
2 Net Additions or (Subtractions) (from page 2, Schedule C)	2			0		0	
3 Total New York Income (line 1, plus or (minus) line 2)	3			25,000		19,800	
4 NY Deduction — CHECK ONLY ONE BOX AND ENTER AMOUNT ▶ See inst. pg. 13. ☑ Standard Deduction OR ☐ Itemized Deduction	4			2,400	—	19,800	—
5 Line 3 minus line 4	5			22,600	—	19,800	—
6 Exemptions: Column A—Enter number claimed 3 x $650 ▶▶▶	6a			1,950	—		
Column B—Enter number claimed 1 x $650 ▶▶▶	6b					650	—
7 New York taxable income (line 5 minus line 6)	7			20,650	—	19,150	—
8 State Tax: a) on amount on line 7 (use NY State Tax Rate Schedule on pg. 14 of inst.)	8a			1,478	—	1,298	—
OR b) Maximum Tax (see inst. pg. 14, complete line 8c and attach Form IT-250)	8b						
c) Personal Service Taxable Income (enter amount from Form IT-250, line 11) 8c	Column A	Column B (only if used above)					
9 State Separate Tax on lump sum distribution (see instructions page 14)	9						
10 Line 8a OR 8b plus line 9	10						
11 Household Credit (see instructions page 15)	11						
12 Line 10 minus line 11	12						
13 Other State Credits (from page 2, Schedule D, line 4)	13						
14 Line 12 minus line 13	14						
15 State Minimum Income Tax (see instructions page 15 and attach Form IT-220)	15						
16 State Unincorporated Business Tax (attach Form IT-202)	16						
17 Total New York State Tax (add lines 14, 15 and 16)	17			1,478	—	1,298	—
18a City of NY Tax on amount on line 7 (Use City of NY Tax Rate Schedule on page 20 of inst.) (Full Year City Residents Only)	18a			506	75	454	25
18b City of NY Nonresident Earnings Tax (attach Form NYC-203)	18b						
18c Other City of NY Taxes (from page 2, Schedule NYC, line 4)	18c						
19 Add lines 17, 18a, 18b and 18c (total NY State and City of NY Tax)	19			1,984	75	1,752	25
Prepayments (attach Wage and Tax Statements to back)	Column A	Column B (only if used above)					
20 Real Property Tax Credit (attach Form IT-214) If any qualified member of household is age 65 or over, check box. ☐	20						
21 State Tax Withheld	21					$3,737.00	
22 State Estimated Tax Paid	22						
23 City Tax Withheld	23						
24 City Estimated Tax Paid (excluding City unincorporated business tax)	24						
25 Total (add lines 20 through 24)	25						
a) Enter line 25 totals in applicable column (see instructions page 18)	25a						
26 If line 19 is larger than line 25a enter Balance Due (Make check or money order payable to "NY State Income Tax")	26						
27 If line 25a is larger than line 19 enter Overpayment	27						
28 Amount of line 27 to be **REFUNDED TO YOU**	28						
29 Amount of line 27 to be cred- NY State	29				For office use only		
30 ited on 1979 estimated tax. City of NY	30						

Sign here ▶ Your signature   Date

▶ Spouse's signature (if filing joint or separately on one return, BOTH must sign)   Date

P

Signature of preparer other than taxpayer   Address   Date

Schedule NYC — Other City of NY Taxes		Column A	Column B
1 Part year City residents enter tax and attach Schedule CR-60.1	1		
2 City of NY Minimum Income Tax (see instructions page 13)	2		
3 City of NY Separate Tax on lump sum distribution (see instructions page 13)	3		
4 Total (add lines 1 through 3) Enter on page 1, line 18c	4		

Schedule A — Income and Adjustments — Complete the Federal Amount Column entering the items as they appear on your Federal return. Transfer the Total Federal Amount from line 16 to page 1, line 1, "Column A". Married Persons who file a joint Federal return and are filing separate NY Returns on **one** form must also complete Columns (A) and (B). Enter the amounts which would have been reportable had you filed separate Federal returns. Transfer line 16 totals to page 1, line 1.

		Federal Amount	A) Husband	B) Wife
1 Wages, salaries, tips, and other employee compensation	1	43,000 —	25,000 —	18,000 —
2 Interest income	2	1,000 —	0	1,000 —
3 Dividends (after exclusion)	3	800 —	0	800 —
4 State and local income tax refunds	4			
5 Alimony received	5			
6 Business income (attach copy of Federal Schedule C, Form 1040)	6			
7 Sale or exchange of capital assets (attach copy of Federal Schedule D, Form 1040)	7			
8 50% of capital gain distributions	8			
9 Sale or exchange of property other than capital assets, etc.	9			
10 Fully taxable pensions and annuities	10			
11a Pensions and annuities	11a			
11b Rents and royalties	11b			
11c Partnerships, estates and trusts and small business corporations	11c			
12 Farm income (attach copy of Federal Schedule F, Form 1040)	12			
13 Other income	13			
14 Total (add lines 1 through 13)	14			
15 Adjustments (including disability income exclusion)	15			
16 Total Income (line 14 minus line 15. Enter on page 1, line 1)	16	44,800 —	25,000 —	19,800 —

NOTE: If husband and wife are filing separate returns on **one** Form and the total of (A) and (B) is not equal to the Federal amount, attach explanation.

Schedule B — Itemized Deductions — Enter on lines 1 through 7 the items below as they appear on your Federal Return and make the applicable modifications on lines 8 and 10.
Disregard if standard deduction is claimed.

1 Medical and dental exp.	
2 Taxes	
3 Interest	
4 Contributions	
5 Casualty or theft losses	
6 Miscellaneous	
7 Total Federal itemized deductions (see inst.)	
8 Subtract income taxes included in line 2	
9 Line 7 minus line 8	
10 Other modifications (see instructions page 9 and attach schedule)	
11 NY itemized deduction Enter on page 1, line 4	

Reminder: Mail your Return to—
NY State Income Tax
The State Campus
Albany, New York 12227

Schedule C — Additions or (Subtractions) — Enter explanation of page 1, line 2 items. If filing status 4 is checked indicate H (husband's) or W (wife's) for page 1, line 2 items. See instructions page 9.

Explanation	Amount
Net Additions or (Subtractions) (Enter on page 1, line 2)	

If you need more space, attach schedule marked Schedule C.

Schedule D — Other NY State Tax Credits (see instructions page 12)

1 Regular Credits	Column A	Column B
a Resident credit—(See inst. pg. 12) (Attach copy of other state return(s). Form IT-112R and, if applicable, Form IT-112.1)		
b Accumulation distribution credit (attach computation)		
c NY State child care credit (from instructions page 12)		
d Catalyst credit (See inst. pg. 12)		
2 Add lines 1a through 1d		
3 Investment credit (attach Form IT-212)		
4 Total credits (line 2 plus line 3) Enter on page 1, line 13		

TAX RATE SCHEDULES: FOR NY STATE SEE PAGE 14 OF INSTRUCTIONS; FOR CITY OF NY SEE PAGE 20.
43 (8/78) 13,000M(0879)

61

WITH $10,000 REAL ESTATE
TAX SHELTER

Form 1040 — U.S. Individual Income Tax Return 1978

Department of the Treasury—Internal Revenue Service

For Privacy Act Notice, see page 3 of Instructions | For the year January 1–December 31, 1978, or other tax year beginning _____, 1978, ending _____, 19 ___.

Use IRS label. Otherwise, please print or type.		
Your first name and initial (if joint return, also give spouse's name and initial) **HENRY + GRETA**	Last name **HASSEL**	Your social security number **000 00 0000**
Present home address (Number and street, including apartment number, or rural route)		Spouse's social security no. **000 00 0000**
City, town or post office, State and ZIP code		Your occupation **PROFESSOR**

Do you want $1 to go to the Presidential Election Campaign Fund? Yes ☐ No ☐
If joint return, does your spouse want $1 to go to this fund? . . Yes ☐ No ☐

Note: Checking Yes will not increase your tax or reduce your refund.

Spouse's occupation **ARTIST**

Filing Status

Check only one box.

1. ☐ Single
2. ✓ Married filing joint return (even if only one had income)
3. ☐ Married filing separate return. If spouse is also filing, give spouse's social security number in the space above and enter full name here ▶
4. ☐ Unmarried head of household. Enter qualifying name ▶ _____. See page 6 of Instructions.
5. ☐ Qualifying widow(er) with dependent child (Year spouse died ▶ 19 ___). See page 6 of Instructions.

Exemptions

Always check the box labeled Yourself. Check other boxes if they apply.

6a ✓ Yourself   ☐ 65 or over   ☐ Blind } Enter number of boxes checked on 6a and b ▶ **2**

b ✓ Spouse   ☐ 65 or over   ☐ Blind

c First names of your dependent children who lived with you ▶ **EDGAR, EMMA** } Enter number of children listed ▶ **2**

d Other dependents: (1) Name	(2) Relationship	(3) Number of months lived in your home	(4) Did dependent have income of $750 or more?	(5) Did you provide more than one-half of dependent's support?	
					Enter number of other dependents ▶

7 Total number of exemptions claimed . . . . } Add numbers entered in boxes above ▶ **4**

Income

Please attach Copy B of your Forms W–2 here.

If you do not have a W–2, see page 5 of Instructions.

Please attach check or money order here.

8 Wages, salaries, tips, and other employee compensation	8	43,000 —
9 Interest income (If over $400, attach Schedule B)	9	1,000 —
10a Dividends (If over $400, attach Schedule B) . 1,000 — , 10b Exclusion 200 —		
10c Subtract line 10b from line 10a	10c	800 —
11 State and local income tax refunds (does not apply unless refund is for year you itemized deductions)	11	0
12 Alimony received	12	0
13 Business income or (loss) (attach Schedule C)	13	
14 Capital gain or (loss) (attach Schedule D)	14	
15 Taxable part of capital gain distributions not reported on Schedule D (see page 9 of Instructions) . .	15	
16 Net gain or (loss) from Supplemental Schedule of Gains and Losses (attach Form 4797)	16	
17 Fully taxable pensions and annuities not reported on Schedule E	17	
18 Pensions, annuities, rents, royalties, partnerships, estates or trusts, etc. (attach Schedule E)	18	(10,000 —)
19 Farm income or (loss) (attach Schedule F)	19	
20 Other income (state nature and source—see page 10 of Instructions) ▶ _____	20	
21 Total income. Add lines 8, 9, and 10c through 20 . . . . ▶	21	34,800 —

Adjustments to Income

22 Moving expense (attach Form 3903)	22	
23 Employee business expenses (attach Form 2106) . .	23	
24 Payments to an IRA (see page 10 of Instructions)	24	
25 Payments to a Keogh (H.R. 10) retirement plan . .	25	
26 Interest penalty due to early withdrawal of savings	26	
27 Alimony paid (see page 10 of Instructions)	27	
28 Total adjustments. Add lines 22 through 27 . . . . ▶	28	0

Adjusted Gross Income

29 Subtract line 28 from line 21	29	34,800 —
30 Disability income exclusion (attach Form 2440)	30	0
31 Adjusted gross income. Subtract line 30 from line 29. If this line is less than $8,000, see page 2 of Instructions. If you want IRS to figure your tax, see page 4 of Instructions . . . . ▶	31	34,800 —

☆ U.S. GOVERNMENT PRINTING OFFICE: 1978—O-263-303 13-2687299

Form 1040 (1978)

Name(s) as shown on Form 1040 (Do not enter name and social security number if shown on other side)	Your social security number
HENRY + GRETA HASSEL	000 00 0000

Part I   Interest Income

1 If you received more than **$400** in interest, **Complete Part I.** Please see page 8 of the instructions to find out what interest to report. Then answer the questions in Part III, below. If you received interest as a nominee for another, or you received or paid accrued interest on securities transferred between interest payment dates, please see page 18 of the instructions.

Name of payer	Amount	
FRIENDLY SAVINGS + LOAN	1,000	—

2 Total interest income. Enter here and on Form 1040, line 9 . . . .

Part II   Dividend Income

3 If you received more than **$400** in gross dividends (including capital gain distributions) and other distributions on stock, **complete Part II.** Please see page 9 of the instructions. Write (H), (W), (J), for stock held by husband, wife, or jointly. Then answer the questions in Part III, below. If you received dividends as a nominee for another, please see page 18 of the instructions.

Name of payer	Amount	
KIDDSTUFF, INC.	500	—
BOARDROOM ENTERPRISES	500	—

	Amount	
4 Total of line 3	1,000	—
5 Capital gain distributions. Enter here and on Schedule D, line 7. See Note below . . .	0	
6 Nontaxable distributions	0	
7 Total (add lines 5 and 6)	0	
8 Dividends before exclusion (subtract line 7 from line 4). Enter here and on Form 1040, line 10a	1,000	—

B

Part III   Foreign Accounts and Foreign Trusts

If you are required to list interest in Part I or dividends in Part II, OR if you had a foreign account or were a grantor of, or a transferor to a foreign trust, you must answer both questions in Part III. Please see page 18 of the instructions.

	Yes	No
A Did you, at any time during the taxable year, have an interest in or signature or other authority over a bank, securities, or other financial account in a foreign country (see page 18 of instructions)? . . .		
B Were you the grantor of, or transferor to, a foreign trust during any taxable year, which foreign trust was in being during the current taxable year, whether or not you have any beneficial interest in such trust? . . If "Yes," you may be required to file Forms 3520, 3520-A, or 926.		

Note: If you received capital gain distributions and do not need Schedule D to report any other gains or losses or to compute the alternative tax, do not file that schedule. Instead, enter the taxable part of capital gain distributions on Form 1040, line 15.

☆ U.S. Government Printing Office: 1978—O—263-309—E.I. # 52-0237640

63

SCHEDULE E
(Form 1040)
Department of the Treasury
Internal Revenue Service

Supplemental Income Schedule

(From pensions and annuities, rents and royalties, partnerships, estates and trusts, etc.)
▶ Attach to Form 1040.   ▶ See Instructions for Schedule E (Form 1040).

1978

Name(s) as shown on Form 1040	Your social security number
HENRY + GRETA HASSEL	000 00 0000

Part I **Pension and Annuity Income.** If fully taxable, do not complete this part. Enter amount on Form 1040, line 17. For one pension or annuity not fully taxable, complete this part. If you have more than one pension or annuity that is not fully taxable, attach a separate sheet listing each one with the appropriate data and enter combined total of taxable portions on line 5.

1 Name of payer ▶ ....

2 Did your employer contribute part of the cost? . . . . ☐ Yes ☐ No

  If "Yes," is your contribution recoverable within 3 years of the annuity starting date? . . . . ☐ Yes ☐ No

  If "Yes," show: Your contribution ▶ $................., Contribution recovered in prior years ▶ | **2** | |

3 Amount received this year . . . . | **3** | |

4 Amount excludable this year . . . . | **4** | |

5 Taxable portion (subtract line 4 from line 3) . . . . | **5** | |

Part II **Rent and Royalty Income.** If you need more space, use Form 4831.

Have you claimed expenses connected with your vacation home (or other dwelling unit) rented to others (see instructions)? . . . . . ☐ Yes ☐ No
If "Yes," did you or a member of your family occupy the vacation home (or other dwelling unit) for more than 14 days during the taxable year? ☐ Yes ☐ No

(a) Kind and location of property If residential, also write "R"	(b) Total amount of rents	(c) Total amount of royalties	(d) Depreciation (explain below) or depletion (attach computation)	(e) Other expenses (Repairs, etc.— explain below)
----------------	--------	--------	--------	--------
----------------	--------	--------	--------	--------
----------------	--------	--------	--------	--------
----------------	--------	--------	--------	--------

6 Totals . . . .

7 Net income or (loss) from rents and royalties (column (b) plus column (c) less columns (d) and (e)) . | **7** | |

8 Net rental income or (loss) (from Form 4831) . . . . | **8** | |

9 Net farm rental profit or (loss) (from Form 4835) . . . . . . | **9** | |

10 Total rent and royalty income or (loss) (add lines 7, 8, and 9) . . . . | **10** | |

Part III **Income or Losses from—**

(a) Name	(b) Employer identification number	(c) Your share of gross farming or fishing income (see instructions)	(d) Loss	(e) Income
Partnerships				
REAL ESTATE PARTNERS	00-0000000	0	(10,000)	0

11 Add amounts in columns (d) and (e) . . . . | **11** | (10,000) | | 0 |
12 Column (e), line 11, less column (d), line 11 . . . . | **12** | | (10,000 —) |
13 Additional first-year depreciation . . . . | **13** | | 0 |
14 Total partnership income or (loss). Combine lines 12 and 13 . . . . | **14** | | (10,000 —) |

Estates or Trusts				

15 Add amounts in columns (d) and (e) . . . . | **15** | |
16 Total estate or trust income or (loss). Column (e), line 15, less column (d), line 15 . . . . . | **16** | |

Small Bus. Corps.				

17 Add amounts in columns (d) and (e) . . . . | **17** | |
18 Total small business corporation income or (loss). (Column (e), line 17, less column (d), line 17 . | **18** | |

19 TOTAL (add lines 5, 10, 14, 16, and 18). Enter here and on Form 1040, line 18 . . . . ▶ | **19** | |

Explanation of Column (e), Part II

Item	Amount	Item	Amount	Item	Amount
--------	--------	--------	--------	--------	--------
--------	--------	--------	--------	--------	--------

Schedule for Depreciation Claimed in Part II above. If you need more space use Form 4562.

(a) Description of property	(b) Date acquired	(c) Cost or other basis	(d) Depreciation allowed or allowable in prior years	(e) Method of computing depreciation	(f) Life or rate	(g) Depreciation for this year	**E**
1 Total additional first-year depreciation (do not include in items below) ▶							
----------------	----	----	----	----	----	----	
----------------	----	----	----	----	----	----	
----------------	----	----	----	----	----	----	
2 Totals	. . . .						

☆ U.S. GOVERNMENT PRINTING OFFICE : 1978-O-203-278-E.I. NO. 52-1074467

Tax Compu-tation	32 Amount from line 31	32	34,800 —
	33 If you do not itemize deductions, enter zero . . . . ⎫ If you itemize, complete Schedule A (Form 1040) and enter the amount from Schedule A, line 41 . . . ⎬	33	0
	Caution: If you have unearned income and can be claimed as a dependent on your parent's return, check here ▶ ☐ and see page 11 of the Instructions. Also see page 11 of the Instructions if: • You are married filing a separate return and your spouse itemizes deductions, OR • You file Form 4563, OR • You are a dual-status alien.		
	34 Subtract line 33 from line 32. Use the amount on line 34 to find your tax from the Tax Tables, or to figure your tax on Schedule TC, Part I . . . . Use Schedule TC, Part I, and the Tax Rate Schedules ONLY if: • The amount on line 34 is more than $20,000 ($40,000 if you checked Filing Status Box 2 or 5), OR • You have more exemptions than those covered in the Tax Table for your filing status, OR • You use any of these forms to figure your tax: Schedule D, Schedule G, or Form 4726. Otherwise, you MUST use the Tax Tables to find your tax.	34	34,800 —
	35 Tax. Enter tax here and check if from ☑ Tax Tables or ☐ Schedule TC MINIMUM TAX	35	7,144 —
	36 Additional taxes. (See page 11 of Instructions.) Enter total and check if from ☐ Form 4970, ⎫ ☐ Form 4972, ☐ Form 5544, ☐ Form 5405, or ☐ Section 72(m)(5) penalty tax . . . ⎬	36	0
	37 **Total.** Add lines 35 and 36 . . . . ▶	37	7,144 —
Credits	38 Credit for contributions to candidates for public office . . [38]		
	39 Credit for the elderly (attach Schedules R&RP) . . . . . . [39]		
	40 Credit for child and dependent care expenses (attach Form 2441) . [40]		
	41 Investment credit (attach Form 3468) . . . . [41]		
	42 Foreign tax credit (attach Form 1116) . . . . [42]		
	43 Work Incentive (WIN) Credit (attach Form 4874) . . . . . [43]		
	44 New jobs credit (attach Form 5884) . . . . [44]		
	45 Residential energy credits (see page 12 of Instructions, attach Form 5695) . . [45]		
	46 **Total credits.** Add lines 38 through 45	46	0
	47 **Balance.** Subtract line 46 from line 37 and enter difference (but not less than zero) . ▶	47	7,144 —
Other Taxes	48 Self-employment tax (attach Schedule SE)	48	
	49 Minimum tax. Check here ▶ ☐ and attach Form 4625	49	
	50 Tax from recomputing prior-year investment credit (attach Form 4255)	50	
	51 Social security (FICA) tax on tip income not reported to employer (attach Form 4137) . .	51	
	52 Uncollected employee FICA and RRTA tax on tips (from Form W–2)	52	
	53 Tax on an IRA (attach Form 5329)	53	
	54 **Total tax.** Add lines 47 through 53 . . . . ▶	54	7,144 —
Payments Attach Forms W–2, W–2G, and W–2P to front.	55 Total Federal income tax withheld . . . . [55]		
	56 1978 estimated tax payments and credit from 1977 return . [56]		
	57 Earned income credit. If line 31 is under $8,000, see page 2 of Instructions. If eligible, enter child's name ▶............... [57]		
	58 Amount paid with Form 4868 . . . . [58]		
	59 Excess FICA and RRTA tax withheld (two or more employers) [59]		
	60 Credit for Federal tax on special fuels and oils (attach Form 4136) . [60]		
	61 Regulated Investment Company credit (attach Form 2439) [61]		
	62 **Total.** Add lines 55 through 61 . . . . ▶	62	
Refund or Due	63 If line 62 is larger than line 54, enter amount OVERPAID . . . . ▶	63	
	64 Amount of line 63 to be REFUNDED TO YOU . . . . ▶	64	
	65 Amount of line 63 to be credited on 1979 estimated tax . ▶ [65]		
	66 If line 54 is larger than line 62, enter BALANCE DUE. Attach check or money order for full amount payable to "Internal Revenue Service." Write your social security number on check or money order . . ▶ (Check ▶ ☐ if Form 2210 (2210F) is attached. See page 14 of instructions.) ▶ $	66	

Please Sign Here

Under penalties of perjury, I declare that I have examined this return, including accompanying schedules and statements, and to the best of my knowledge and belief, it is true, correct, and complete. Declaration of preparer (other than taxpayer) is based on all information of which preparer has any knowledge.

▶ Your signature	Date	▶ Spouse's signature (if filing jointly, BOTH must sign even if only one had income)

Paid Preparer's Information	Preparer's signature ▶		Preparer's social security no.	Check if self-employed ▶ ☐
	Firm's name (or yours, if self-employed), address and ZIP code ▶		E.I. No. ▶	
			Date ▶	

65

IT-201/208 New York State Income Tax **1978**
Resident Return

New York State Department of Taxation and Finance

With City of New York Personal Income Tax & Nonresident Earnings Tax

R

Or Fiscal Year Ended 1979

Page 1

PRINT OR TYPE	First name and initial (if joint or combined return, enter both) Last name	Your social security number	Occupation(s)
	HENRY + GRETA HASSEL	000 00 0000	PROFESSOR, ARTIST
	Home address (number and street or rural route) Apt. No.	Spouse's social security number	School district name
		000 00 0000	
	City, village, post office and state ZIP code	County of residence	School district code

A) Change of State Residence—If you were a New York State resident for only part of the year, enter the number of months of residence in the box and attach Schedule CR-60.1 (see instructions page 18) ▶   [number of months]

B) Filing Status — Check Only **One** Box —
(1) ☐ Single   (2) ☐ Unmarried Head of Household or Qualifying Widow(er) with dependent child
(3) ☐ Married filing joint Return   (4) ☑ Married filing separately on **one** Return   (5) ☐ Married filing separate Returns (on separate Forms)

If filing status (4) is checked, use Col. A and B. All others use Col. A.

			Federal Amount	Column A	Column B
1	Total Income (from page 2, Schedule A, line 16)	1	34,800 —	20,000 —	14,800 —
2	Net Additions or (Subtractions) (from page 2, Schedule C)	2		0	0
3	Total New York Income (line 1, plus or (minus) line 2)	3		20,000 —	14,800 —
4	NY Deduction — CHECK ONLY ONE BOX AND ENTER AMOUNT ▶ See inst. pg. 13. ☑ Standard Deduction **OR** ☐ Itemized Deduction	4		2,400 —	0 —
5	Line 3 minus line 4	5		17,600 —	14,800 —
6	Exemptions: Column A—Enter number claimed 3 x $650 ▶▶▶	6a		1,950 —	
	Column B—Enter number claimed 1 x $650 ▶▶▶	6b			650 —
7	New York taxable income (line 5 minus line 6)	7		15,650 —	14,150 —
8	State Tax: a) on amount on line 7 (use NY State Tax Rate Schedule on pg. 14 of inst.)	8a		925 —	783 50
	OR b) Maximum Tax (see inst. pg. 14, complete line 8c and attach Form IT-250)	8b			
	c) Personal Service Taxable Income (enter amount from Form IT-250, line 11) Column A Column B (only if used above)	8c			
9	State Separate Tax on lump sum distribution (see instructions page 14)	9			
10	Line 8a OR 8b plus line 9	10			
11	Household Credit (see instructions page 15)	11			
12	Line 10 minus line 11	12			
13	Other State Credits (from page 2, Schedule D, line 4)	13			
14	Line 12 minus line 13	14			
15	State Minimum Income Tax (see instructions page 15 and attach Form IT-220)	15			
16	State Unincorporated Business Tax (attach Form IT-202)	16			
17	Total New York State Tax (add lines 14, 15 and 16)	17		925 —	783 50
18a	City of NY Tax on amount on line 7 (Use City of NY Tax Rate Schedule on page 20 of inst.) (Full Year City Residents Only)	18a		341 15	296 35
18b	City of NY Nonresident Earnings Tax (attach Form NYC-203)	18b			
18c	Other City of NY Taxes (from page 2, Schedule NYC, line 4)	18c			
19	Add lines 17, 18a, 18b and 18c (total NY State and City of NY Tax)	19		1,266 15	1,079 85

Prepayments (attach Wage and Tax Statements to back)   Column A   Column B (only if used above)

20	Real Property Tax Credit (attach Form IT-214) If any qualified member of household is age 65 or over, check box. ☐	20		
21	State Tax Withheld	21		$2,346.00
22	State Estimated Tax Paid	22		
23	City Tax Withheld	23		
24	City Estimated Tax Paid (excluding City unincorporated business tax)	24		
25	Total (add lines 20 through 24)	25		
	a) Enter line 25 totals in applicable column (see instructions page 18)	25a		
26	If line 19 is larger than line 25a enter Balance Due (Make check or money order payable to "NY State Income Tax")	26		
27	If line 25a is larger than line 19 enter Overpayment	27		
28	Amount of line 27 to be REFUNDED TO YOU	28		
29	Amount of line 27 to be credited on 1979 estimated tax. NY State	29		For office use only
30	City of NY	30		

Sign here ▶ Your signature   Date

Spouse's signature (if filing joint or separately on one return, BOTH must sign)   Date

Signature of preparer other than taxpayer   Address   Date   P

66

Schedule NYC — Other City of NY Taxes		Column A	Column B
1 Part year City residents enter tax and attach Schedule CR-60.1	1		
2 City of NY Minimum Income Tax (see instructions page 13)	2		
3 City of NY Separate Tax on lump sum distribution (see instructions page 13)	3		
4 Total (add lines 1 through 3) Enter on page 1, line 18c	4		

Schedule A — Income and Adjustments — Complete the Federal Amount Column entering the items as they appear on your Federal return. Transfer the Total Federal Amount from line 16 to page 1, line 1, "Column A". <u>Married Persons</u> who file a joint Federal return and are filing separate NY Returns on <u>one</u> form must also complete Columns (A) and (B). Enter the amounts which would have been reportable had you filed separate Federal returns. Transfer line 16 totals to page 1, line 1.

		Federal Amount	A) Husband	B) Wife
1 Wages, salaries, tips, and other employee compensation	1	43,000 —	25,000 —	18,000 —
2 Interest income	2	1,000 —	0	1,000 —
3 Dividends (after exclusion)	3	800 —	0	800 —
4 State and local income tax refunds	4			
5 Alimony received	5			
6 Business income (attach copy of Federal Schedule C, Form 1040)	6			
7 Sale or exchange of capital assets (attach copy of Federal Schedule D, Form 1040)	7			
8 50% of capital gain distributions	8			
9 Sale or exchange of property other than capital assets, etc.	9			
10 Fully taxable pensions and annuities	10			
11a Pensions and annuities — Enter the appropriate amounts	11a			
11b Rents and royalties — from Federal Schedule E, Form	11b			
11c Partnerships, estates and trusts and small business corporations — 1040 on lines 11a, 11b and 11c and attach a copy of Schedule E.	11c	(10,000 —)	(5,000 —)	(5,000 —)
12 Farm income (attach copy of Federal Schedule F, Form 1040)	12			
13 Other income	13			
14 Total (add lines 1 through 13)	14			
15 Adjustments (including disability income exclusion)	15			
16 Total Income (line 14 minus line 15. Enter on page 1, line 1)	16	34,800 —	20,000 —	14,800 —

NOTE: If husband and wife are filing separate returns on <u>one</u> Form and the total of (A) and (B) is not equal to the Federal amount, attach explanation.

Schedule B — Itemized Deductions — Enter on lines 1 through 7 the items below as they appear on your Federal Return and make the applicable modifications on lines 8 and 10.
Disregard if standard deduction is claimed.

1 Medical and dental exp.		
2 Taxes		
3 Interest		
4 Contributions		
5 Casualty or theft losses		
6 Miscellaneous		
7 Total Federal itemized deductions (see inst.)		
8 Subtract income taxes included in line 2		
9 Line 7 minus line 8		
10 Other modifications (see instructions page 9 and attach schedule)		
11 NY itemized deduction Enter on page 1, line 4		

Reminder: Mail your Return to—
NY State Income Tax
The State Campus
Albany, New York 12227

Schedule C — Additions or (Subtractions) — Enter explanation of page 1, line 2 items. If filing status 4 is checked indicate H (husband's) or W (wife's) for page 1, line 2 items. See instructions page 9.

Explanation	Amount

Net Additions or (Subtractions)(Enter on page 1, line 2)
If you need more space, attach schedule marked Schedule C.

Schedule D — Other NY State Tax Credits (see instructions page 12)

1 Regular Credits	Column A	Column B
a Resident credit—(See inst. pg. 12) (Attach copy of other state return(s), Form IT-112R and, if applicable, Form IT-112.1)		
b Accumulation distribution credit (attach computation)		
c NY State child care credit (from instructions page 12)		
d Catalyst credit (See inst. pg. 12)		
2 Add lines 1a through 1d		
3 Investment credit (attach Form IT-212)		
4 Total credits (line 2 plus line 3) Enter on page 1, line 13		

TAX RATE SCHEDULES: FOR NY STATE SEE PAGE 14 OF INSTRUCTIONS; FOR CITY OF NY SEE PAGE 20.
◄●▬ 43   (8/78) 13,000M(0879)

Form 1040

Department of the Treasury—Internal Revenue Service

U.S. Individual Income Tax Return 1978

| For Privacy Act Notice, see page 3 of Instructions | For the year January 1–December 31, 1978, or other tax year beginning | , 1978, ending | , 19 . |

Use IRS label. Otherwise, please print or type.	Your first name and initial (if joint return, also give spouse's name and initial) MARIA	Last name BEAUMONT	Your social security number 000 00 0000
	Present home address (Number and street, including apartment number, or rural route)		Spouse's social security no.
	City, town or post office, State and ZIP code		Your occupation INVESTOR
			Spouse's occupation

Do you want $1 to go to the Presidential Election Campaign Fund?   Yes ☐   No ☐
If joint return, does your spouse want $1 to go to this fund? . .   Yes ☐   No ☐

Note: Checking Yes will not increase your tax or reduce your refund.

Filing Status

Check only one box.

1 ☐ Single
2 ☐ Married filing joint return (even if only one had income)
3 ☐ Married filing separate return. If spouse is also filing, give spouse's social security number in the space above and enter full name here ▶
4 ☐ Unmarried head of household. Enter qualifying name ▶ . . . . See page 6 of Instructions.
5 ☐ Qualifying widow(er) with dependent child (Year spouse died ▶ 19). See page 6 of Instructions.

Exemptions

Always check the box labeled Yourself. Check other boxes if they apply.

6a ☑ Yourself   ☐ 65 or over   ☐ Blind   } Enter number of boxes checked on 6a and b ▶ | 1 |

b ☐ Spouse   ☐ 65 or over   ☐ Blind

c First names of your dependent children who lived with you ▶ . . . . } Enter number of children listed ▶

d Other dependents: (1) Name	(2) Relationship	(3) Number of months lived in your home	(4) Did dependent have income of $750 or more?	(5) Did you provide more than one-half of dependent's support?

Enter number of other dependents ▶

Add numbers entered in boxes above ▶ | 1 |

7 Total number of exemptions claimed . . . .

Income

Please attach Copy B of your Forms W–2 here.

If you do not have a W–2, see page 5 of Instructions.

Please attach check or money order here.

8	Wages, salaries, tips, and other employee compensation	8	0
9	Interest income (If over $400, attach Schedule B)	9	10,000 —
10a	Dividends (If over $400, attach Schedule B) . . 40,000 —, 10b Exclusion . . 100		
10c	Subtract line 10b from line 10a	10c	39,900 —
11	State and local income tax refunds (does not apply unless refund is for year you itemized deductions)	11	0
12	Alimony received	12	0
13	Business income or (loss) (attach Schedule C)	13	0
14	Capital gain or (loss) (attach Schedule D)	14	0
15	Taxable part of capital gain distributions not reported on Schedule D (see page 9 of Instructions) . .	15	0
16	Net gain or (loss) from Supplemental Schedule of Gains and Losses (attach Form 4797)	16	0
17	Fully taxable pensions and annuities not reported on Schedule E	17	0
18	Pensions, annuities, rents, royalties, partnerships, estates or trusts, etc. (attach Schedule E)	18	0
19	Farm income or (loss) (attach Schedule F)	19	0
20	Other income (state nature and source—see page 10 of Instructions) ▶	20	0
21	Total income. Add lines 8, 9, and 10c through 20 . . . . ▶	21	49,900 —

Adjustments to Income

22	Moving expense (attach Form 3903)	22	
23	Employee business expenses (attach Form 2106) . .	23	
24	Payments to an IRA (see page 10 of Instructions)	24	
25	Payments to a Keogh (H.R. 10) retirement plan . . .	25	
26	Interest penalty due to early withdrawal of savings	26	
27	Alimony paid (see page 10 of Instructions)	27	
28	Total adjustments. Add lines 22 through 27 . . . . ▶	28	0

Adjusted Gross Income

29	Subtract line 28 from line 21	29	49,900 —
30	Disability income exclusion (attach Form 2440)	30	0
31	Adjusted gross income. Subtract line 30 from line 29. If this line is less than $8,000, see page 2 of Instructions. If you want IRS to figure your tax, see page 4 of Instructions . . . . ▶	31	49,900 —

☆ U.S. GOVERNMENT PRINTING OFFICE: 1978—O-263-303 13-2687299

Form 1040 (1978)

68

Name(s) as shown on Form 1040 (Do not enter name and social security number if shown on other side) | Your social security number

MARIA BEAUMONT   000 00 0000

Part I   Interest Income

1 If you received more than $400 in interest, Complete Part I. Please see page 8 of the instructions to find out what interest to report. Then answer the questions in Part III, below. If you received interest as a nominee for another, or you received or paid accrued interest on securities transferred between interest payment dates, please see page 18 of the instructions.

Name of payer	Amount	
ABC BANK	3,500	—
DEF BANK	3,500	—
GHI BANK	650	—
JKL 4¼s OF 2001	850	—
MNO 8s OF 1984	800	—
PQR 7s OF 1984	700	—

| 2 Total interest income. Enter here and on Form 1040, line 9 . . . . | 10,000 | — |

Part II   Dividend Income

3 If you received more than $400 in gross dividends (including capital gain distributions) and other distributions on stock, complete Part II. Please see page 9 of the instructions. Write (H), (W), (J), for stock held by husband, wife, or jointly. Then answer the questions in Part III, below. If you received dividends as a nominee for another, please see page 18 of the instructions.

Name of payer	Amount	
ABC INDUSTRIES	5,000	—
DEF, INC.	5,000	—
GHI SONICS	5,000	—
GENERAL INCORPORATED	5,000	—
BOVASONICS	10,000	—
KIDDSTUFF, INC.	10,000	—

4 Total of line 3	40,000	—
5 Capital gain distributions. Enter here and on Schedule D, line 7. See Note below . . .	0	
6 Nontaxable distributions	0	
7 Total (add lines 5 and 6)	0	
8 Dividends before exclusion (subtract line 7 from line 4). Enter here and on Form 1040, line 10a	40,000	—

B

Part III   Foreign Accounts and Foreign Trusts

If you are required to list interest in Part I or dividends in Part II, OR if you had a foreign account or were a grantor of, or a transferor to a foreign trust, you must answer both questions in Part III. Please see page 18 of the instructions.

	Yes	No
A Did you, at any time during the taxable year, have an interest in or signature or other authority over a bank, securities, or other financial account in a foreign country (see page 18 of instructions)? . . .		
B Were you the grantor of, or transferor to, a foreign trust during any taxable year, which foreign trust was in being during the current taxable year, whether or not you have any beneficial interest in such trust? . If "Yes," you may be required to file Forms 3520, 3520–A, or 926.		

Note: If you received capital gain distributions and do not need Schedule D to report any other gains or losses or to compute the alternative tax, do not file that schedule. Instead, enter the taxable part of capital gain distributions on Form 1040, line 15.

☆ U.S. Government Printing Office: 1978—O—263-309—E.I. # 52-0237640

SCHEDULE TC
(Form 1040)
Department of the Treasury
Internal Revenue Service

Tax Computation Schedule

▶ Attach to Form 1040.

1978

Name(s) as shown on Form 1040	Your social security number
MARIA BEAUMONT	000 : 00 : 0000

Part I   Computation of Tax for Taxpayers Who Cannot Use the Tax Tables

Use this part to figure your tax if:

● Your income on Form 1040, line 34, is more than $20,000 and you checked Filing Status Box 1, 3, or 4 on Form 1040.
● Your income on Form 1040, line 34, is more than $40,000 and you checked Filing Status Box 2 or 5 on Form 1040.

● You had more exemptions than were covered in the Tax Table for your filing status.
● You figure your tax using the alternative tax computation on Schedule D (Capital Gains and Losses), Schedule G (Income Averaging), or Form 4726 (Maximum Tax on Personal Service Income).

1 Enter the amount from Form 1040, line 34	**1**	49,900	—
2 Multiply $750 by the total number of exemptions claimed on Form 1040, line 7	**2**	750	—
3 Taxable Income. Subtract line 2 from line 1. (Figure your tax on this amount by using the Tax Rate Schedules or one of the other methods listed on line 4.)	**3**	49,150	—
4 Income Tax. Enter tax and check if from: ☑ Tax Rate Schedule X, Y, or Z, ☐ Schedule D, ☐ Schedule G, or ☐ Form 4726	**4**	18,360	—

General Tax Credit

5 Multiply $35 by the total number of exemptions claimed on Form 1040, line 7. (If you are married filing a separate return, skip lines 6 through 9 and enter the amount from line 5 on line 10.)	**5**	35 —			
6 Enter the amount from line 3, above	**6**	49,150 —			
7 Enter { $3,200 if you are married filing a joint return or a qualifying widow(er) / $2,200 if you are single or an unmarried head of household . . . }	**7**	2,200 —			
8 Subtract line 7 from line 6	**8**	46,950 —			
9 Enter 2% of line 8 (but do not enter more than $180)	**9**	180 —			

10 General tax credit. Enter the amount from line 5 or line 9, whichever is larger	**10**	180	—
11 Tax. Subtract line 10 from line 4. (If $0 or less, enter $0.) Enter this amount on Form 1040, line 35 . . . . ▶	**11**	18,180	—

Part II   Computation for Certain Taxpayers Who Must Itemize Deductions

If you are included in one of the groups below, you MUST itemize. If you must itemize and the amount on Schedule A (Form 1040), line 40, is more than your itemized deductions on Schedule A, line 39, you must complete Part II before figuring your tax.

You MUST itemize your deductions if:

A. You can be claimed as a dependent on your parent's return and had interest, dividends, or other unearned income of $750 or more and less than $2,200 of earned income if single (less than $1,600 if married filing a separate return).

Note: If your earned income is more than your itemized deductions on Schedule A, line 39, enter your earned income in Part II, line 3, of this schedule, unless you are married filing a separate return and your spouse itemizes deductions. Generally, your earned income is the total of any amounts on Form 1040, lines 8,

13, and 19. See page 11 of the Instructions for Form 1040 for more details.

B. You are married filing a separate return and your spouse itemizes deductions. (There is an exception to this rule. You don't have to itemize if your spouse must itemize only because he or she is described in A and enters earned income instead of itemized deductions on Part II, line 3, of this schedule. If this is the case, don't complete Part II. Go back to Form 1040, line 33, and enter $0. Then go to Form 1040, line 34.)

C. You file Form 4563 to exclude income from sources in U.S. possessions. (Please see Form 4563, and Publication 570, Tax Guide for U.S. Citizens Employed in U.S. Possessions, for more details.)

D. You had dual status as a nonresident alien for part of 1978, and during the rest of the year you were either a resident alien or a U.S. citizen. However, you don't have to itemize if at the end of 1978, you were married to a U.S. resident or citizen and file a joint return reporting your combined worldwide income.

1 Enter the amount from Form 1040, line 31	**1**	
2 Enter the amount from Schedule A, line 40	**2**	
3 Enter the amount from Schedule A, line 39	**3**	
Caution: If you can be claimed as a dependent on your parent's return, see the Note above. Be sure you check the box below line 33 of Form 1040.		
4 Subtract line 3 from line 2	**4**	
5 Add lines 1 and 4. Enter here and on Form 1040, line 34. (Leave Form 1040, line 33 blank. Disregard the instruction to subtract line 33 from line 32. Follow the rest of the instructions for Form 1040, line 34.) . . . . ▶	**5**	

☆ U.S. GOVERNMENT PRINTING OFFICE: 1978— 263-331   23-188-5979

70

Tax Compu-tation	32 Amount from line 31	32	49,900 —
	33 If you do not itemize deductions, enter zero . . . . } If you itemize, complete Schedule A (Form 1040) and enter the amount from Schedule A, line 41 . . . . }	33	0
	Caution: If you have unearned income and can be claimed as a dependent on your parent's return, check here ▶ ☐ and see page 11 of the Instructions. Also see page 11 of the Instructions if: • You are married filing a separate return and your spouse itemizes deductions, OR • You file Form 4563, OR • You are a dual-status alien.		
	34 Subtract line 33 from line 32. Use the amount on line 34 to find your tax from the Tax Tables, or to figure your tax on Schedule TC, Part I . . . . Use Schedule TC, Part I, and the Tax Rate Schedules ONLY if: • The amount on line 34 is more than $20,000 ($40,000 if you checked Filing Status Box 2 or 5), OR • You have more exemptions than those covered in the Tax Table for your filing status, OR • You use any of these forms to figure your tax: Schedule D, Schedule G, or Form 4726. Otherwise, you MUST use the Tax Tables to find your tax.	34	49,900 —
	35 Tax. Enter tax here and check if from ☐ Tax Tables or ☑ Schedule TC	35	18,180 —
	36 Additional taxes. (See page 11 of Instructions.) Enter total and check if from ☐ Form 4970, } ☐ Form 4972, ☐ Form 5544, or ☐ Section 72(m)(5) penalty tax . . . }	36	0
	37 Total. Add lines 35 and 36 . . . . ▶	37	18,180 —
Credits	38 Credit for contributions to candidates for public office . .	38		
	39 Credit for the elderly (attach Schedules R&RP)	39		
	40 Credit for child and dependent care expenses (attach Form 2441) .	40		
	41 Investment credit (attach Form 3468)	41		
	42 Foreign tax credit (attach Form 1116)	42		
	43 Work Incentive (WIN) Credit (attach Form 4874)	43		
	44 New jobs credit (attach Form 5884)	44		
	45 Residential energy credits (see page 12 of Instructions, attach Form 5695) . .	45		
	46 Total credits. Add lines 38 through 45	46	0
	47 Balance. Subtract line 46 from line 37 and enter difference (but not less than zero) . ▶	47	18,180 —
Other Taxes	48 Self-employment tax (attach Schedule SE)	48	
	49 Minimum tax. Check here ▶ ☐ and attach Form 4625	49	
	50 Tax from recomputing prior-year investment credit (attach Form 4255)	50	
	51 Social security (FICA) tax on tip income not reported to employer (attach Form 4137) . .	51	
	52 Uncollected employee FICA and RRTA tax on tips (from Form W–2)	52	
	53 Tax on an IRA (attach Form 5329)	53	
	54 Total tax. Add lines 47 through 53 . . . . ▶	54	18,180 —
Payments Attach Forms W–2, W–2G, and W–2P to front.	55 Total Federal income tax withheld	55		
	56 1978 estimated tax payments and credit from 1977 return .	56		
	57 Earned income credit. If line 31 is under $8,000, see page 2 of Instructions. If eligible, enter child's name ▶...............	57		
	58 Amount paid with Form 4868	58		
	59 Excess FICA and RRTA tax withheld (two or more employers)	59		
	60 Credit for Federal tax on special fuels and oils (attach Form 4136) .	60		
	61 Regulated Investment Company credit (attach Form 2439)	61		
	62 Total. Add lines 55 through 61 . . . . ▶	62	
Refund or Due	63 If line 62 is larger than line 54, enter amount OVERPAID . . . . ▶	63	
	64 Amount of line 63 to be REFUNDED TO YOU . . . . ▶	64	
	65 Amount of line 63 to be credited on 1979 estimated tax. ▶	65		
	66 If line 54 is larger than line 62, enter BALANCE DUE. Attach check or money order for full amount payable to "Internal Revenue Service." Write your social security number on check or money order . . ▶ (Check ▶ ☐ if Form 2210 (2210F) is attached. See page 14 of instructions.) ▶ $	66	

Under penalties of perjury, I declare that I have examined this return, including accompanying schedules and statements, and to the best of my knowledge and belief, it is true, correct, and complete. Declaration of preparer (other than taxpayer) is based on all information of which preparer has any knowledge.

Please Sign Here

▶ Your signature	Date	▶ Spouse's signature (if filing jointly, BOTH must sign even if only one had income)

Paid Preparer's Information	Preparer's ▶ signature		Preparer's social security no.	Check if self-employed ▶ ☐
	Firm's name (or yours, if self-employed), address and ZIP code ▶		E.I. No. ▶	
			Date ▶	

Form 1040 U.S. Individual Income Tax Return 1978

Department of the Treasury—Internal Revenue Service

WITH $25,000 MUNICIPAL-BOND INCOME AS TAX SHELTER

For Privacy Act Notice, see page 3 of Instructions | For the year January 1–December 31, 1978, or other tax year beginning ____, 1978, ending ____, 19 ____.

Use IRS label. Otherwise, please print or type.	Your first name and initial (if joint return, also give spouse's name and initial) MARIA Last name BEAUMONT	Your social security number 000 00 0000
	Present home address (Number and street, including apartment number, or rural route)	Spouse's social security no.
	City, town or post office, State and ZIP code	Your occupation INVESTOR
		Spouse's occupation

Do you want $1 to go to the Presidential Election Campaign Fund? ... Yes ☐ No ☐
If joint return, does your spouse want $1 to go to this fund? .. Yes ☐ No ☐

Note: Checking Yes will not increase your tax or reduce your refund.

Filing Status

Check only one box.

1 ✔ Single
2 ☐ Married filing joint return (even if only one had income)
3 ☐ Married filing separate return. If spouse is also filing, give spouse's social security number in the space above and enter full name here ▶ ....
4 ☐ Unmarried head of household. Enter qualifying name ▶ .... See page 6 of Instructions.
5 ☐ Qualifying widow(er) with dependent child (Year spouse died ▶ 19). See page 6 of Instructions.

Exemptions

Always check the box labeled Yourself. Check other boxes if they apply.

6a ☐ Yourself ☐ 65 or over ☐ Blind } Enter number of boxes checked on 6a and b ▶ 1
b ☐ Spouse ☐ 65 or over ☐ Blind

c First names of your dependent children who lived with you ▶ .... Enter number of children listed ▶

d Other dependents: (1) Name	(2) Relationship	(3) Number of months lived in your home	(4) Did dependent have income of $750 or more?	(5) Did you provide more than one-half of dependent's support?

Enter number of other dependents ▶

Add numbers entered in boxes above ▶ 1

7 Total number of exemptions claimed ....

Income

Please attach Copy B of your Forms W–2 here.

If you do not have a W–2, see page 5 of Instructions.

Please attach check or money order here.

8	Wages, salaries, tips, and other employee compensation	8	0
9	Interest income (If over $400, attach Schedule B)................	9	5,000 —
10a	Dividends (If over $400, attach Schedule B)...20,000 —, 10b Exclusion...100 —		
10c	Subtract line 10b from line 10a	10c	19,900 —
11	State and local income tax refunds (does not apply unless refund is for year you itemized deductions)..................	11	0
12	Alimony received	12	0
13	Business income or (loss) (attach Schedule C)...............	13	0
14	Capital gain or (loss) (attach Schedule D).................	14	0
15	Taxable part of capital gain distributions not reported on Schedule D (see page 9 of Instructions) ..	15	0
16	Net gain or (loss) from Supplemental Schedule of Gains and Losses (attach Form 4797)	16	0
17	Fully taxable pensions and annuities not reported on Schedule E	17	0
18	Pensions, annuities, rents, royalties, partnerships, estates or trusts, etc. (attach Schedule E)	18	0
19	Farm income or (loss) (attach Schedule F)...............	19	0
20	Other income (state nature and source—see page 10 of Instructions) ▶	20	0
21	Total income. Add lines 8, 9, and 10c through 20 ....▶	21	24,900 —

Adjustments to Income

22	Moving expense (attach Form 3903)	22	
23	Employee business expenses (attach Form 2106) ..	23	
24	Payments to an IRA (see page 10 of Instructions)	24	
25	Payments to a Keogh (H.R. 10) retirement plan ...	25	
26	Interest penalty due to early withdrawal of savings	26	
27	Alimony paid (see page 10 of Instructions)	27	
28	Total adjustments. Add lines 22 through 27 ....▶	28	0

Adjusted Gross Income

29	Subtract line 28 from line 21	29	24,900 —
30	Disability income exclusion (attach Form 2440)	30	0
31	Adjusted gross income. Subtract line 30 from line 29. If this line is less than $8,000, see page 2 of Instructions. If you want IRS to figure your tax, see page 4 of Instructions ....▶	31	24,900 —

☆ U.S. GOVERNMENT PRINTING OFFICE: 1978—O-263-303 13-2687299

Form 1040 (1978)

Name(s) as shown on Form 1040 (Do not enter name and social security number if shown on other side) | **Your social security number**

MARIA BEAUMONT   000 00 0000

Part I — Interest Income

1 If you received more than $400 in interest, **Complete Part I.** Please see page 8 of the instructions to find out what interest to report. Then answer the questions in Part III, below. If you received interest as a nominee for another, or you received or paid accrued interest on securities transferred between interest payment dates, please see page 18 of the instructions.

Name of payer	Amount
ABC BANK	1,000 —
DEF BANK	1,000 —
GHI BANK	650 —
JKL 4¼s OF 2001	850 —
MNO 8s OF 1984	800 —
PQR 7s OF 1984	700 —

2 Total interest income. Enter here and on Form 1040, line 9 . . . . | **5,000 —**

Part II — Dividend Income

3 If you received more than $400 in gross dividends (including capital gain distributions) and other distributions on stock, complete **Part II.** Please see page 9 of the instructions. Write (H), (W), (J), for stock held by husband, wife, or jointly. Then answer the questions in Part III, below. If you received dividends as a nominee for another, please see page 18 of the instructions.

Name of payer	Amount
ABC INDUSTRIES	5,000 —
DEF, INC.	5,000 —
GHI SONICS	5,000 —
GENERAL INCORPORATED	5,000 —

4 Total of line 3 . . . . 20,000 —

5 Capital gain distributions. Enter here and on Schedule D, line 7. See Note below . . .   0

6 Nontaxable distributions   0

7 Total (add lines 5 and 6)   0

8 Dividends before exclusion (subtract line 7 from line 4). Enter here and on Form 1040, line 10a . . . . 20,000 —

Note: If you received capital gain distributions and do not need Schedule D to report any other gains or losses or to compute the alternative tax, do not file that schedule. Instead, enter the taxable part of capital gain distributions on Form 1040, line 15.

Part III — Foreign Accounts and Foreign Trusts

If you are required to list interest in Part I or dividends in Part II, OR if you had a foreign account or were a grantor of, or a transferor to a foreign trust, you must answer both questions in Part III. Please see page 18 of the instructions.

	Yes	No
A Did you, at any time during the taxable year, have an interest in or signature or other authority over a bank, securities, or other financial account in a foreign country (see page 18 of instructions)? . . .		
B Were you the grantor of, or transferor to, a foreign trust during any taxable year, which foreign trust was in being during the current taxable year, whether or not you have any beneficial interest in such trust? . If "Yes," you may be required to file Forms 3520, 3520–A, or 926.		

☆ U.S. Government Printing Office: 1978—O—263-309—E.I. # 52-0237640

73

SCHEDULE TC
(Form 1040)
Department of the Treasury
Internal Revenue Service

Tax Computation Schedule

▶ Attach to Form 1040.

1978

Name(s) as shown on Form 1040	Your social security number
MARIA BEAUMONT	000 00 0000

Part I — Computation of Tax for Taxpayers Who Cannot Use the Tax Tables

Use this part to figure your tax if:

- Your income on Form 1040, line 34, is more than $20,000 and you checked Filing Status Box 1, 3, or 4 on Form 1040.
- Your income on Form 1040, line 34, is more than $40,000 and you checked Filing Status Box 2 or 5 on Form 1040.

- You had more exemptions than were covered in the Tax Table for your filing status.
- You figure your tax using the alternative tax computation on Schedule D (Capital Gains and Losses), Schedule G (Income Averaging), or Form 4726 (Maximum Tax on Personal Service Income).

1 Enter the amount from Form 1040, line 34	**1**	24,900 —
2 Multiply $750 by the total number of exemptions claimed on Form 1040, line 7	**2**	750 —
3 Taxable Income. Subtract line 2 from line 1. (Figure your tax on this amount by using the Tax Rate Schedules or one of the other methods listed on line 4.)	**3**	24,150 —
4 Income Tax. Enter tax and check if from: ☐ Tax Rate Schedule X, Y, or Z, ☐ Schedule D, ☐ Schedule G, or ☐ Form 4726	**4**	5,971 —

General Tax Credit

5 Multiply $35 by the total number of exemptions claimed on Form 1040, line 7. (If you are married filing a separate return, skip lines 6 through 9 and enter the amount from line 5 on line 10.)	**5**	35 —	
6 Enter the amount from line 3, above	**6**	24,150 —	
7 Enter { $3,200 if you are married filing a joint return or a qualifying widow(er) } { $2,200 if you are single or an unmarried head of household } . . .	**7**	2,200 —	**TC**
8 Subtract line 7 from line 6	**8**	21,950 —	
9 Enter 2% of line 8 (but do not enter more than $180)	**9**	180 —	

10 General tax credit. Enter the amount from line 5 or line 9, whichever is larger	**10**	180 —
11 Tax. Subtract line 10 from line 4. (If $0 or less, enter $0.) Enter this amount on Form 1040, line 35 . . . . ▶	**11**	5,791 —

Part II — Computation for Certain Taxpayers Who Must Itemize Deductions

If you are included in one of the groups below, you MUST itemize. If you must itemize and the amount on Schedule A (Form 1040), line 40, is more than your itemized deductions on Schedule A, line 39, you must complete Part II before figuring your tax.

You MUST itemize your deductions if:

A. You can be claimed as a dependent on your parent's return and had interest, dividends, or other unearned income of $750 or more and less than $2,200 of earned income if single (less than $1,600 if married filing a separate return).

Note: If your earned income is more than your itemized deductions on Schedule A, line 39, enter your earned income in Part II, line 3, above unless you are married filing a separate return and your spouse itemizes deductions. Generally, your earned income is the total of any amounts on Form 1040, lines 8,

13, and 19. See page 11 of the Instructions for Form 1040 for more details.

B. You are married filing a separate return and your spouse itemizes deductions. (There is an exception to this rule. You don't have to itemize if your spouse must itemize only because he or she is described in A and enters earned income instead of itemized deductions on Part II, line 3, of this schedule. If this is the case, don't complete Part II. Go back to Form 1040, line 33, and enter $0. Then go to Form 1040, line 34.)

C. You file Form 4563 to exclude income from sources in U.S. possessions. (Please see Form 4563, and Publication 570, Tax Guide for U.S. Citizens Employed in U.S. Possessions, for more details.)

D. You had dual status as a nonresident alien for part of 1978, and during the rest of the year you were either a resident alien or a U.S. citizen. However, you don't have to itemize if at the end of 1978, you were married to a U.S. resident or citizen and file a joint return reporting your combined worldwide income.

1 Enter the amount from Form 1040, line 31		**1**
2 Enter the amount from Schedule A, line 40	**2**	
3 Enter the amount from Schedule A, line 39	**3**	
Caution: If you can be claimed as a dependent on your parent's return, see the Note above. Be sure you check the box below line 33 of Form 1040.		
4 Subtract line 3 from line 2		**4**
5 Add lines 1 and 4. Enter here and on Form 1040, line 34. (Leave Form 1040, line 33 blank. Disregard the instruction to subtract line 33 from line 32. Follow the rest of the instructions for Form 1040, line 34.) . . . . ▶		**5**

Tax Compu-tation	32 Amount from line 31	32	24,900 —
	33 If you do not itemize deductions, enter zero . . . . } If you itemize, complete Schedule A (Form 1040) and enter the amount from Schedule A, line 41	33	0
	Caution: If you have unearned income and can be claimed as a dependent on your parent's return, check here ▶ ☐ and see page 11 of the Instructions. Also see page 11 of the Instructions if: • You are married filing a separate return and your spouse itemizes deductions, OR • You file Form 4563, OR • You are a dual-status alien.		
	34 Subtract line 33 from line 32. Use the amount on line 34 to find your tax from the Tax Tables, or to figure your tax on Schedule TC, Part I . . . . Use Schedule TC, Part I, and the Tax Rate Schedules ONLY if: • The amount on line 34 is more than $20,000 ($40,000 if you checked Filing Status Box 2 or 5), OR • You have more exemptions than those covered in the Tax Table for your filing status, OR • You use any of these forms to figure your tax: Schedule D, Schedule G, or Form 4726. Otherwise, you MUST use the Tax Tables to find your tax.	34	24,900 —
	35 Tax. Enter tax here and check if from ☐ Tax Tables or ☑ Schedule TC	35	5,791 —
	36 Additional taxes. (See page 11 of Instructions.) Enter total and check if from ☐ Form 4970, } ☐ Form 4972, ☐ Form 5544, ☐ Form 5405, or ☐ Section 72(m)(5) penalty tax . . .	36	0
	37 Total. Add lines 35 and 36 . . . . ▶	37	5,791 —
Credits	38 Credit for contributions to candidates for public office . .	38		
	39 Credit for the elderly (attach Schedules R&RP)	39		
	40 Credit for child and dependent care expenses (attach Form 2441) .	40		
	41 Investment credit (attach Form 3468)	41		
	42 Foreign tax credit (attach Form 1116)	42		
	43 Work Incentive (WIN) Credit (attach Form 4874)	43		
	44 New jobs credit (attach Form 5884)	44		
	45 Residential energy credits (see page 12 of Instructions, attach Form 5695). . .	45		
	46 Total credits. Add lines 38 through 45 . . . . ▶	46	0
	47 Balance. Subtract line 46 from line 37 and enter difference (but not less than zero) . ▶	47	5,791 —
Other Taxes	48 Self-employment tax (attach Schedule SE)	48	
	49 Minimum tax. Check here ▶ ☐ and attach Form 4625	49	
	50 Tax from recomputing prior-year investment credit (attach Form 4255)	50	
	51 Social security (FICA) tax on tip income not reported to employer (attach Form 4137) . .	51	
	52 Uncollected employee FICA and RRTA tax on tips (from Form W–2)	52	
	53 Tax on an IRA (attach Form 5329)	53	
	54 Total tax. Add lines 47 through 53 . . . . ▶	54	5,791 —
Payments Attach Forms W–2, W–2G, and W–2P to front.	55 Total Federal income tax withheld	55		
	56 1978 estimated tax payments and credit from 1977 return .	56		
	57 Earned income credit. If line 31 is under $8,000, see page 2 of Instructions. If eligible, enter child's name ▶........................	57		
	58 Amount paid with Form 4868	58		
	59 Excess FICA and RRTA tax withheld (two or more employers)	59		
	60 Credit for Federal tax on special fuels and oils (attach Form 4136) .	60		
	61 Regulated Investment Company credit (attach Form 2439)	61		
	62 Total. Add lines 55 through 61 . . . . ▶	62	
Refund or Due	63 If line 62 is larger than line 54, enter amount OVERPAID . . . . ▶	63	
	64 Amount of line 63 to be REFUNDED TO YOU . . . . ▶	64	
	65 Amount of line 63 to be credited on 1979 estimated tax . ▶	65		
	66 If line 54 is larger than line 62, enter BALANCE DUE. Attach check or money order for full amount payable to "Internal Revenue Service." Write your social security number on check or money order . . ▶ (Check ▶ ☐ if Form 2210 (2210F) is attached. See page 14 of instructions.) ▶ $	66	

Please Sign Here

Under penalties of perjury, I declare that I have examined this return, including accompanying schedules and statements, and to the best of my knowledge and belief, it is true, correct, and complete. Declaration of preparer (other than taxpayer) is based on all information of which preparer has any knowledge.

▶ Your signature	Date	▶ Spouse's signature (if filing jointly, BOTH must sign even if only one had income)

Paid Preparer's Information	Preparer's signature ▶	Preparer's social security no.	Check if self-employed ▶ ☐
	Firm's name (or yours, if self-employed), address and ZIP code ▶	E.I. No. ▶	
		Date ▶	

75

Form 1040

Department of the Treasury—Internal Revenue Service
U.S. Individual Income Tax Return **1978**

For Privacy Act Notice, see page 3 of Instructions | For the year January 1–December 31, 1978, or other tax year beginning _____ , 1978, ending _____ , 19___ .

Use IRS label. Other-wise, please print or type.	Your first name and initial (if joint return, also give spouse's name and initial) BEN + BARBARA	Last name REICH	Your social security number 000 00 0000
	Present home address (Number and street, including apartment number, or rural route)		Spouse's social security no. 000 00 0000
	City, town or post office, State and ZIP code		Your occupation EXECUTIVE

Do you want $1 to go to the Presidential Election Campaign Fund? **Yes** ☐ **No** ☐
If joint return, does your spouse want $1 to go to this fund? . . **Yes** ☐ **No** ☐

Note: Checking Yes will not increase your tax or reduce your refund.

Spouse's occupation HOUSEWIFE

Filing Status

Check only one box.

1 ☐ Single
2 ☑ Married filing joint return (even if only one had income)
3 ☐ Married filing separate return. If spouse is also filing, give spouse's social security number in the space above and enter full name here ▶ --------------------
4 ☐ Unmarried head of household. Enter qualifying name ▶ ----------------- See page 6 of Instructions.
5 ☐ Qualifying widow(er) with dependent child (Year spouse died ▶ 19___). See page 6 of Instructions.

Exemptions

Always check the box labeled Yourself. Check other boxes if they apply.

6a ☑ Yourself ☐ 65 or over ☐ Blind
b ☑ Spouse ☐ 65 or over ☐ Blind

Enter number of boxes checked on 6a and b ▶ **2**

c First names of your dependent children who lived with you ▶ -----------------

Enter number of children listed ▶ ☐

d Other dependents: (1) Name	(2) Relationship	(3) Number of months lived in your home	(4) Did dependent have income of $750 or more?	(5) Did you provide more than one-half of dependent's support?

Enter number of other dependents ▶ ☐

Add numbers entered in boxes above ▶ **2**

Income

Please attach Copy B of your Forms W–2 here.

If you do not have a W–2, see page 5 of Instructions.

7	Total number of exemptions claimed		**2**
8	Wages, salaries, tips, and other employee compensation	8	100,000 —
9	Interest income (If over $400, attach Schedule B)	9	0
10a	Dividends (If over $400, attach Schedule B) _____ , 10b Exclusion _____		
10c	Subtract line 10b from line 10a	10c	0
11	State and local income tax refunds (does not apply unless refund is for year you itemized deductions)	11	0
12	Alimony received	12	0
13	Business income or (loss) (attach Schedule C)	13	0
14	Capital gain or (loss) (attach Schedule D)	14	8,000
15	Taxable part of capital gain distributions not reported on Schedule D (see page 9 of Instructions) . .	15	0
16	Net gain or (loss) from Supplemental Schedule of Gains and Losses (attach Form 4797)	16	0
17	Fully taxable pensions and annuities not reported on Schedule E	17	0
18	Pensions, annuities, rents, royalties, partnerships, estates or trusts, etc. (attach Schedule E)	18	5,000 —
19	Farm income or (loss) (attach Schedule F)	19	0
20	Other income (state nature and source—see page 10 of Instructions) ▶ -----------------	20	0
21	Total income. Add lines 8, 9, and 10c through 20 . . . . ▶	21	113,000

Adjustments to Income

22	Moving expense (attach Form 3903)	22	
23	Employee business expenses (attach Form 2106) . .	23	
24	Payments to an IRA (see page 10 of Instructions)	24	
25	Payments to a Keogh (H.R. 10) retirement plan . . .	25	
26	Interest penalty due to early withdrawal of savings	26	
27	Alimony paid (see page 10 of Instructions)	27	
28	Total adjustments. Add lines 22 through 27 . . . . ▶	28	0

Adjusted Gross Income

29	Subtract line 28 from line 21	29	113,000 —
30	Disability income exclusion (attach Form 2440)	30	0
31	Adjusted gross income. Subtract line 30 from line 29. If this line is less than $8,000, see page 2 of Instructions. If you want IRS to figure your tax, see page 4 of Instructions . . . . ▶	31	113,000 —

☆ U.S. GOVERNMENT PRINTING OFFICE: 1978—O-263-303 13-2687299

Form 1040 (1978)

| SCHEDULE D (Form 1040) Department of the Treasury Internal Revenue Service | **Capital Gains and Losses** (Examples of property to be reported on this Schedule are gains and losses on stocks, bonds, and similar investments, and gains (but not losses) on personal assets such as a home or jewelry.) ▶ Attach to Form 1040. ▶ See Instructions for Schedule D (Form 1040.) | 1978 |

Name(s) as shown on Form 1040	Your social security number
BEN + BARBARA REICH	000 00 0000

Part I — Short-term Capital Gains and Losses—Assets Held One Year or Less D

a. Kind of property and description (Example, 100 shares of "Z" Co.)	b. Date acquired (Mo., day, yr.)	c. Date sold (Mo., day, yr.)	d. Gross sales price less expense of sale	e. Cost or other basis, as adjusted (see instructions page 19)	f. Gain or (loss) from all sales during entire tax year (d less e)	g. Enter gain or (loss) from sales after 10/31/78
1						

2 Enter your share of net short-term gain or (loss) from partnerships and fiduciaries	2	
3 Enter net gain or (loss), combine lines 1 and 2	3	
4 Short-term capital loss carryover attributable to years beginning after 1969 (see Instructions page 19)	4 ( )	
5 Net short-term gain or (loss), combine lines 3 and 4, column (f)	5	0

Part II — Long-term Capital Gains and Losses—Assets Held More Than One Year

a.	b.	c.	d.	e.	f.	g.
61,000 MONARCH IND.	12/13/74	12/16/78	40,000—	20,000—	20,000	— 20,000 —

7 Capital gain distributions	7	0	0
8 Enter gain, if applicable, from Form 4797, line 6(a)(1) (see Instructions page 19)	8	0	0
9 Enter your share of net long-term gain or (loss) from partnerships and fiduciaries	9	0	0
10 Enter your share of net long-term gain from small business corporations (Subchapter S)	10	0	0
11 Net gain or (loss), combine lines 6 through 10	11	20,000 —	20,000 —
12 Long-term capital loss carryover attributable to years beginning after 1969 (see Instructions page 19)	12 ( )		
13 Net long-term gain or (loss), combine lines 11 and 12, column (f)	13	20,000 —	

NOTE: If you have capital loss carryovers from years beginning before 1970, do not complete Parts III, IV, or VI. See Form 4798 instead.

Part III — Computation of Capital Gain Deduction
(Complete this part only if line 14 shows a gain)

14 Combine lines 5 and 13, column (f), and enter here. If result is zero or a loss, do not complete the rest of this part. Instead skip to Part IV, line 24 on page 2	14	20,000 —
15 Enter line 13, column (f) or line 14, whichever is smaller. If zero or a loss, enter zero and skip to line 23	15	20,000 —
16 If line 11, column (g) is a gain, combine lines 3 and 11, column (g), and enter here. If this line or line 11, column (g) shows a loss or zero, enter a zero and skip to line 20	16	20,000 —
17 Enter line 11, column (g) or line 16, whichever is smaller	17	20,000 —
18 Enter line 15 or line 17, whichever is smaller	18	20,000 —
19 Enter 60% of amount on line 18	19	12,000 —
20 Subtract line 18 from line 15	20	0
21 Enter 50% of amount on line 20	21	0
22 Add line 19 and line 21. This is your capital gain deduction	22	12,000 —
23 Subtract line 22 from line 14. Enter this amount on Form 1040, line 14	23	8,000 —

77

Part IV Computation of Capital Loss Deduction
(Complete this part only if line 14, page 1 shows a loss)

24 If line 14 shows a loss—
  a Enter one of the following amounts:
    (i) If line 5, column (f) is zero or a net gain, enter 50% of line 14;
    (ii) If line 13, column (f) is zero or a net gain, enter line 14; or
    (iii) If line 5, column (f) and line 13 are net losses, enter amount on line 5, column (f) added to
      50% of amount on line 13, column (f) . . . . | **24a** |

  b Enter here and enter as a (loss) on Form 1040, line 14, the smallest of:
    (i) The amount on line 24a;
    (ii) $3,000 ($1,500 if married and filing a separate return); or
    (iii) Taxable income, as adjusted (see Instructions page 20) . . . . | **24b** |

Part V Computation of Alternative Tax *TOO HIGH - 4726 CALCULATION USED INSTEAD*
(See instructions page 20 to see if the alternative tax will benefit you)

25 Enter amount from Schedule TC (Form 1040), Part I, line 3	**25**	111,500 —
26 Subtract line 22 from line 15 (or Form 4798, line 15 from line 7) and enter here	**26**	8,000 —
27 Subtract line 26 from line 25 (if line 26 is more than line 25, do not complete the rest of this part. The Alternative Tax will not benefit you)	**27**	103,500 —
Note: If line 15 is not more than $50,000 ($25,000, if married, filing separately), skip lines 28 through 31, and enter zero on line 32.		
28 Divide line 26 by line 15. Multiply the result by $50,000 ($25,000, if married filing separately), and enter here	**28**	
29 Add lines 27 and 28	**29**	
30 Tax on amount on line 25 (use Tax Rate Schedule in instructions) . . . **30**		
31 Tax on amount on line 29 (use Tax Rate Schedule in instructions) . . . **31**		
32 Subtract line 31 from line 30	**32**	0
33 Tax on amount on line 27 (use Tax Rate Schedule in instructions)	**33**	45,366 —
34 Enter 25% of line 15 but not more than $12,500 ($6,250, if married filing separately)	**34**	5,000 —
35 Alternative Tax—add lines 32, 33, and 34. If less than the tax figured on the amount on Schedule TC (Form 1040), Part I, line 3, enter this alternative tax on Schedule TC (Form 1040), Part I, line 4. Also check the Schedule D box on Schedule TC (Form 1040), Part I, line 4	**35**	50,366 —

Part VI Computation of Post-1969 Capital Loss Carryovers from 1978 to 1979
(Complete this part if the loss on line 24a is more than the loss shown on line 24b)

Section A.—Short-term Capital Loss Carryover

36 Enter loss shown on line 5; if none enter zero and skip lines 37 through 41—then go to line 42 . . .	**36**	
37 Enter gain shown on line 13. If that line is blank or shows a loss, enter zero	**37**	
38 Reduce any loss on line 36 to the extent of any gain on line 37	**38**	
39 Enter amount shown on line 24b	**39**	
40 Enter smaller of line 38 or 39	**40**	
41 Subtract line 40 from line 38	**41**	

    Note: The amount on line 41 is the part of your short-term capital loss carryover from 1978 to 1979 that is attributable to years beginning after 1969.

Section B.—Long-term Capital Loss Carryover

42 Subtract line 40 from line 39 (**Note:** If you skipped lines 37 through 41, enter amount from line 24b) .	**42**	
43 Enter loss from line 13; if none, enter zero and skip lines 44 through 47	**43**	
44 Enter gain shown on line 5. If that line is blank or shows a loss, enter a zero	**44**	
45 Reduce any loss on line 43 to the extent of any gain on line 44	**45**	
46 Multiply amount on line 42 by 2	**46**	
47 Subtract line 46 from line 45	**47**	

    Note: The amount on line 47 is the part of your long-term capital loss carryover from 1978 to 1979 that is attributable to years beginning after 1969.

☆ U.S GOVERNMENT PRINTING OFFICE :1978-O-263-276—E.I. NO. 52-1074467

78

SCHEDULE E
(Form 1040)
Department of the Treasury
Internal Revenue Service

Supplemental Income Schedule

(From pensions and annuities, rents and royalties, partnerships, estates and trusts, etc.)
▶ Attach to Form 1040.   ▶ See Instructions for Schedule E (Form 1040).

1978

Name(s) as shown on Form 1040	Your social security number
BEN + BARBARA REICH	000 00 0000

Part I   Pension and Annuity Income. If fully taxable, do not complete this part. Enter amount on Form 1040, line 17.
For one pension or annuity not fully taxable, complete this part. If you have more than one pension or annuity that is not fully taxable, attach a separate sheet listing each one with the appropriate data and enter combined total of taxable portions on line 5.

1 Name of payer ▶ ....
2 Did your employer contribute part of the cost? . . . . ☐ Yes ☐ No
   If "Yes," is your contribution recoverable within 3 years of the annuity starting date? . . . . ☐ Yes ☐ No
   If "Yes," show: Your contribution ▶ $...................., Contribution recovered in prior years ▶ | 2 | |
3 Amount received this year . . . . | 3 | |
4 Amount excludable this year . . . . | 4 | |
5 Taxable portion (subtract line 4 from line 3) . . . . | 5 | |

Part II   Rent and Royalty Income. If you need more space, use Form 4831.
Have you claimed expenses connected with your vacation home (or other dwelling unit) rented to others (see instructions)? . . . . . ☐ Yes ☐ No
If "Yes," did you or a member of your family occupy the vacation home (or other dwelling unit) for more than 14 days during the taxable year? ☐ Yes ☐ No

(a) Kind and location of property If residential, also write "R"	(b) Total amount of rents	(c) Total amount of royalties	(d) Depreciation (explain below) or depletion (attach computation)	(e) Other expenses (Repairs, etc.— explain below)

6 Totals . . . .
7 Net income or (loss) from rents and royalties (column (b) plus column (c) less columns (d) and (e)) . | 7 | |
8 Net rental income or (loss) (from Form 4831) . . . . | 8 | |
9 Net farm rental profit or (loss) (from Form 4835) . . . . | 9 | |
10 Total rent and royalty income or (loss) (add lines 7, 8, and 9) . . . . | 10 | |

Part III   Income or Losses from—

(a) Name	(b) Employer identification number	(c) Your share of gross farming or fishing income (see instructions)	(d) Loss	(e) Income

Partnerships

11 Add amounts in columns (d) and (e) . . . . | 11 | | |
12 Column (e), line 11, less column (d), line 11 . . . . | 12 | |
13 Additional first-year depreciation . . . . | 13 | |
14 Total partnership income or (loss). Combine lines 12 and 13 . . . . | 14 | |

Estates or Trusts

D'COURTNEY ITF BARBARA REICH	00-0000000			5,000 —

15 Add amounts in columns (d) and (e) . . . . | 15 | | |
16 Total estate or trust income or (loss). Column (e), line 15, less column (d), line 15 . . . . . | 16 | 5,000 — |

Small Bus. Corps.

17 Add amounts in columns (d) and (e) . . . . | 17 | | |
18 Total small business corporation income or (loss). (Column (e), line 17, less column (d), line 17 . | 18 | |

19 TOTAL (add lines 5, 10, 14, 16, and 18). Enter here and on Form 1040, line 18 . . . . ▶ | 19 | |

Explanation of Column (e), Part II

Item	Amount	Item	Amount	Item	Amount

Schedule for Depreciation Claimed in Part II above. If you need more space use Form 4562.

(a) Description of property	(b) Date acquired	(c) Cost or other basis	(d) Depreciation allowed or allowable in prior years	(e) Method of computing depreciation	(f) Life or rate	(g) Depreciation for this year
1 Total additional first-year depreciation (do not include in items below) ——————————————————▶						
2 Totals						

☆ U.S. GOVERNMENT PRINTING OFFICE: 1978—263-318

23-188-5979

SCHEDULE TC
(Form 1040)
Department of the Treasury
Internal Revenue Service

Tax Computation Schedule

▶ Attach to Form 1040.

1978

Name(s) as shown on Form 1040

BEN + BARBARA REICH

Your social security number

000 00 0000

Part I — Computation of Tax for Taxpayers Who Cannot Use the Tax Tables

Use this part to figure your tax if:

- Your income on Form 1040, line 34, is more than $20,000 and you checked Filing Status Box 1, 3, or 4 on Form 1040.
- Your income on Form 1040, line 34, is more than $40,000 and you checked Filing Status Box 2 or 5 on Form 1040.

- You had more exemptions than were covered in the Tax Table for your filing status.
- You figure your tax using the alternative tax computation on Schedule D (Capital Gains and Losses), Schedule G (Income Averaging), or Form 4726 (Maximum Tax on Personal Service Income).

1 Enter the amount from Form 1040, line 34	**1**	113,000 —
2 Multiply $750 by the total number of exemptions claimed on Form 1040, line 7	**2**	1,500 —
3 Taxable Income. Subtract line 2 from line 1. (Figure your tax on this amount by using the Tax Rate Schedules or one of the other methods listed on line 4.)	**3**	111,500 —
4 Income Tax. Enter tax and check if from: ☐ Tax Rate Schedule X, Y, or Z, ☐ Schedule D, ☐ Schedule G, or ☑ Form 4726	**4**	47,658 —

General Tax Credit

5 Multiply $35 by the total number of exemptions claimed on Form 1040, line 7. (If you are married filing a separate return, skip lines 6 through 9 and enter the amount from line 5 on line 10.)	**5**	70 —
6 Enter the amount from line 3, above	**6**	111,500 —
7 Enter { $3,200 if you are married filing a joint return or a qualifying widow(er) } { $2,200 if you are single or an unmarried head of household . . . }	**7**	3,200 —
8 Subtract line 7 from line 6	**8**	108,300 —
9 Enter 2% of line 8 (but do not enter more than $180)	**9**	180 —
10 General tax credit. Enter the amount from line 5 or line 9, whichever is larger	**10**	180 —
11 Tax. Subtract line 10 from line 4. (If $0 or less, enter $0.) Enter this amount on Form 1040, line 35 . . . . ▶	**11**	47,478 —

TC

Part II — Computation for Certain Taxpayers Who Must Itemize Deductions

If you are included in one of the groups below, you MUST itemize. If you must itemize and the amount on Schedule A (Form 1040), line 40, is more than your itemized deductions on Schedule A, line 39, you must complete Part II before figuring your tax.

You MUST itemize your deductions if:

A. You can be claimed as a dependent on your parent's return and had interest, dividends, or other unearned income of $750 or more and less than $2,200 of earned income if single (less than $1,600 if married filing a separate return).

Note: If your earned income is more than your itemized deductions on Schedule A, line 39, enter your earned income in Part II, line 3, of this schedule, unless you are married filing a separate return and your spouse itemizes deductions. Generally, your earned income is the total of any amounts on Form 1040, lines 8,

13, and 19. See page 11 of the Instructions for Form 1040 for more details.

B. You are married filing a separate return and your spouse itemizes deductions. (There is an exception to this rule. You don't have to itemize if your spouse must itemize only because he or she has earned income instead of itemized deductions on Part II, line 3, of this schedule. If this is the case, don't complete Part II. Go back to Form 1040, line 33, and enter $0. Then go to Form 1040, line 34.)

C. You file Form 4563 to exclude income from sources in U.S. possessions. (Please see Form 4563, and Publication 570, Tax Guide for U.S. Citizens Employed in U.S. Possessions, for more details.)

D. You had dual status as a nonresident alien for part of 1978, and during the rest of the year you were either a resident alien or a U.S. citizen. However, you don't have to itemize if at the end of 1978, you were married to a U.S. resident or citizen and file a joint return reporting your combined worldwide income.

1 Enter the amount from Form 1040, line 31		**1**
2 Enter the amount from Schedule A, line 40	**2**	
3 Enter the amount from Schedule A, line 39	**3**	
Caution: If you can be claimed as a dependent on your parent's return, see the Note above. Be sure you check the box below line 33 of Form 1040.		
4 Subtract line 3 from line 2		**4**
5 Add lines 1 and 4. Enter here and on Form 1040, line 34. (Leave Form 1040, line 33 blank. Disregard the instruction to subtract line 33 from line 32. Follow the rest of the instructions for Form 1040, line 34.) . . . . ▶		**5**

Form **4726**
Department of the Treasury
Internal Revenue Service

Maximum Tax on Personal Service Income
▶ Attach to Form 1040 (or Form 1041).

1978

Name(s) as shown on Form 1040 (or Form 1041)

BEN + BARBARA REICH

Identifying number

000-00-0000

Do not complete this form if—(a) Taxable income or personal service taxable income is:

$40,200 or less, and on Form 1040, you checked box 1 or box 4,

$55,200 or less, and on Form 1040, you checked box 2 or box 5,

$26,000 or less and this is an Estate or Trust return (Form 1041);

(b) You elected income averaging; or

(c) On Form 1040, you checked box 3.

A—Personal Service Income		B—Deductions Against Personal Service Income	
Total personal service income	100,000 —	Total deductions against personal service income . .	0

1 Personal service net income—Subtract total amount in column B from total amount in column A . .	**1**	100,000 —	
2 Enter your adjusted gross income (see instructions)	**2**	113,000 —	
3 Divide the amount on line 1 by the amount on line 2. Enter percentage result here, but not more than 100%. Round to nearest 4 numbers (see instructions)	**3**	88.50 %	
4 Enter your taxable income (see instructions)	**4**	111,500 —	
5 Multiply the amount on line 4 by the percentage on line 3	**5**	98,678 —	
6 Enter the total of your 1978 tax preference items (see instructions) . NOT APPLICABLE . . .	**6**		
7 Personal service taxable income. Subtract line 6 from line 5 (see instructions)	**7**		
8 If: on Form 1040, you checked box 1 or box 4, enter $40,200 . . . . on Form 1040, you checked box 2 or box 5, enter $55,200 . . Estate or Trust, enter $26,000	**8**	55,200 —	
9 Subtract line 8 from line 7 (if zero or less, do not complete rest of form)	**9**	43,478 —	
10 Enter 50% of line 9	**10**	21,739 —	
11 Tax on amount on line 4 . . . . **11**	50,326 —		
12 Tax on amount on line 7 . . . . **12**	42,467 —		
13 Subtract line 12 from line 11	**13**	7,859 —	
14 If the amount on line 8 is: $40,200, enter $13,290 ($12,240 if unmarried head of household) . . $55,200, enter $18,060 . . . . $26,000, enter $9,030	**14**	18,060 —	
15 Add lines 10, 13, and 14. This is your maximum tax (see instructions)	**15**	47,658 —	

Computation of Alternative Tax

16 Amount from line 4	**16**	111,500 —	
17 Enter amount reportable on Schedule D (Form 1040), line 26 or Schedule D (Form 1041), line 20* . .	**17**	8,000 —	
18 Subtract line 17 from line 16	**18**	103,500 —	
Note: If Schedule D (Form 1040), line 15; Form 4798, line 7; or Schedule D (Form 1041), line 17(e) or 31 is not more than $50,000, skip lines 19 through 23.			
19 Enter amount reportable on Schedule D (Form 1040), line 28 or Schedule D (Form 1041), line 22 . .	**19**		
20 Add lines 18 and 19	**20**		
21 Enter amount from line 11	**21**		
22 Tax on amount on line 20	**22**		
23 Subtract line 22 from line 21	**23**		
24 Tax on amount on line 18. Caution: If line 7 is more than line 18, enter instead, amount on line 12 less 50% of the excess of line 7 over line 18	**24**	45,366 —	
25 Subtract line 24 from line 11	**25**	4,960 —	
26 Subtract line 25 from line 15	**26**	42,698 —	
27 Enter 25% of Schedule D (Form 1040), line 15; Form 4798, line 7; or Schedule D (Form 1041), line 17(e) or 31, but not more than $12,500	**27**	5,000 —	
28 Add lines 23 (if applicable), 26 and 27	**28**	47,698 —	

*If you reported capital gain distributions but did not use Schedule D (Form 1040), enter on line 17 the amount shown on Form 1040, line 15.

263–165–1

Form **4726** (1978)

81

Tax Compu- tation	32 Amount from line 31	32	113,000 —
	33 If you do not itemize deductions, enter zero		
	If you itemize, complete Schedule A (Form 1040) and enter the amount from Schedule A, line 41	33	0
	Caution: If you have unearned income and can be claimed as a dependent on your parent's return, check here ▶ ☐ and see page 11 of the Instructions. Also see page 11 of the Instructions if:		
	• You are married filing a separate return and your spouse itemizes deductions, OR		
	• You file Form 4563, OR		
	• You are a dual-status alien.		
	34 Subtract line 33 from line 32. Use the amount on line 34 to find your tax from the Tax Tables, or to figure your tax on Schedule TC, Part I	34	113,000 —
	Use Schedule TC, Part I, and the Tax Rate Schedules ONLY if:		
	• The amount on line 34 is more than $20,000 ($40,000 if you checked Filing Status Box 2 or 5), OR		
	• You have more exemptions than those covered in the Tax Table for your filing status, OR		
	• You use any of these forms to figure your tax: Schedule D, Schedule G, or Form 4726.		
	Otherwise, you MUST use the Tax Tables to find your tax.		
	35 Tax. Enter tax here and check if from ☐ Tax Tables or ☑ Schedule TC	35	47,478 —
	36 Additional taxes. (See page 11 of Instructions.) Enter total and check if from ☐ Form 4970, ☐ Form 4972, ☐ Form 5544, or ☐ Form 5405, or ☐ Section 72(m)(5) penalty tax . . .	36	
	37 Total. Add lines 35 and 36 . . . . ▶	37	47,478 —
Credits	38 Credit for contributions to candidates for public office . .	38		
	39 Credit for the elderly (attach Schedules R&RP)	39		
	40 Credit for child and dependent care expenses (attach Form 2441) .	40		
	41 Investment credit (attach Form 3468)	41		
	42 Foreign tax credit (attach Form 1116)	42		
	43 Work Incentive (WIN) Credit (attach Form 4874)	43		
	44 New jobs credit (attach Form 5884)	44		
	45 Residential energy credits (see page 12 of Instructions, attach Form 5695) . .	45		
	46 Total credits. Add lines 38 through 45	46	0
	47 Balance. Subtract line 46 from line 37 and enter difference (but not less than zero) . ▶	47	47,478 —
Other Taxes	48 Self-employment tax (attach Schedule SE)	48	
	49 Minimum tax. Check here ▶ ☐ and attach Form 4625	49	
	50 Tax from recomputing prior-year investment credit (attach Form 4255)	50	
	51 Social security (FICA) tax on tip income not reported to employer (attach Form 4137) . .	51	
	52 Uncollected employee FICA and RRTA tax on tips (from Form W–2)	52	
	53 Tax on an IRA (attach Form 5329)	53	
	54 Total tax. Add lines 47 through 53 . . . . ▶	54	47,478 —
Payments Attach Forms W–2, W–2G, and W–2P to front.	55 Total Federal income tax withheld	55		
	56 1978 estimated tax payments and credit from 1977 return .	56		
	57 Earned income credit. If line 31 is under $8,000, see page 2 of Instructions. If eligible, enter child's name ▶	57		
	58 Amount paid with Form 4868	58		
	59 Excess FICA and RRTA tax withheld (two or more employers)	59		
	60 Credit for Federal tax on special fuels and oils (attach Form 4136) .	60		
	61 Regulated Investment Company credit (attach Form 2439)	61		
	62 Total. Add lines 55 through 61 . . . . ▶	62	
Refund or Due	63 If line 62 is larger than line 54, enter amount OVERPAID . . . . ▶	63	
	64 Amount of line 63 to be REFUNDED TO YOU . . . . ▶	64	
	65 Amount of line 63 to be credited on 1979 estimated tax . ▶	65		
	66 If line 54 is larger than line 62, enter BALANCE DUE. Attach check or money order for full amount payable to "Internal Revenue Service." Write your social security number on check or money order . . ▶ (Check ▶ ☐ if Form 2210 (2210F) is attached. See page 14 of instructions.) ▶ $	66	

Please Sign Here

Under penalties of perjury, I declare that I have examined this return, including accompanying schedules and statements, and to the best of my knowledge and belief, it is true, correct, and complete. Declaration of preparer (other than taxpayer) is based on all information of which preparer has any knowledge.

▶ Your signature   Date   ▶ Spouse's signature (if filing jointly, BOTH must sign even if only one had income)

Paid Preparer's Information

Preparer's signature ▶		Preparer's social security no.	Check if self-employed ▶ ☐
Firm's name (or yours, if self-employed), address and ZIP code ▶		E.I. No. ▶	
		Date ▶	

82

Form 1040 Department of the Treasury—Internal Revenue Service
U.S. Individual Income Tax Return **1978**

For Privacy Act Notice, see page 3 of Instructions | For the year January 1–December 31, 1978, or other tax year beginning _____, 1978, ending _____, 19___.

Use IRS label. Other-wise, please print or type.	Your first name and initial (if joint return, also give spouse's name and initial) BEN + BARBARA	Last name REICH	Your social security number 000 00 0000
	Present home address (Number and street, including apartment number, or rural route)		Spouse's social security no. 000 00 0000
	City, town or post office, State and ZIP code		Your occupation EXECUTIVE

Do you want $1 to go to the Presidential Election Campaign Fund? Yes ☐ No ☐
If joint return, does your spouse want $1 to go to this fund? Yes ☐ No ☐
Note: Checking Yes will not increase your tax or reduce your refund.
Spouse's occupation HOUSEWIFE

Filing Status
Check only one box.

1 ☐ Single
2 ☑ Married filing joint return (even if only one had income)
3 ☐ Married filing separate return. If spouse is also filing, give spouse's social security number in the space above and enter full name here ▶
4 ☐ Unmarried head of household. Enter qualifying name ▶ _____ See page 6 of Instructions.
5 ☐ Qualifying widow(er) with dependent child (Year spouse died ▶ 19___). See page 6 of Instructions.

Exemptions
Always check the box labeled Yourself. Check other boxes if they apply.

6a ☑ Yourself ☐ 65 or over ☐ Blind | Enter number of boxes checked on 6a and b ▶ 2
b ☑ Spouse ☐ 65 or over ☐ Blind |
c First names of your dependent children who lived with you ▶ _____ | Enter number of children listed ▶ ☐

d Other dependents:

(1) Name	(2) Relationship	(3) Number of months lived in your home	(4) Did dependent have income of $750 or more?	(5) Did you provide more than one-half of dependent's support?

Enter number of other dependents ▶ ☐

Add numbers entered in boxes above ▶ 2

7 Total number of exemptions claimed

Income
Please attach Copy B of your Forms W-2 here. If you do not have a W-2, see page 5 of Instructions.

8 Wages, salaries, tips, and other employee compensation	8	100,000 —
9 Interest income (If over $400, attach Schedule B)	9	0
10a Dividends (If over $400, attach Schedule B) _____, 10b Exclusion _____		
10c Subtract line 10b from line 10a	10c	0
11 State and local income tax refunds (does not apply unless refund is for year you itemized deductions)	11	0
12 Alimony received	12	0
13 Business income or (loss) (attach Schedule C)	13	0
14 Capital gain or (loss) (attach Schedule D)	14	8,000 —
15 Taxable part of capital gain distributions not reported on Schedule D (see page 9 of Instructions)	15	
16 Net gain or (loss) from Supplemental Schedule of Gains and Losses (attach Form 4797)	16	0
17 Fully taxable pensions and annuities not reported on Schedule E	17	0
18 Pensions, annuities, rents, royalties, partnerships, estates or trusts, etc. (attach Schedule E)	18	(17,500) —
19 Farm income or (loss) (attach Schedule F)	19	0
20 Other income (state nature and source—see page 10 of Instructions) ▶	20	0
21 Total income. Add lines 8, 9, and 10c through 20 ▶	21	90,500 —

Please attach check or money order here.

Adjustments to Income

22 Moving expense (attach Form 3903)	22	
23 Employee business expenses (attach Form 2106)	23	
24 Payments to an IRA (see page 10 of Instructions)	24	
25 Payments to a Keogh (H.R. 10) retirement plan	25	
26 Interest penalty due to early withdrawal of savings	26	
27 Alimony paid (see page 10 of Instructions)	27	
28 Total adjustments. Add lines 22 through 27 ▶	28	

Adjusted Gross Income

29 Subtract line 28 from line 21	29	
30 Disability income exclusion (attach Form 2440)	30	
31 Adjusted gross income. Subtract line 30 from line 29. If this line is less than $8,000, see page 2 of Instructions. If you want IRS to figure your tax, see page 4 of Instructions ▶	31	

☆ U.S. GOVERNMENT PRINTING OFFICE: 1978—O-263-303 13-2687299

Form 1040 (1978)

SCHEDULE D
(Form 1040)
Department of the Treasury
Internal Revenue Service

Capital Gains and Losses
(Examples of property to be reported on this Schedule are gains and losses on stocks, bonds, and similar investments, and gains (but not losses) on personal assets such as a home or jewelry.)
▶ Attach to Form 1040.   ▶ See Instructions for Schedule D (Form 1040.)

1978

Name(s) as shown on Form 1040	Your social security number
BEN + BARBARA REICH	000 00 0000

Part I Short-term Capital Gains and Losses—Assets Held One Year or Less   **D**

a. Kind of property and description (Example, 100 shares of "Z" Co.)	b. Date acquired (Mo., day, yr.)	c. Date sold (Mo., day, yr.)	d. Gross sales price less expense of sale	e. Cost or other basis, as adjusted (see instructions page 19)	f. Gain or (loss) from all sales during entire tax year (d less e)	g. Enter gain or (loss) from sales after 10/31/78
1						

2 Enter your share of net short-term gain or (loss) from partnerships and fiduciaries	**2**		
3 Enter net gain or (loss), combine lines 1 and 2	**3**		
4 Short-term capital loss carryover attributable to years beginning after 1969 (see Instructions page 19).	**4** (	)	
5 Net short-term gain or (loss), combine lines 3 and 4, column (f)	**5**	0	

Part II Long-term Capital Gains and Losses—Assets Held More Than One Year

a. Kind of property and description	b. Date acquired	c. Date sold	d. Gross sales price less expense	e. Cost or other basis	f. Gain or (loss) from all sales	g. Enter gain or (loss) from sales after 10/31/78
6 1,000 MONARCH IND.	12/13/74	12/16/78	40,000 —	20,000 —	20,000 —	20,000 —

7 Capital gain distributions	**7**	0	0
8 Enter gain, if applicable, from Form 4797, line 6(a)(1) (see Instructions page 19)	**8**	0	0
9 Enter your share of net long-term gain or (loss) from partnerships and fiduciaries	**9**	0	0
10 Enter your share of net long-term gain from small business corporations (Subchapter S)	**10**	0	0
11 Net gain or (loss), combine lines 6 through 10	**11**	20,000 —	20,000 —
12 Long-term capital loss carryover attributable to years beginning after 1969 (see Instructions page 19)	**12** (	)	
13 Net long-term gain or (loss), combine lines 11 and 12, column (f)	**13**	20,000 —	

NOTE: If you have capital loss carryovers from years beginning before 1970, do not complete Parts III, IV, or VI. See Form 4798 instead.

Part III Computation of Capital Gain Deduction
(Complete this part only if line 14 shows a gain)

14 Combine lines 5 and 13, column (f), and enter here. If result is zero or a loss, do not complete the rest of this part. Instead skip to Part IV, line 24 on page 2	**14**	20,000 —
15 Enter line 13, column (f) or line 14, whichever is smaller. If zero or a loss, enter zero and skip to line 23 .	**15**	20,000 —
16 If line 11, column (g) is a gain, combine lines 3 and 11, column (g), and enter here. If this line or line 11, column (g) shows a loss or zero, enter a zero and skip to line 20	**16**	20,000 —
17 Enter line 11, column (g) or line 16, whichever is smaller	**17**	20,000 —
18 Enter line 15 or line 17, whichever is smaller	**18**	20,000 —
19 Enter 60% of amount on line 18	**19**	12,000 —
20 Subtract line 18 from line 15	**20**	0
21 Enter 50% of amount on line 20	**21**	0
22 Add line 19 and line 21. This is your capital gain deduction	**22**	12,000 —
23 Subtract line 22 from line 14. Enter this amount on Form 1040, line 14	**23**	8,000 —

Part IV — **Computation of Capital Loss Deduction**
(Complete this part only if line 14, page 1 shows a loss)

24 If line 14 shows a loss—
 a Enter one of the following amounts:
  (i) If line 5, column (f) is zero or a net gain, enter 50% of line 14;
  (ii) If line 13, column (f) is zero or a net gain, enter line 14; or
  (iii) If line 5, column (f) and line 13 are net losses, enter amount on line 5, column (f) added to 50% of amount on line 13, column (f) . . . .
	24a	

b Enter here and enter as a (loss) on Form 1040, line 14, the smallest of:
  (i) The amount on line 24a;
  (ii) $3,000 ($1,500 if married and filing a separate return); or
  (iii) Taxable income, as adjusted (see Instructions page 20) . . . .
	24b	

Part V — **Computation of Alternative Tax**
(See instructions page 20 to see if the alternative tax will benefit you)

25 Enter amount from Schedule TC (Form 1040), Part I, line 3	**25**	89,000	—
26 Subtract line 22 from line 15 (or Form 4798, line 15 from line 7) and enter here	**26**	8,000	—
27 Subtract line 26 from line 25 (if line 26 is more than line 25, do not complete the rest of this part. The Alternative Tax will not benefit you)	**27**	81,000	—
Note: *If line 15 is not more than $50,000 ($25,000, if married, filing separately), skip lines 28 through 31, and enter zero on line 32.*			
28 Divide line 26 by line 15. Multiply the result by $50,000 ($25,000, if married filing separately), and enter here	**28**	20,000	—
29 Add lines 27 and 28	**29**	101,000	—
30 Tax on amount on line 25 (use Tax Rate Schedule in instructions) . . . 　**30**　36,704 —			
31 Tax on amount on line 29 (use Tax Rate Schedule in instructions) . . . 　**31**　43,860 —			
32 Subtract line 31 from line 30	**32**	0	
33 Tax on amount on line 27 (use Tax Rate Schedule in instructions)	**33**	32,064	—
34 Enter 25% of line 15 but not more than $12,500 ($6,250, if married filing separately) . . .	**34**	5,000	—
35 Alternative Tax—add lines 32, 33, and 34. If less than the tax figured on the amount on Schedule TC (Form 1040), Part I, line 3, enter this alternative tax on Schedule TC (Form 1040), Part I, line 4. Also check the Schedule D box on Schedule TC (Form 1040), Part I, line 4	**35**	37,064	—

Part VI — **Computation of Post-1969 Capital Loss Carryovers from 1978 to 1979**
(Complete this part if the loss on line 24a is more than the loss shown on line 24b)

Section A.—Short-term Capital Loss Carryover

36 Enter loss shown on line 5; if none enter zero and skip lines 37 through 41—then go to line 42 . . .	**36**	
37 Enter gain shown on line 13. If that line is blank or shows a loss, enter zero	**37**	
38 Reduce any loss on line 36 to the extent of any gain on line 37	**38**	
39 Enter amount shown on line 24b	**39**	
40 Enter smaller of line 38 or 39	**40**	
41 Subtract line 40 from line 38	**41**	
Note: *The amount on line 41 is the part of your short-term capital loss carryover from 1978 to 1979 that is attributable to years beginning after 1969.*		

Section B.—Long-term Capital Loss Carryover

42 Subtract line 40 from line 39 **(Note:** *If you skipped lines 37 through 41, enter amount from line 24b)* .	**42**	
43 Enter loss from line 13; if none, enter zero and skip lines 44 through 47	**43**	
44 Enter gain shown on line 5. If that line is blank or shows a loss, enter a zero	**44**	
45 Reduce any loss on line 43 to the extent of any gain on line 44	**45**	
46 Multiply amount on line 42 by 2	**46**	
47 Subtract line 46 from line 45	**47**	
Note: *The amount on line 47 is the part of your long-term capital loss carryover from 1978 to 1979 that is attributable to years beginning after 1969.*		

☆ U.S. GOVERNMENT PRINTING OFFICE : 1978—O-263-276—E.I. NO. 52-1074467

85

SCHEDULE E (Form 1040) Department of the Treasury Internal Revenue Service	**Supplemental Income Schedule** (From pensions and annuities, rents and royalties, partnerships, estates and trusts, etc.) ▶ Attach to Form 1040. ▶ See Instructions for Schedule E (Form 1040).	19**78**

Name(s) as shown on Form 1040   **Your social security number**

BEN + BARBARA REICH   000 : 00 : 0000

Part I   Pension and Annuity Income. If **fully taxable**, do not complete this part. Enter amount on Form 1040, line 17. For one pension or annuity not fully taxable, complete this part. If you have more than one pension or annuity that is not fully taxable, attach a separate sheet listing each one with the appropriate data and enter combined total of taxable portions on line 5.

1 Name of payer ▶

2 Did your employer contribute part of the cost? . . . . ☐ Yes ☐ No

  If "Yes," is your contribution recoverable within 3 years of the annuity starting date? . . . . ☐ Yes ☐ No

  If "Yes," show: Your contribution ▶ $.................., Contribution recovered in prior years ▶ | 2 |

3 Amount received this year . . . . | 3 |

4 Amount excludable this year . . . . | 4 |

5 Taxable portion (subtract line 4 from line 3) . . . . | 5 |

Part II   Rent and Royalty Income. If you need more space, use Form 4831.

Have you claimed expenses connected with your vacation home (or other dwelling unit) rented to others (see instructions)? . . . . ☐ Yes ☐ No

If "Yes," did you or a member of your family occupy the vacation home (or other dwelling unit) for more than 14 days during the taxable year? ☐ Yes ☐ No

(a) Kind and location of property If residential, also write "R"	(b) Total amount of rents	(c) Total amount of royalties	(d) Depreciation (explain below) or depletion (attach computation)	(e) Other expenses (Repairs, etc.— explain below)

6 Totals . . . .

7 Net income or (loss) from rents and royalties (column (b) plus column (c) less columns (d) and (e)) . | 7 |

8 Net rental income or (loss) (from Form 4831) . . . . | 8 |

9 Net farm rental profit or (loss) (from Form 4835) . . . . | 9 |

10 Total rent and royalty income or (loss) (add lines 7, 8, and 9) . . . . | 10 |

Part III	Income or Losses from— (a) Name	(b) Employer identification number	(c) Your share of gross farming or fishing income (see instructions)	(d) Loss	(e) Income
Partnerships	GUSHER OIL EXPLORERS	000-00-0000		(9,000-)	0
	BONANZA DRILLING	000-00-0000		(9,000-)	0
	PETROCHEMICAL EXPLORATION, LTD.	000-00-0000		(4,500-)	0
	11 Add amounts in columns (d) and (e)	11	(22,500-)	0
	12 Column (e), line 11, less column (d), line 11	12	(22,500 -)
	13 Additional first-year depreciation	13	0
	14 Total partnership income or (loss). Combine lines 12 and 13	14	(22,500 -)
Estates or Trusts	D'COURTNEY ITF BARBARA REICH	00-0000000			5,000 —
	15 Add amounts in columns (d) and (e)	15		
	16 Total estate or trust income or (loss). Column (e), line 15, less column (d), line 15	16	5,000 —
Small Bus. Corps.					
	17 Add amounts in columns (d) and (e)	17		
	18 Total small business corporation income or (loss). (Column (e), line 17, less column (d), line 17 .	18	

19 **TOTAL** (add lines 5, 10, 14, 16, and 18. Enter here and on Form 1040, line 18 . . . . ▶ | 19 | (17,500 -) |

Explanation of Column (e), Part II

Item	Amount	Item	Amount	Item	Amount

Schedule for Depreciation Claimed in Part II above. If you need more space use Form 4562.

(a) Description of property	(b) Date acquired	(c) Cost or other basis	(d) Depreciation allowed or allowable in prior years	(e) Method of computing depreciation	(f) Life or rate	(g) Depreciation for this year	**E**
1 Total additional first-year depreciation (do not include in items below) ▶							
2 Totals			. . . .		

Form **4726** Department of the Treasury Internal Revenue Service	**Maximum Tax on Personal Service Income** ▶ Attach to Form 1040 (or Form 1041).	**1978**

Name(s) as shown on Form 1040 (or Form 1041) BEN + BARBARA REICH	Identifying number 000-00-0000

Do not complete this form if—(a) Taxable income or personal service taxable income is:

$40,200 or less, and on Form 1040, you checked box 1 or box 4,

$55,200 or less, and on Form 1040, you checked box 2 or box 5,

$26,000 or less and this is an Estate or Trust return (Form 1041);

(b) You elected income averaging; or

(c) On Form 1040, you checked box 3.

A—Personal Service Income		B—Deductions Against Personal Service Income	
Total personal service income	100,000—	Total deductions against personal service income	0

1 Personal service net income—Subtract total amount in column B from total amount in column A	1	100,000—
2 Enter your adjusted gross income (see instructions)	2	90,500—
3 Divide the amount on line 1 by the amount on line 2. Enter percentage result here, but not more than 100%. Round to nearest 4 numbers (see instructions)	3	.905
4 Enter your taxable income (see instructions)	4	89,000—
5 Multiply the amount on line 4 by the percentage on line 3	5	80,545—
6 Enter the total of your 1978 tax preference items (see instructions)	6	22,500—
7 Personal service taxable income. Subtract line 6 from line 5 (see instructions)	7	58,045—
8 If: on Form 1040, you checked box 1 or box 4, enter $40,200 on Form 1040, you checked box 2 or box 5, enter $55,200 Estate or Trust, enter $26,000	8	55,200—
9 Subtract line 8 from line 7 (if zero or less, do not complete rest of form)	9	2,845—
10 Enter 50% of line 9	10	1,422—
11 Tax on amount on line 4 . . . 11	36,704—	
12 Tax on amount on line 7 . . . 12	19,568—	
13 Subtract line 12 from line 11	13	17,136—
14 If the amount on line 8 is: $40,200, enter $13,290 ($12,240 if unmarried head of household) $55,200, enter $18,060 $26,000, enter $9,030	14	18,060—
15 Add lines 10, 13, and 14. This is your maximum tax (see instructions)	15	(36,618—)

Computation of Alternative Tax

16 Amount from line 4	16	89,000—
17 Enter amount reportable on Schedule D (Form 1040), line 26 or Schedule D (Form 1041), line 20*	17	8,000—
18 Subtract line 17 from line 16	18	81,000—
Note: If Schedule D (Form 1040), line 15; Form 4798, line 7; or Schedule D (Form 1041), line 17(e) or 31 is not more than $50,000, skip lines 19 through 23.		
19 Enter amount reportable on Schedule D (Form 1040), line 28 or Schedule D (Form 1041), line 22	19	10,000—
20 Add lines 18 and 19	20	91,000—
21 Enter amount from line 11	21	36,704—
22 Tax on amount on line 20	22	37,864—
23 Subtract line 22 from line 21	23	0
24 Tax on amount on line 18. **Caution:** If line 7 is more than line 18, enter instead, amount on line 12 less 50% of the excess of line 7 over line 18	24	32,064—
25 Subtract line 24 from line 11	25	4,640—
26 Subtract line 25 from line 15	26	31,978—
27 Enter 25% of Schedule D (Form 1040), line 15; Form 4798, line 7; or Schedule D (Form 1041), line 17(e) or 31, but not more than $12,500	27	5,000—
28 Add lines 23 (if applicable), 26 and 27	28	36,978

*If you reported capital gain distributions but did not use Schedule D (Form 1040), enter on line 17 the amount shown on Form 1040, line 15.

263-165-1

Form **4726** (1978)

SCHEDULE TC
(Form 1040)
Department of the Treasury
Internal Revenue Service

Tax Computation Schedule

▶ Attach to Form 1040.

1978

Name(s) as shown on Form 1040

BEN + BARBARA REICH

Your social security number

000 00 0000

Part I — Computation of Tax for Taxpayers Who Cannot Use the Tax Tables

Use this part to figure your tax if:
- Your income on Form 1040, line 34, is more than $20,000 and you checked Filing Status Box 1, 3, or 4 on Form 1040.
- Your income on Form 1040, line 34, is more than $40,000 and you checked Filing Status Box 2 or 5 on Form 1040.

- You had more exemptions than were covered in the Tax Table for your filing status.
- You figure your tax using the alternative tax computation on Schedule D (Capital Gains and Losses), Schedule G (Income Averaging), or Form 4726 (Maximum Tax on Personal Service Income).

1 Enter the amount from Form 1040, line 34	1	90,500 —
2 Multiply $750 by the total number of exemptions claimed on Form 1040, line 7	2	1,500 —
3 Taxable Income. Subtract line 2 from line 1. (Figure your tax on this amount by using the Tax Rate Schedules or one of the other methods listed on line 4.)	3	89,000 —
4 Income Tax. Enter tax and check if from: ☐ Tax Rate Schedule X, Y, or Z, ☐ Schedule D, ☐ Schedule G, or ☑ Form 4726	4	36,618 —

General Tax Credit

5 Multiply $35 by the total number of exemptions claimed on Form 1040, line 7. (If you are married filing a separate return, skip lines 6 through 9 and enter the amount from line 5 on line 10.)	5	70 —	
6 Enter the amount from line 3, above	6	89,000 —	
7 Enter { $3,200 if you are married filing a joint return or a qualifying widow(er) } { $2,200 if you are single or an unmarried head of household . . . }	7	3,200 —	
8 Subtract line 7 from line 6	8	85,800 —	
9 Enter 2% of line 8 (but do not enter more than $180)	9	180 —	
10 General tax credit. Enter the amount from line 5 or line 9, whichever is larger	10	180 —	
11 Tax. Subtract line 10 from line 4. (If $0 or less, enter $0.) Enter this amount on Form 1040, line 35 . . . . ▶	11	36,438 —	

TC

Part II — Computation for Certain Taxpayers Who Must Itemize Deductions

If you are included in one of the groups below, you MUST itemize. If you must itemize and the amount on Schedule A (Form 1040), line 40, is more than your itemized deductions on Schedule A, line 39, you must complete Part II before figuring your tax.

You MUST itemize your deductions if:

A. You can be claimed as a dependent on your parent's return and had interest, dividends, or other unearned income of $750 or more and less than $2,200 of earned income if single (less than $1,600 if married filing a separate return).

Note: If your earned income is more than your itemized deductions on Schedule A, line 39, enter your earned income in Part II, line 3, of this schedule, unless you are married filing a separate return and your spouse itemizes deductions. Generally, your earned income is the total of any amounts on Form 1040, lines 8,

13, and 19. See page 11 of the Instructions for Form 1040 for more details.

B. You are married filing a separate return and your spouse itemizes deductions. (There is an exception to this rule. You don't have to itemize if your spouse must itemize only because he or she is described in A and enters earned income instead of itemized deductions on Part II, line 3, of this schedule. If this is the case, don't complete Part II. Go back to Form 1040, line 33, and enter $0. Then go to Form 1040, line 34.)

C. You file Form 4563 to exclude income from sources in U.S. possessions. (Please see Form 4563, and Publication 570, Tax Guide for U.S. Citizens Employed in U.S. Possessions, for more details.)

D. You had dual status as a nonresident alien for part of 1978, and during the rest of the year you were either a resident alien or a U.S. citizen. However, you don't have to itemize if at the end of 1978, you were married to a U.S. resident or citizen and file a joint return reporting your combined worldwide income.

1 Enter the amount from Form 1040, line 31			1
2 Enter the amount from Schedule A, line 40	2		
3 Enter the amount from Schedule A, line 39	3		
Caution: If you can be claimed as a dependent on your parent's return, see the Note above. Be sure you check the box below line 33 of Form 1040.			
4 Subtract line 3 from line 2			4
5 Add lines 1 and 4. Enter here and on Form 1040, line 34. (Leave Form 1040, line 33 blank. Disregard the instruction to subtract line 33 from line 32. Follow the rest of the instructions for Form 1040, line 34.) . . . . ▶			5

Tax Compu- tation	32 Amount from line 31	32	90,500 —
	33 If you do not itemize deductions, enter zero . . . . } If you itemize, complete Schedule A (Form 1040) and enter the amount from Schedule A, line 41	33	0
	Caution: If you have unearned income and can be claimed as a dependent on your parent's return, check here ▶ ☐ and see page 11 of the Instructions. Also see page 11 of the Instructions if: ● You are married filing a separate return and your spouse itemizes deductions, OR ● You file Form 4563, OR ● You are a dual-status alien.		
	34 Subtract line 33 from line 32. Use the amount on line 34 to find your tax from the Tax Tables, or to figure your tax on Schedule TC, Part I . . . . Use Schedule TC, Part I, and the Tax Rate Schedules ONLY if: ● The amount on line 34 is more than $20,000 ($40,000 if you checked Filing Status Box 2 or 5), OR ● You have more exemptions than those covered in the Tax Table for your filing status, OR ● You use any of these forms to figure your tax: Schedule D, Schedule G, or Form 4726. Otherwise, you MUST use the Tax Tables to find your tax.	34	90,500 —
	35 Tax. Enter tax here and check if from ☐ Tax Tables or ☑ Schedule TC	35	36,438 —
	36 Additional taxes. (See page 11 of Instructions.) Enter total and check if from ☐ Form 4970, } ☐ Form 4972, ☐ Form 5544, ☐ Form 5405, or ☐ Section 72(m)(5) penalty tax . . .	36	0
	37 Total. Add lines 35 and 36 . . . . ▶	37	36,438 —
Credits	38 Credit for contributions to candidates for public office . .	38		
	39 Credit for the elderly (attach Schedules R&RP)	39		
	40 Credit for child and dependent care expenses (attach Form 2441)	40		
	41 Investment credit (attach Form 3468)	41		
	42 Foreign tax credit (attach Form 1116)	42		
	43 Work Incentive (WIN) Credit (attach Form 4874)	43		
	44 New jobs credit (attach Form 5884)	44		
	45 Residential energy credits (see page 12 of Instructions, attach Form 5695) . . .	45		
	46 Total credits. Add lines 38 through 45 . . . . ▶	46	0
	47 Balance. Subtract line 46 from line 37 and enter difference (but not less than zero) . ▶	47	36,438 —
Other Taxes	48 Self-employment tax (attach Schedule SE)	48	
	49 Minimum tax. Check here ▶ ☐ and attach Form 4625 TAX LIABILITY EXCEEDED PREFERENCE ITEMS	49	0
	50 Tax from recomputing prior-year investment credit (attach Form 4255)	50	
	51 Social security (FICA) tax on tip income not reported to employer (attach Form 4137) . .	51	
	52 Uncollected employee FICA and RRTA tax on tips (from Form W–2)	52	
	53 Tax on an IRA (attach Form 5329)	53	
	54 Total tax. Add lines 47 through 53 . . . . ▶	54	36,438 —
Payments Attach Forms W–2, W–2G, and W–2P to front.	55 Total Federal income tax withheld	55		
	56 1978 estimated tax payments and credit from 1977 return .	56		
	57 Earned income credit. If line 31 is under $8,000, see page 2 of Instructions. If eligible, enter child's name ▶..............	57		
	58 Amount paid with Form 4868	58		
	59 Excess FICA and RRTA tax withheld (two or more employers)	59		
	60 Credit for Federal tax on special fuels and oils (attach Form 4136) .	60		
	61 Regulated Investment Company credit (attach Form 2439)	61		
	62 Total. Add lines 55 through 61 . . . . ▶	62	
Refund or Due	63 If line 62 is larger than line 54, enter amount OVERPAID . . . . ▶	63	
	64 Amount of line 63 to be REFUNDED TO YOU . . . . ▶	64	
	65 Amount of line 63 to be credited on 1979 estimated tax. ▶	65	
	66 If line 54 is larger than line 62, enter BALANCE DUE. Attach check or money order for full amount payable to "Internal Revenue Service." Write your social security number on check or money order . . ▶ (Check ▶ ☐ if Form 2210 (2210F) is attached. See page 14 of instructions.) ▶ $	66	

Please Sign Here	Under penalties of perjury, I declare that I have examined this return, including accompanying schedules and statements, and to the best of my knowledge and belief, it is true, correct, and complete. Declaration of preparer (other than taxpayer) is based on all information of which preparer has any knowledge.		
	▶ Your signature	Date	Spouse's signature (if filing jointly, BOTH must sign even if only one had income)
	Paid Preparer's Information	Preparer's signature ▶	Preparer's social security no.	Check if self-employed ▶ ☐
		Firm's name (or yours, if self-employed), address and ZIP code ▶	E.I. No. ▶
			Date ▶

Form 1040

Department of the Treasury—Internal Revenue Service

U.S. Individual Income Tax Return 1978

For Privacy Act Notice, see page 3 of Instructions | For the year January 1–December 31, 1978, or other tax year beginning _____ , 1978, ending _____ , 19 ___ .

Use IRS label. Otherwise, please print or type.	Your first name and initial (if joint return, also give spouse's name and initial)	Last name	Your social security number
	OLIVIA	PRESTEIGN	000 00 0000
	Present home address (Number and street, including apartment number, or rural route)		Spouse's social security no.
	City, town or post office, State and ZIP code		Your occupation EXECUTIVE
			Spouse's occupation

Do you want $1 to go to the Presidential Election Campaign Fund? **Yes** ☐ **No** ☐
If joint return, does your spouse want $1 to go to this fund? . . **Yes** ☐ **No** ☐
Note: Checking Yes will not increase your tax or reduce your refund.

Filing Status
Check only one box.

1. ✓ Single
2. ☐ Married filing joint return (even if only one had income)
3. ☐ Married filing separate return. If spouse is also filing, give spouse's social security number in the space above and enter full name here ▶ _____
4. ☐ Unmarried head of household. Enter qualifying name ▶ _____ See page 6 of Instructions.
5. ☐ Qualifying widow(er) with dependent child (Year spouse died ▶ 19 ___). See page 6 of Instructions.

Exemptions
Always check the box labeled Yourself.
Check other boxes if they apply.

6a ✓ Yourself ☐ 65 or over ☐ Blind

Enter number of boxes checked on 6a and b ▶ **1**

b ☐ Spouse ☐ 65 or over ☐ Blind

c First names of your dependent children who lived with you ▶ _____

Enter number of children listed ▶

d Other dependents:

(1) Name	(2) Relationship	(3) Number of months lived in your home	(4) Did dependent have income of $750 or more?	(5) Did you provide more than one-half of dependent's support?

Enter number of other dependents ▶

Add numbers entered in boxes above ▶ **1**

7. Total number of exemptions claimed . . . .

Income
Please attach Copy B of your Forms W–2 here.

If you do not have a W–2, see page 5 of Instructions.

8	Wages, salaries, tips, and other employee compensation	8	40,000
9	Interest income (If over $400, attach Schedule B)	9	0
10a	Dividends (If over $400, attach Schedule B) _____ , 10b Exclusion _____		
10c	Subtract line 10b from line 10a	10c	0
11	State and local income tax refunds (does not apply unless refund is for year you itemized deductions)	11	0
12	Alimony received	12	0
13	Business income or (loss) (attach Schedule C)	13	0
14	Capital gain or (loss) (attach Schedule D)	14	0
15	Taxable part of capital gain distributions not reported on Schedule D (see page 9 of Instructions) . .	15	0
16	Net gain or (loss) from Supplemental Schedule of Gains and Losses (attach Form 4797)	16	0
17	Fully taxable pensions and annuities not reported on Schedule E	17	0
18	Pensions, annuities, rents, royalties, partnerships, estates or trusts, etc. (attach Schedule E)	18	0
19	Farm income or (loss) (attach Schedule F)	19	0
20	Other income (state nature and source—see page 10 of Instructions) ▶ _____	20	0
21	Total income. Add lines 8, 9, and 10c through 20 . . . . ▶	21	40,000

Please attach check or money order here.

Adjustments to Income

22	Moving expense (attach Form 3903)	22	
23	Employee business expenses (attach Form 2106) . . .	23	
24	Payments to an IRA (see page 10 of Instructions)	24	
25	Payments to a Keogh (H.R. 10) retirement plan . . .	25	
26	Interest penalty due to early withdrawal of savings	26	
27	Alimony paid (see page 10 of Instructions)	27	
28	Total adjustments. Add lines 22 through 27 . . . . ▶	28	0

Adjusted Gross Income

29	Subtract line 28 from line 21	29	40,000
30	Disability income exclusion (attach Form 2440)	30	0
31	Adjusted gross income. Subtract line 30 from line 29. If this line is less than $8,000, see page 2 of Instructions. If you want IRS to figure your tax, see page 4 of Instructions . . . . ▶	31	40,000

☆ U.S. GOVERNMENT PRINTING OFFICE: 1978—O-263-303   13-2587299

Form 1040 (1978)

Tax Computation Schedule

SCHEDULE TC
(Form 1040)
Department of the Treasury
Internal Revenue Service

▶ Attach to Form 1040.

1978

Name(s) as shown on Form 1040

OLIVIA PRESTEIGN

Your social security number

000 00 0000

Part I — Computation of Tax for Taxpayers Who Cannot Use the Tax Tables

Use this part to figure your tax if:
- Your income on Form 1040, line 34, is more than $20,000 and you checked Filing Status Box 1, 3, or 4 on Form 1040.
- Your income on Form 1040, line 34, is more than $40,000 and you checked Filing Status Box 2 or 5 on Form 1040.

- You had more exemptions than were covered in the Tax Table for your filing status.
- You figure your tax using the alternative tax computation on Schedule D (Capital Gains and Losses), Schedule G (Income Averaging), or Form 4726 (Maximum Tax on Personal Service Income).

1 Enter the amount from Form 1040, line 34	**1**	40,000 —
2 Multiply $750 by the total number of exemptions claimed on Form 1040, line 7	**2**	750 —
3 Taxable Income. Subtract line 2 from line 1. (Figure your tax on this amount by using the Tax Rate Schedules or one of the other methods listed on line 4.)	**3**	39,250 —
4 Income Tax. Enter tax and check it from: ☑ Tax Rate Schedule X, Y, or Z, ☐ Schedule D, ☐ Schedule G, or ☐ Form 4726	**4**	12,815 —

General Tax Credit

5 Multiply $35 by the total number of exemptions claimed on Form 1040, line 7. (If you are married filing a separate return, skip lines 6 through 9 and enter the amount from line 5 on line 10.)	**5**	35 —	
6 Enter the amount from line 3, above	**6**	39,250 —	
7 Enter { $3,200 if you are married filing a joint return or a qualifying widow(er)	$2,200 if you are single or an unmarried head of household . . . }	**7**	2,200 —	
8 Subtract line 7 from line 6	**8**	37,050 —	
9 Enter 2% of line 8 (but do not enter more than $180)	**9**	180 —	
10 General tax credit. Enter the amount from line 5 or line 9, whichever is larger	**10**	180 —
11 Tax. Subtract line 10 from line 4. (If $0 or less, enter $0.) Enter this amount on Form 1040, line 35 . . . . ▶	**11**	12,635 —

TC

Part II — Computation for Certain Taxpayers Who Must Itemize Deductions

If you are included in one of the groups below, you MUST itemize. If you must itemize and the amount on Schedule A (Form 1040), line 40, is more than your itemized deductions on Schedule A, line 39, you must complete Part II before figuring your tax.

You MUST itemize your deductions if:

A. You can be claimed as a dependent on your parent's return and had interest, dividends, or other unearned income of $750 or more and less than $2,200 of earned income if single (less than $1,600 if married filing a separate return).

Note: If your earned income is more than your itemized deductions on Schedule A, line 39, enter your earned income in Part II, line 3, of this schedule, unless you are married filing a separate return and your spouse itemizes deductions. Generally, your earned income is the total of any amounts on Form 1040, lines 8,

13, and 19. See page 11 of the Instructions for Form 1040 for more details.

B. You are married filing a separate return and your spouse itemizes deductions. (There is an exception to this rule. You don't have to itemize if your spouse must itemize only because he or she is described in A and enters earned income instead of itemized deductions on Part II, line 3, of this schedule. If this is the case, don't complete Part II. Go back to Form 1040, line 33, and enter $0. Then go to Form 1040, line 34.)

C. You file Form 4563 to exclude income from sources in U.S. possessions. (Please see Form 4563, and Publication 570, Tax Guide for U.S. Citizens Employed in U.S. Possessions, for more details.)

D. You had dual status as a nonresident alien for part of 1978, and during the rest of the year you were either a resident alien or a U.S. citizen. However, you don't have to itemize if at the end of 1978, you were married to a U.S. resident or citizen and file a joint return reporting your combined worldwide income.

1 Enter the amount from Form 1040, line 31		**1**	
2 Enter the amount from Schedule A, line 40	**2**		
3 Enter the amount from Schedule A, line 39	**3**		
Caution: If you can be claimed as a dependent on your parent's return, see the Note above. Be sure you check the box below line 33 of Form 1040.			
4 Subtract line 3 from line 2		**4**	
5 Add lines 1 and 4. Enter here and on Form 1040, line 34. (Leave Form 1040, line 33 blank. Disregard the instruction to subtract line 33 from line 32. Follow the rest of the instructions for Form 1040, line 34.) . . . . ▶		**5**	

☆U.S. GOVERNMENT PRINTING OFFICE: 1978—263-331

23-188-5979

91

Tax Compu- tation	32 Amount from line 31	32	40,000 —
	33 If you do not itemize deductions, enter zero . . . . ⎫ If you itemize, complete Schedule A (Form 1040) and enter the amount from Schedule A, line 41 . . . . ⎬	33	0
	Caution: If you have unearned income and can be claimed as a dependent on your parent's return, check here ▶ ☐ and see page 11 of the Instructions. Also see page 11 of the Instructions if: • You are married filing a separate return and your spouse itemizes deductions, OR • You file Form 4563, OR • You are a dual-status alien.		
	34 Subtract line 33 from line 32. Use the amount on line 34 to find your tax from the Tax Tables, or to figure your tax on Schedule TC, Part I . . . . Use Schedule TC, Part I, and the Tax Rate Schedules ONLY if: • The amount on line 34 is more than $20,000 ($40,000 if you checked Filing Status Box 2 or 5), OR • You have more exemptions than those covered in the Tax Table for your filing status, OR • You use any of these forms to figure your tax: Schedule D, Schedule G, or Form 4726. Otherwise, you MUST use the Tax Tables to find your tax.	34	40,000
	35 Tax. Enter tax here and check if from ☐ Tax Tables or ☑ Schedule TC	35	12,635 —
	36 Additional taxes. (See page 11 of Instructions.) Enter total and check if from ☐ Form 4970, ⎫ ☐ Form 4972, ☐ Form 5544, ☐ Form 5405, or ☐ Section 72(m)(5) penalty tax . . . ⎬	36	0
	37 **Total.** Add lines 35 and 36 . . . . ▶	37	12,635 —
Credits	38 Credit for contributions to candidates for public office . .	38		
	39 Credit for the elderly (attach Schedules R&RP)	39		
	40 Credit for child and dependent care expenses (attach Form 2441) .	40		
	41 Investment credit (attach Form 3468)	41		
	42 Foreign tax credit (attach Form 1116)	42		
	43 Work Incentive (WIN) Credit (attach Form 4874)	43		
	44 New jobs credit (attach Form 5884)	44		
	45 Residential energy credits (see page 12 of Instructions, attach Form 5695) . .	45		
	46 Total credits. Add lines 38 through 45	46	0
	47 **Balance.** Subtract line 46 from line 37 and enter difference (but not less than zero) . ▶	47	12,635 —
Other Taxes	48 Self-employment tax (attach Schedule SE)	48		
	49 Minimum tax. Check here ▶ ☐ and attach Form 4625	49		
	50 Tax from recomputing prior-year investment credit (attach Form 4255)	50		
	51 Social security (FICA) tax on tip income not reported to employer (attach Form 4137) . .	51		
	52 Uncollected employee FICA and RRTA tax on tips (from Form W–2)	52		
	53 Tax on an IRA (attach Form 5329)	53		
	54 **Total tax.** Add lines 47 through 53 . . . . ▶	54	12,635 —
Payments Attach Forms W–2, W–2G, and W–2P to front.	55 Total Federal income tax withheld	55		
	56 1978 estimated tax payments and credit from 1977 return .	56		
	57 Earned income credit. If line 31 is under $8,000, see page 2 of Instructions. If eligible, enter child's name ▶	57		
	58 Amount paid with Form 4868	58		
	59 Excess FICA and RRTA tax withheld (two or more employers)	59		
	60 Credit for Federal tax on special fuels and oils (attach Form 4136) .	60		
	61 Regulated Investment Company credit (attach Form 2439)	61		
	62 **Total.** Add lines 55 through 61 . . . . ▶	62		
Refund or Due	63 If line 62 is larger than line 54, enter amount **OVERPAID** . . . . ▶	63		
	64 Amount of line 63 to be **REFUNDED TO YOU** . . . . ▶	64		
	65 Amount of line 63 to be credited on 1979 estimated tax . ▶	65		
	66 If line 54 is larger than line 62, enter **BALANCE DUE.** Attach check or money order for full amount payable to "Internal Revenue Service." Write your social security number on check or money order . . ▶ (Check ▶ ☐ if Form 2210 (2210F) is attached. See page 14 of instructions.) ▶ $	66		

Please Sign Here

Under penalties of perjury, I declare that I have examined this return, including accompanying schedules and statements, and to the best of my knowledge and belief, it is true, correct, and complete. Declaration of preparer (other than taxpayer) is based on all information of which preparer has any knowledge.

▶ Your signature	Date	▶ Spouse's signature (if filing jointly, BOTH must sign even if only one had income)

Paid Preparer's Information	Preparer's signature ▶	Preparer's social security no.	Check if self-employed ▶ ☐
	Firm's name (or yours, if self-employed), address and ZIP code ▶	E.I. No. ▶	
		Date ▶	

92

Form **1040** Department of the Treasury—Internal Revenue Service
U.S. Individual Income Tax Return 1978

| For Privacy Act Notice, see page 3 of Instructions | For the year January 1–December 31, 1978, or other tax year beginning | , 1978, ending | , 19 |

Use IRS label. Other-wise, please print or type.	Your first name and initial (if joint return, also give spouse's name and initial)	Last name	Your social security number
	OLIVIA	PRESTEIGN	000 00 0000
	Present home address (Number and street, including apartment number, or rural route)		Spouse's social security no.
	City, town or post office, State and ZIP code		Your occupation EXECUTIVE

Do you want $1 to go to the Presidential Election Campaign Fund? **Yes** / **No**
If joint return, does your spouse want $1 to go to this fund? . . **Yes** / **No**

Note: Checking Yes will not increase your tax or reduce your refund.

Spouse's occupation

Filing Status
Check only one box.

1. ✓ Single
2. ☐ Married filing joint return (even if only one had income)
3. ☐ Married filing separate return. If spouse is also filing, give spouse's social security number in the space above and enter full name here ▶
4. ☐ Unmarried head of household. Enter qualifying name ▶ . See page 6 of Instructions.
5. ☐ Qualifying widow(er) with dependent child (Year spouse died ▶ 19). See page 6 of Instructions.

Exemptions
Always check the box labeled Yourself.
Check other boxes if they apply.

6a ✓ Yourself ☐ 65 or over ☐ Blind
  } Enter number of boxes checked on 6a and b ▶ ✓

b ☐ Spouse ☐ 65 or over ☐ Blind

c First names of your dependent children who lived with you ▶ .... } Enter number of children listed ▶

d Other dependents:

(1) Name	(2) Relationship	(3) Number of months lived in your home	(4) Did dependent have income of $750 or more?	(5) Did you provide more than one-half of dependent's support?

Enter number of other dependents ▶

Add numbers entered in boxes above ▶ | 1

Income

Please attach Copy B of your Forms W–2 here.

If you do not have a W–2, see page 5 of Instructions.

7	Total number of exemptions claimed		
8	Wages, salaries, tips, and other employee compensation	8	40,000 —
9	Interest income (If over $400, attach Schedule B)	9	0
10a	Dividends (If over $400, attach Schedule B)............|....., 10b Exclusion....|....		
10c	Subtract line 10b from line 10a	10c	0
11	State and local income tax refunds (does not apply unless refund is for year you itemized deductions)	11	0
12	Alimony received	12	0
13	Business income or (loss) (attach Schedule C)	13	0
14	Capital gain or (loss) (attach Schedule D)	14	0
15	Taxable part of capital gain distributions not reported on Schedule D (see page 9 of Instructions) . .	15	0
16	Net gain or (loss) from Supplemental Schedule of Gains and Losses (attach Form 4797)	16	0
17	Fully taxable pensions and annuities not reported on Schedule E	17	0
18	Pensions, annuities, rents, royalties, partnerships, estates or trusts, etc. (attach Schedule E)	18	(5,000)
19	Farm income or (loss) (attach Schedule F)	19	0
20	Other income (state nature and source—see page 10 of Instructions) ▶	20	0
21	Total income. Add lines 8, 9, and 10c through 20 . . . . ▶	21	35,000 —

Please attach check or money order here.

Adjustments to Income

22	Moving expense (attach Form 3903)	22	
23	Employee business expenses (attach Form 2106) . .	23	
24	Payments to an IRA (see page 10 of Instructions)	24	
25	Payments to a Keogh (H.R. 10) retirement plan . . .	25	
26	Interest penalty due to early withdrawal of savings	26	
27	Alimony paid (see page 10 of Instructions)	27	
28	Total adjustments. Add lines 22 through 27 . . . . ▶	28	0

Adjusted Gross Income

29	Subtract line 28 from line 21	29	35,000 —
30	Disability income exclusion (attach Form 2440)	30	0
31	Adjusted gross income. Subtract line 30 from line 29. If this line is less than $8,000, see page 2 of Instructions. If you want IRS to figure your tax, see page 4 of Instructions . . . . ▶	31	35,000 —

☆ U.S. GOVERNMENT PRINTING OFFICE: 1978—O-263-303 13-2687299

Form 1040 (1978)

SCHEDULE E
(Form 1040)

Department of the Treasury
Internal Revenue Service

Supplemental Income Schedule

(From pensions and annuities, rents and royalties, partnerships, estates and trusts, etc.)
▶ Attach to Form 1040.   ▶ See Instructions for Schedule E (Form 1040).

19**78**

Name(s) as shown on Form 1040   Your social security number

OLIVIA PRESTEIGN   000 00 0000

Part I   Pension and Annuity Income. If fully taxable, do not complete this part. Enter amount on Form 1040, line 17.
For one pension or annuity not fully taxable, complete this part. If you have more than one pension or annuity that is not fully taxable, attach a separate sheet listing each one with the appropriate data and enter combined total of taxable portions on line 5.

1 Name of payer ▶ ....
2 Did your employer contribute part of the cost? . . . . □ Yes □ No
   If "Yes," is your contribution recoverable within 3 years of the annuity starting date? . . . . . . □ Yes □ No
   If "Yes," show: Your contribution ▶ $................., Contribution recovered in prior years ▶ | 2 | |
3 Amount received this year . . . . | 3 | |
4 Amount excludable this year . . . . | 4 | |
5 Taxable portion (subtract line 4 from line 3) . . . . | 5 | |

Part II   Rent and Royalty Income. If you need more space, use Form 4831.

Have you claimed expenses connected with your vacation home (or other dwelling unit) rented to others (see instructions)? . . . . . □ Yes □ No
If "Yes," did you or a member of your family occupy the vacation home (or other dwelling unit) for more than 14 days during the taxable year? □ Yes □ No

(a) Kind and location of property If residential, also write "R"	(b) Total amount of rents	(c) Total amount of royalties	(d) Depreciation (explain below) or depletion (attach computation)	(e) Other expenses (Repairs, etc.— explain below)

6 Totals . . . .
7 Net income or (loss) from rents and royalties (column (b) plus column (c) less columns (d) and (e)) . | 7 | |
8 Net rental income or (loss) (from Form 4831) . . . . | 8 | |
9 Net farm rental profit or (loss) (from Form 4835) . . . . | 9 | |
10 Total rent and royalty income or (loss) (add lines 7, 8, and 9) . . . . | 10 | |

Part III   Income or Losses from—

(a) Name	(b) Employer identification number	(c) Your share of gross farming or fishing income (see instructions)	(d) Loss	(e) Income
Partnerships BEAUTEOUS GARDEN APARTMENTS	00-0000000		(5,000)	0

11 Add amounts in columns (d) and (e) . . . . | 11 | (5,000) | 0 |
12 Column (e), line 11, less column (d), line 11 . . . . | 12 | (5,000 ▶) |
13 Additional first-year depreciation . . . . | 13 | 0 |
14 Total partnership income or (loss). Combine lines 12 and 13 . . . . | 14 | (5,000 ▶) |

Estates or Trusts

15 Add amounts in columns (d) and (e) . . . . | 15 | |
16 Total estate or trust income or (loss). Column (e), line 15, less column (d), line 15 . . . . . | 16 | |

Small Bus. Corps.

17 Add amounts in columns (d) and (e) . . . . | 17 | |
18 Total small business corporation income or (loss). (Column (e), line 17, less column (d), line 17 . | 18 | |
19 TOTAL (add lines 5, 10, 14, 16, and 18). Enter here and on Form 1040, line 18 . . . . ▶ | 19 | |

Explanation of Column (e), Part II

Item	Amount	Item	Amount	Item	Amount

Schedule for Depreciation Claimed in Part II above. If you need more space use Form 4562.

(a) Description of property	(b) Date acquired	(c) Cost or other basis	(d) Depreciation allowed or allowable in prior years	(e) Method of computing depreciation	(f) Life or rate	(g) Depreciation for this year
1 Total additional first-year depreciation (do not include in items below) ▶						
2 Totals						

☆U.S. GOVERNMENT PRINTING OFFICE 1978 - 263 318   23-188-5979

SCHEDULE TC
(Form 1040)
Department of the Treasury
Internal Revenue Service

Tax Computation Schedule

▶ Attach to Form 1040.

1978

Name(s) as shown on Form 1040	Your social security number
OLIVIA PRESTEIGN	000 00 0000

Part I Computation of Tax for Taxpayers Who Cannot Use the Tax Tables

Use this part to figure your tax if:
- Your income on Form 1040, line 34, is more than $20,000 and you checked Filing Status Box 1, 3, or 4 on Form 1040.
- Your income on Form 1040, line 34, is more than $40,000 and you checked Filing Status Box 2 or 5 on Form 1040.

- You had more exemptions than were covered in the Tax Table for your filing status.
- You figure your tax using the alternative tax computation on Schedule D (Capital Gains and Losses), Schedule G (Income Averaging), or Form 4726 (Maximum Tax on Personal Service Income).

1 Enter the amount from Form 1040, line 34	1	35,000 —
2 Multiply $750 by the total number of exemptions claimed on Form 1040, line 7	2	750 —
3 Taxable Income. Subtract line 2 from line 1. (Figure your tax on this amount by using the Tax Rate Schedules or one of the other methods listed on line 4.)	3	34,250 —
4 Income Tax. Enter tax and check if from: ☑ Tax Rate Schedule X, Y, or Z, ☐ Schedule D, ☐ Schedule G, or ☐ Form 4726	4	10,315 —

General Tax Credit

5 Multiply $35 by the total number of exemptions claimed on Form 1040, line 7. (If you are married filing a separate return, skip lines 6 through 9 and enter the amount from line 10 on line 5.) . . .	5	35 —		
6 Enter the amount from line 3, above	6	34,250 —		
7 Enter { $3,200 if you are married filing a joint return or a qualifying widow(er) } { $2,200 if you are single or an unmarried head of household } . . .	7	2,200 —		
8 Subtract line 7 from line 6	8	32,050 —		
9 Enter 2% of line 8 (but do not enter more than $180)	9	180 —		
10 General tax credit. Enter the amount from line 5 or line 9, whichever is larger	10	180 —		
11 Tax. Subtract line 10 from line 4. (If $0 or less, enter $0.) Enter this amount on Form 1040, line 35 . . . . ▶	11	10,135 —		

TC

Part II Computation for Certain Taxpayers Who Must Itemize Deductions

If you are included in one of the groups below, you MUST itemize. If you must itemize and the amount on Schedule A (Form 1040), line 40, is more than your itemized deductions on Schedule A, line 39, you must complete Part II before figuring your tax.

You MUST itemize your deductions if:

A. You can be claimed as a dependent on your parent's return and had interest, dividends, or other unearned income of $750 or more and less than $2,200 of earned income if single (less than $1,600 if married filing a separate return).

Note: If your earned income is more than your itemized deductions on Schedule A, line 39, enter your earned income in Part II, line 3, of this schedule, unless you are married filing a separate return and your spouse itemizes deductions. Generally, your earned income is the total of any amounts on Form 1040, lines 8,

13, and 19. See page 11 of the Instructions for Form 1040 for more details.

B. You are married filing a separate return and your spouse itemizes deductions. (There is an exception to this rule. You don't have to itemize if your spouse must itemize only because he or she is described in A and enters earned income instead of itemized deductions on Part II, line 3, of this schedule. If this is the case, don't complete Part II. Go back to Form 1040, line 33, and enter $0. Then go to Form 1040, line 34.)

C. You file Form 4563 to exclude income from sources in U.S. possessions. (Please see Form 4563, and Publication 570, Tax Guide for U.S. Citizens Employed in U.S. Possessions, for more details.)

D. You had dual status as a nonresident alien for part of 1978, and during the rest of the year you were either a resident alien or a U.S. citizen. However, you don't have to itemize if at the end of 1978, you were married to a U.S. resident or citizen and file a joint return reporting your combined worldwide income.

1 Enter the amount from Form 1040, line 31	1	
2 Enter the amount from Schedule A, line 40	2	
3 Enter the amount from Schedule A, line 39	3	
Caution: If you can be claimed as a dependent on your parent's return, see the Note above. Be sure you check the box below line 33 of Form 1040.		
4 Subtract line 3 from line 2	4	
5 Add lines 1 and 4. Enter here and on Form 1040, line 34. (Leave Form 1040, line 33 blank. Disregard the instruction to subtract line 33 from line 32. Follow the rest of the instructions for Form 1040, line 34.) . . . . ▶	5	

☆ U.S. GOVERNMENT PRINTING OFFICE: 1978—263-331

23-188-5979

Tax Compu- tation	32 Amount from line 31	32	35,000 —
	33 If you do not itemize deductions, enter zero . . . . ⎫		
	If you itemize, complete Schedule A (Form 1040) and enter the amount from Schedule A, line 41 . . . . ⎬	33	0
	Caution: If you have unearned income and can be claimed as a dependent on your parent's return, check here ▶ ☐ and see page 11 of the Instructions. Also see page 11 of the Instructions if: • You are married filing a separate return and your spouse itemizes deductions, OR • You file Form 4563, OR • You are a dual-status alien.		
	34 Subtract line 33 from line 32. Use the amount on line 34 to find your tax from the Tax Tables, or to figure your tax on Schedule TC, Part I . . . . Use Schedule TC, Part I, and the Tax Rate Schedules ONLY if: • The amount on line 34 is more than $20,000 ($40,000 if you checked Filing Status Box 2 or 5), OR • You have more exemptions than those covered in the Tax Table for your filing status, OR • You use any of these forms to figure your tax: Schedule D, Schedule G, or Form 4726. Otherwise, you MUST use the Tax Tables to find your tax.	34	35,000 —
	35 Tax. Enter tax here and check if from ☐ Tax Tables or ☑ Schedule TC	35	10,135 —
	36 Additional taxes. (See page 11 of Instructions.) Enter total and check if from ☐ Form 4970, ⎫ ☐ Form 4972, ☐ Form 5544, ☐ Form 5405, or ☐ Section 72(m)(5) penalty tax . . . ⎬	36	0
	37 Total. Add lines 35 and 36 . . . . ▶	37	10,135 —
Credits	38 Credit for contributions to candidates for public office . .	38		
	39 Credit for the elderly (attach Schedules R&RP)	39		
	40 Credit for child and dependent care expenses (attach Form 2441) .	40		
	41 Investment credit (attach Form 3468)	41		
	42 Foreign tax credit (attach Form 1116)	42		
	43 Work Incentive (WIN) Credit (attach Form 4874)	43		
	44 New jobs credit (attach Form 5884)	44		
	45 Residential energy credits (see page 12 of Instructions, attach Form 5695) . .	45		
	46 Total credits. Add lines 38 through 45	46	0
	47 Balance. Subtract line 46 from line 37 and enter difference (but not less than zero) . ▶	47	10,135 —
Other Taxes	48 Self-employment tax (attach Schedule SE)	48	
	49 Minimum tax. Check here ▶ ☐ and attach Form 4625	49	
	50 Tax from recomputing prior-year investment credit (attach Form 4255)	50	
	51 Social security (FICA) tax on tip income not reported to employer (attach Form 4137) . .	51	
	52 Uncollected employee FICA and RRTA tax on tips (from Form W–2)	52	
	53 Tax on an IRA (attach Form 5329)	53	
	54 Total tax. Add lines 47 through 53 . . . . ▶	54	10,
Payments Attach Forms W–2, W–2G, and W–2P to front.	55 Total Federal income tax withheld	55		
	56 1978 estimated tax payments and credit from 1977 return .	56		
	57 Earned income credit. If line 31 is under $8,000, see page 2 of Instructions. If eligible, enter child's name ▶...............	57		
	58 Amount paid with Form 4868	58		
	59 Excess FICA and RRTA tax withheld (two or more employers)	59		
	60 Credit for Federal tax on special fuels and oils (attach Form 4136) .	60		
	61 Regulated Investment Company credit (attach Form 2439)	61		
	62 Total. Add lines 55 through 61 . . . . ▶	62	
Refund or Due	63 If line 62 is larger than line 54, enter amount OVERPAID . . . . ▶	63	
	64 Amount of line 63 to be REFUNDED TO YOU . . . . ▶	64	
	65 Amount of line 63 to be credited on 1979 estimated tax. ▶	65	
	66 If line 54 is larger than line 62, enter BALANCE DUE. Attach check or money order for full amount payable to "Internal Revenue Service." Write your social security number on check or money order . . ▶ (Check ▶ ☐ if Form 2210 (2210F) is attached. See page 14 of instructions.) ▶ $	66	

Please Sign Here	Under penalties of perjury, I declare that I have examined this return, including accompanying schedules and statements, and to the best of my knowledge and belief, it is true, correct, and complete. Declaration of preparer (other than taxpayer) is based on all information of which preparer has any knowledge.

Your signature	Date	Spouse's signature (if filing jointly, BOTH must sign even if only one had income)

Paid Preparer's Information	Preparer's signature ▶	Preparer's social security no.	Check if self-employed ▶ ☐
	Firm's name (or yours, if self-employed), address and ZIP code ▶	E.I. No. ▶	
		Date ▶	

96

Form 1040 Department of the Treasury—Internal Revenue Service
U.S. Individual Income Tax Return **1978**

For Privacy Act Notice, see page 3 of Instructions | For the year January 1–December 31, 1978, or other tax year beginning ____, 1978, ending ____, 19 __.

Use IRS label. Otherwise, please print or type.	Your first name and initial (if joint return, also give spouse's name and initial) ODYSSEUS	Last name GAUL	Your social security number 000 00 0000
	Present home address (Number and street, including apartment number, or rural route)		Spouse's social security no.
	City, town or post office, State and ZIP code		Your occupation RETIRED

Do you want $1 to go to the Presidential Election Campaign Fund? Yes ☐ No ☐
If joint return, does your spouse want $1 to go to this fund? Yes ☐ No ☐
Note: Checking Yes will not increase your tax or reduce your refund.

Spouse's occupation

Filing Status
Check only one box.

1 ✓ Single
2 ☐ Married filing joint return (even if only one had income)
3 ☐ Married filing separate return. If spouse is also filing, give spouse's social security number in the space above and enter full name here ▶
4 ☐ Unmarried head of household. Enter qualifying name ▶ .... See page 6 of Instructions.
5 ☐ Qualifying widow(er) with dependent child (Year spouse died ▶ 19). See page 6 of Instructions.

Exemptions

Always check the box labeled Yourself. Check other boxes if they apply.

6a ✓ Yourself ✓ 65 or over ☐ Blind
   Enter number of boxes checked on 6a and b ▶ 2
b ☐ Spouse ☐ 65 or over ☐ Blind
c First names of your dependent children who lived with you ▶
   Enter number of children listed ▶

d Other dependents:

(1) Name	(2) Relationship	(3) Number of months lived in your home	(4) Did dependent have income of $750 or more?	(5) Did you provide more than one-half of dependent's support?

Enter number of other dependents ▶

Add numbers entered in boxes above ▶ 2

7 Total number of exemptions claimed ....

Income

Please attach Copy B of your Forms W-2 here.

If you do not have a W-2, see page 5 of Instructions.

Please attach check or money order here.

8	Wages, salaries, tips, and other employee compensation	8	0
9	Interest income (If over $400, attach Schedule B)	9	2,500 —
10a	Dividends (If over $400, attach Schedule B) ...., 10b Exclusion........		
10c	Subtract line 10b from line 10a	10c	0
11	State and local income tax refunds (does not apply unless refund is for year you itemized deductions)	11	0
12	Alimony received	12	0
13	Business income or (loss) (attach Schedule C)	13	0
14	Capital gain or (loss) (attach Schedule D)	14	0
15	Taxable part of capital gain distributions not reported on Schedule D (see page 9 of Instructions)	15	0
16	Net gain or (loss) from Supplemental Schedule of Gains and Losses (attach Form 4797)	16	0
17	Fully taxable pensions and annuities not reported on Schedule E	17	15,000 —
18	Pensions, annuities, rents, royalties, partnerships, estates or trusts, etc. (attach Schedule E)	18	0
19	Farm income or (loss) (attach Schedule F)	19	0
20	Other income (state nature and source—see page 10 of Instructions) ▶	20	0
21	Total income. Add lines 8, 9, and 10c through 20 ▶	21	17,500 —

Adjustments to Income

22	Moving expense (attach Form 3903)	22	
23	Employee business expenses (attach Form 2106)	23	
24	Payments to an IRA (see page 10 of Instructions)	24	
25	Payments to a Keogh (H.R. 10) retirement plan	25	
26	Interest penalty due to early withdrawal of savings	26	
27	Alimony paid (see page 10 of Instructions)	27	
28	Total adjustments. Add lines 22 through 27 ▶	28	0

Adjusted Gross Income

29	Subtract line 28 from line 21	29	17,500 —
30	Disability income exclusion (attach Form 2440)	30	0
31	Adjusted gross income. Subtract line 30 from line 29. If this line is less than $8,000, see page 2 of Instructions. If you want IRS to figure your tax, see page 4 of Instructions ▶	31	17,500 —

☆ U.S. GOVERNMENT PRINTING OFFICE: 1978—O-263-303 13-2687299

Form 1040 (1978)

Name(s) as shown on Form 1040 (Do not enter name and social security number if shown on other side) | Your social security number

ODYSSEUS GAUL   000 00 0000

Part I   Interest Income

1 If you received more than $400 in interest, Complete Part I. Please see page 8 of the instructions to find out what interest to report. Then answer the questions in Part III, below. If you received interest as a nominee for another, or you received or paid accrued interest on securities transferred between interest payment dates, please see page 18 of the instructions.

Part II   Dividend Income

3 If you received more than $400 in gross dividends (including capital gain distributions) and other distributions on stock, complete Part II. Please see page 9 of the instructions. Write (H), (W), (J), for stock held by husband, wife, or jointly. Then answer the questions in Part III, below. If you received dividends as a nominee for another, please see page 18 of the instructions.

Name of payer	Amount		Name of payer	Amount
ABSCONDERS + DEFAULTERS	2,500 —			
NATIONAL BANK				
2 Total interest income. Enter here and on Form 1040, line 9				

Part III   Foreign Accounts and Foreign Trusts

If you are required to list interest in Part I or dividends in Part II, OR if you had a foreign account or were a grantor of, or a transferor to a foreign trust, you must answer both questions in Part III. Please see page 18 of the instructions.

	Yes	No
A Did you, at any time during the taxable year, have an interest in or signature or other authority over a bank, securities, or other financial account in a foreign country (see page 18 of instructions)? . . .		
B Were you the grantor of, or transferor to, a foreign trust during any taxable year, which foreign trust was in being during the current taxable year, whether or not you have any beneficial interest in such trust? . If "Yes," you may be required to file Forms 3520, 3520-A, or 926.		

4 Total of line 3 . . . .

5 Capital gain distributions. Enter here and on Schedule D, line 7. See Note below . . .

6 Nontaxable distributions . . . . .

7 Total (add lines 5 and 6) . . . . . .

8 Dividends before exclusion (subtract line 7 from line 4). Enter here and on Form 1040, line 10a . . . .

B

Note: *If you received capital gain distributions and do not need Schedule D to report any other gains or losses or to compute the alternative tax, do not file that schedule. Instead, enter the taxable part of capital gain distributions on Form 1040, line 15.*

☆ U.S. Government Printing Office: 1978-O-263-309-E.I. # 52-0237640

Tax Compu-tation	32 Amount from line 31	32	17,500 —
	33 If you do not itemize deductions, enter zero . . . . } If you itemize, complete Schedule A (Form 1040) and enter the amount from Schedule A, line 41 . . . . }	33	0
	Caution: If you have unearned income and can be claimed as a dependent on your parent's return, check here ▶ ☐ and see page 11 of the Instructions. Also see page 11 of the Instructions if: • You are married filing a separate return and your spouse itemizes deductions, OR • You file Form 4563, OR • You are a dual-status alien.		
	34 Subtract line 33 from line 32. Use the amount on line 34 to find your tax from the Tax Tables, or to figure your tax on Schedule TC, Part I . . . . Use Schedule TC, Part I, and the Tax Rate Schedules ONLY if: • The amount on line 34 is more than $20,000 ($40,000 if you checked Filing Status Box 2 or 5), OR • You have more exemptions than those covered in the Tax Table for your filing status, OR • You use any of these forms to figure your tax: Schedule D, Schedule G, or Form 4726. Otherwise, you MUST use the Tax Tables to find your tax.	34	17,500 —
	35 Tax. Enter tax here and check if from ☑ Tax Tables or ☐ Schedule TC	35	2,965 —
	36 Additional taxes. (See page 11 of Instructions.) Enter total and check if from ☐ Form 4970, } ☐ Form 4972, ☐ Form 5544, ☐ Form 5405, or ☐ Section 72(m)(5) penalty tax . . . }	36	0
	37 **Total.** Add lines 35 and 36 . . . . ▶	37	2,965 —

Credits	38 Credit for contributions to candidates for public office . .	38		
	39 Credit for the elderly (attach Schedules R&RP)	39		
	40 Credit for child and dependent care expenses (attach Form 2441) .	40		
	41 Investment credit (attach Form 3468)	41		
	42 Foreign tax credit (attach Form 1116)	42		
	43 Work Incentive (WIN) Credit (attach Form 4874)	43		
	44 New jobs credit (attach Form 5884)	44		
	45 Residential energy credits (see page 12 of Instructions, attach Form 5695) . .	45		
	46 **Total credits.** Add lines 38 through 45	46	0
	47 **Balance.** Subtract line 46 from line 37 and enter difference (but not less than zero) . ▶	47	2,965 —

Other Taxes	48 Self-employment tax (attach Schedule SE)	48	
	49 Minimum tax. Check here ▶ ☐ and attach Form 4625	49	
	50 Tax from recomputing prior-year investment credit (attach Form 4255)	50	
	51 Social security (FICA) tax on tip income not reported to employer (attach Form 4137) . . .	51	
	52 Uncollected employee FICA and RRTA tax on tips (from Form W–2)	52	
	53 Tax on an IRA (attach Form 5329)	53	
	54 **Total tax.** Add lines 47 through 53 . . . . ▶	54	2,965 —

Payments Attach Forms W–2, W–2G, and W–2P to front.	55 Total Federal income tax withheld	55	
	56 1978 estimated tax payments and credit from 1977 return .	56	
	57 Earned income credit. If line 31 is under $8,000, see page 2 of Instructions. If eligible, enter child's name ▶...............	57	
	58 Amount paid with Form 4868	58	
	59 Excess FICA and RRTA tax withheld (two or more employers)	59	
	60 Credit for Federal tax on special fuels and oils (attach Form 4136) .	60	
	61 Regulated Investment Company credit (attach Form 2439)	61	
	62 **Total.** Add lines 55 through 61 . . . . ▶	62	

Refund or Due	63 If line 62 is larger than line 54, enter amount **OVERPAID** . . . . ▶	63	
	64 Amount of line 63 to be **REFUNDED TO YOU** . . . . ▶	64	
	65 Amount of line 63 to be credited on 1979 estimated tax. ▶	65	
	66 If line 54 is larger than line 62, enter **BALANCE DUE.** Attach check or money order for full amount payable to "Internal Revenue Service." Write your social security number on check or money order . . ▶ (Check ▶ ☐ if Form 2210 (2210F) is attached. See page 14 of instructions.) ▶ $	66	

Please Sign Here

Under penalties of perjury, I declare that I have examined this return, including accompanying schedules and statements, and to the best of my knowledge and belief, it is true, correct, and complete. Declaration of preparer (other than taxpayer) is based on all information of which preparer has any knowledge.

Your signature	Date	Spouse's signature (if filing jointly, BOTH must sign even if only one had income)

Paid Preparer's Information	Preparer's signature ▶	Preparer's social security no.	Check if self-employed ▶ ☐
	Firm's name (or yours, if self-employed), address and ZIP code ▶	E.I. No. ▶	
		Date ▶	

99

Form 1040

Department of the Treasury—Internal Revenue Service
U.S. Individual Income Tax Return 1978

For Privacy Act Notice, see page 3 of Instructions | For the year January 1–December 31, 1978, or other tax year beginning , 1978, ending , 19 .

Use IRS label. Other-wise, please print or type.	Your first name and initial (if joint return, also give spouse's name and initial) ODYSSEUS	Last name GAUL	Your social security number 000 00 0000
	Present home address (Number and street, including apartment number, or rural route)		Spouse's social security no.
	City, town or post office, State and ZIP code		Your occupation RETIRED

Do you want $1 to go to the Presidential Election Campaign Fund? ☐ Yes ☐ No
If joint return, does your spouse want $1 to go to this fund? . . ☐ Yes ☐ No

Note: Checking Yes will not increase your tax or reduce your refund.

Spouse's occupation

Filing Status

Check only one box.

1 ✔ Single
2 ☐ Married filing joint return (even if only one had income)
3 ☐ Married filing separate return. If spouse is also filing, give spouse's social security number in the space above and enter full name here ▶
4 ☐ Unmarried head of household. Enter qualifying name ▶ . See page 6 of Instructions.
5 ☐ Qualifying widow(er) with dependent child (Year spouse died ▶ 19). See page 6 of Instructions.

Exemptions

Always check the box labeled Yourself. Check other boxes if they apply.

6a ✔ Yourself ✔ 65 or over ☐ Blind } Enter number of boxes checked on 6a and b ▶ **2**

b ☐ Spouse ☐ 65 or over ☐ Blind

c First names of your dependent children who lived with you ▶ -------- Enter number of children listed ▶

d Other dependents: (1) Name	(2) Relationship	(3) Number of months lived in your home	(4) Did dependent have income of $750 or more?	(5) Did you provide more than one-half of dependent's support?

Enter number of other dependents ▶

7 Total number of exemptions claimed . . . . Add numbers entered in boxes above ▶ **2**

Income

Please attach Copy B of your Forms W–2 here.

If you do not have a W–2, see page 5 of Instructions.

Please attach check or money order here.

8	Wages, salaries, tips, and other employee compensation	8	O
9	Interest income (If over $400, attach Schedule B)	9	O
10a	Dividends (If over $400, attach Schedule B) . . . . . , 10b Exclusion		
10c	Subtract line 10b from line 10a	10c	O
11	State and local income tax refunds (does not apply unless refund is for year you itemized deductions)	11	O
12	Alimony received	12	O
13	Business income or (loss) (attach Schedule C)	13	O
14	Capital gain or (loss) (attach Schedule D)	14	O
15	Taxable part of capital gain distributions not reported on Schedule D (see page 9 of Instructions) . .	15	O
16	Net gain or (loss) from Supplemental Schedule of Gains and Losses (attach Form 4797)	16	O
17	Fully taxable pensions and annuities not reported on Schedule E	17	15,000 —
18	Pensions, annuities, rents, royalties, partnerships, estates or trusts, etc. (attach Schedule E)	18	c
19	Farm income or (loss) (attach Schedule F)	19	O
20	Other income (state nature and source—see page 10 of Instructions) ▶ --------	20	O
21	Total income. Add lines 8, 9, and 10c through 20 . . . . ▶	21	15,000

Adjustments to Income

22	Moving expense (attach Form 3903)	22		
23	Employee business expenses (attach Form 2106) . .	23		
24	Payments to an IRA (see page 10 of Instructions)	24		
25	Payments to a Keogh (H.R. 10) retirement plan . . .	25		
26	Interest penalty due to early withdrawal of savings	26		
27	Alimony paid (see page 10 of Instructions)	27		
28	Total adjustments. Add lines 22 through 27 . . . . ▶		28	O

Adjusted Gross Income

29	Subtract line 28 from line 21	29	15,000 —
30	Disability income exclusion (attach Form 2440)	30	O
31	Adjusted gross income. Subtract line 30 from line 29. If this line is less than $8,000, see page 2 of Instructions. If you want IRS to figure your tax, see page 4 of Instructions . . . . ▶	31	15,000 —

☆ U.S. GOVERNMENT PRINTING OFFICE: 1978—O-263-303 13-2687299

Form 1040 (1978)

Form 1040 (1978)   Page **2**

Tax Compu- tation	32 Amount from line 31	32	15,000 —
	33 If you do not itemize deductions, enter zero . . . . }		
	If you itemize, complete Schedule A (Form 1040) and enter the amount from Schedule A, line 41	33	0
	Caution: If you have unearned income and can be claimed as a dependent on your parent's return, check here ▶ ☐ and see page 11 of the Instructions. Also see page 11 of the Instructions if: • You are married filing a separate return and your spouse itemizes deductions, OR • You file Form 4563, OR • You are a dual-status alien.		
	34 Subtract line 33 from line 32. Use the amount on line 34 to find your tax from the Tax Tables, or to figure your tax on Schedule TC, Part I	34	15,000 —
	Use Schedule TC, Part I, and the Tax Rate Schedules ONLY if: • The amount on line 34 is more than $20,000 ($40,000 if you checked Filing Status Box 2 or 5), OR • You have more exemptions than those covered in the Tax Table for your filing status, OR • You use any of these forms to figure your tax: Schedule D, Schedule G, or Form 4726. Otherwise, you MUST use the Tax Tables to find your tax.		
	35 Tax. Enter tax here and check if from ☑ Tax Tables or ☐ Schedule TC	35	2,254 —
	36 Additional taxes. (See page 11 of Instructions.) Enter total and check if from ☐ Form 4970, } ☐ Form 4972, ☐ Form 5544, ☐ Form 5405, or ☐ Section 72(m)(5) penalty tax . . . }	36	0
	37 **Total.** Add lines 35 and 36 . . . . ▶	37	2,254 —
Credits	38 Credit for contributions to candidates for public office . . `38`		
	39 Credit for the elderly (attach Schedules R&RP) . . . . . `39`		
	40 Credit for child and dependent care expenses (attach Form 2441) . `40`		
	41 Investment credit (attach Form 3468) . . . . `41`		
	42 Foreign tax credit (attach Form 1116) . . . . `42`		
	43 Work Incentive (WIN) Credit (attach Form 4874) . . . . . `43`		
	44 New jobs credit (attach Form 5884) . . . . `44`		
	45 Residential energy credits (see page 12 of Instructions, attach Form 5695) . . `45`		
	46 **Total credits.** Add lines 38 through 45	46	0
	47 **Balance.** Subtract line 46 from line 37 and enter difference (but not less than zero) . ▶	47	2,254 —
Other Taxes	48 Self-employment tax (attach Schedule SE)	48	
	49 Minimum tax. Check here ▶ ☐ and attach Form 4625	49	
	50 Tax from recomputing prior-year investment credit (attach Form 4255)	50	
	51 Social security (FICA) tax on tip income not reported to employer (attach Form 4137) . .	51	
	52 Uncollected employee FICA and RRTA tax on tips (from Form W–2)	52	
	53 Tax on an IRA (attach Form 5329)	53	
	54 **Total tax.** Add lines 47 through 53 . . . . ▶	54	2,254 —
Payments Attach Forms W–2, W–2G, and W–2P to front.	55 Total Federal income tax withheld . . . . `55`		
	56 1978 estimated tax payments and credit from 1977 return . `56`		
	57 Earned income credit. If line 31 is under $8,000, see page 2 of Instructions. If eligible, enter child's name ▶................... `57`		
	58 Amount paid with Form 4868 . . . . `58`		
	59 Excess FICA and RRTA tax withheld (two or more employers) `59`		
	60 Credit for Federal tax on special fuels and oils (attach Form 4136) . `60`		
	61 Regulated Investment Company credit (attach Form 2439) `61`		
	62 **Total.** Add lines 55 through 61 . . . . ▶	62	
Refund or Due	63 If line 62 is larger than line 54, enter amount **OVERPAID** . . . . ▶	63	
	64 Amount of line 63 to be **REFUNDED TO YOU** . . . . ▶	64	
	65 Amount of line 63 to be credited on 1979 estimated tax. ▶ `65`		
	66 If line 54 is larger than line 62, enter **BALANCE DUE.** Attach check or money order for full amount payable to "Internal Revenue Service." Write your social security number on check or money order . . ▶ (Check ▶ ☐ if Form 2210 (2210F) is attached. See page 14 of instructions.) ▶ $	66	

Under penalties of perjury, I declare that I have examined this return, including accompanying schedules and statements, and to the best of my knowledge and belief, it is true, correct, and complete. Declaration of preparer (other than taxpayer) is based on all information of which preparer has any knowledge.

▶ Your signature	Date ▶	▶ Spouse's signature (if filing jointly, BOTH must sign even if only one had income)

Paid Preparer's Information	Preparer's signature ▶		Preparer's social security no.	Check if self- employed ▶ ☐
	Firm's name (or yours, if self-employed), address and ZIP code ▶		E.I. No. ▶	
			Date ▶	

Please Sign Here

101

Part
TWO: CONSERVATIVE
TAX SHELTERS

5 For Widows and Orphans: Tax-Exempt Securities

Although tax shelters are almost always thought of in connection with professionals—high-income investors who can afford big risks—there are many tax shelters "safe" enough for the prudent trustee's shibboleth: widows and orphans. ("Safe" is in quotes because none of these investments offers protection against interest-rate risk or inflation.) Of these, tax-exempt securities (also called municipal bonds) are probably the best known.

Municipal bonds can be issued by state and local governments, including counties and cities, and by legally created municipal agencies (e.g., housing finance, health and hospitals, power authorities). There are two major types of municipal bonds: general obligation bonds and revenue bonds.

General obligation bonds (often abbreviated GO in financial newspapers and journals) are issued by a political subdivision (state, county, city) where the issuer has the power to tax property—a power which generally stems from the state itself. The state's ability to tax property at an unspecified rate (whatever it takes to pay the debt) is pledged as a source of security. This concept is referred to as the "full faith and credit" of the issuing agent.

Revenue bonds are secured by a stream of income from a specific project—for example, construction of a baseball stadium whose users pay the city, a municipally owned electric power plant which sells the electricity it produces—anything that has a revenue stream. Interest payments and bond redemptions are secured by that revenue. If the bond is payable only from that revenue stream and the revenue becomes insufficient, the issuer will not be able to pay the principal and the interest on the bond. Failure on the part of the issuer to pay debt service when due is called *default* and has been resorted to by several state turnpike authorities in the past.

Sometimes a revenue bond is also secured by the issuer's full faith and credit. This guarantee is an advantage, especially during the first few years of the project's life; if an unexpected cash-flow problem arises, the guarantee is especially important. Such a bond is called a "double-barreled bond"; its being secured by both project revenues and the issuer's general obligations makes it a stronger investment than either a straight revenue or a general obligation bond. For this reason, these bonds usually pay less interest than traditional revenue bonds. The State of Florida Hillsborough Expressway bonds are an example of this category; they are secured first by tolls and gasoline taxes, and also by Florida's full faith and credit.

Industrial development bonds and pollution-control bonds are also revenue bonds that are tax-exempt. Since corporations cannot issue tax-exempt bonds, the bonds are issued by the municipality where the facilities are to be located. However, the bonds are secured only by the corporation's ability to pay. The municipality has no responsibility for debt service (interest and repayment of principal). Because of this, these bonds are generally only as good as the corporation issuing them, and the bond ratings are based solely on the corporation's financial strength.

Industrial development bonds are generally sold to

help a corporation build a plant in a community by providing inexpensive financing. Because these bonds are tax-exempt, they will cost the corporation less in interest charges—often 2% to 3%, or $20 to $30 per $1,000 per year. Similarly, for companies with existing facilities, the tax-exempt feature of pollution-control revenue bonds provides an economic incentive to build such pollution-control facilities as scrubbers and water-treatment equipment.

NOTE: For all bond investments, analysis of how senior the bond is (how many other bond issues must be paid off before it) is important in determining the safety or risk of the investment. A brokerage house's bond research department will do this for customers and prospects.

Bond maturities—the date the borrower must repay the money that the bond represents—are an important factor in municipal investments. A borrower can redeem bonds prior to maturity in two ways: through call provisions or through a sinking fund, options which are printed on the bond.

The *call date* is the first date that the bonds can be retired by the issuer, an option for which the issuer will usually pay a premium. Thus a bond that matures in 2010 may be callable beginning in 1985 at a price of 103 (103% of par value, or $1,030). Called bonds are chosen by lottery—usually in inverse order, with the longest maturities chosen first so that the issuer saves on debt service. Otherwise the issuer would have to pay interest on those bonds for the longest period of time.

An issuer can also use a *sinking fund* to redeem bonds before they fall due. In this instance, the issuer puts away funds, on a semiannual basis, to redeem a predetermined number of bonds, chosen by lot. This procedure reduces the total debt and improves the debt coverage on the remaining bonds. This improves the quality of the outstanding bonds. Unfortunately, unlike a called bond, which is redeemed at a premium, a bond called through a sinking fund is usually redeemed at par (written as 100, and meaning 100% of each $1,000 of debt).

Bond ratings have been mentioned earlier in passing.

Standard & Poor's and Moody's ratings are the best known. Fitch's, another rating service, is active primarily in the Midwest.

Investors should be aware that Standard & Poor's and Moody's ratings can differ widely. For example, Allegheny County (Pittsburgh area) bonds are rated Baa-1 by Moody's and AA by Standard & Poor's—a substantial difference.

Moral obligation bonds are also rated differently by the two services. Unlike general obligation bonds, which are backed by the full faith and credit of the issuer, moral obligation bonds provide that if there is a deficit in the project's debt-service reserve fund, the project administrator must certify the deficit to the governor, who may decide for or against appropriating state funds to cure the deficit. The state legislature then votes on appropriating money for that purpose. Although the governor or state legislature could turn down the request, such a veto would probably adversely affect the state's future credibility in the bond markets and is therefore unlikely to occur. Accordingly, Standard & Poor's will automatically rate any moral obligation bond one notch below its corresponding general obligation bond; for example, the service rates New York State general obligation bonds AA and its moral obligation bonds A. On the other hand, Moody's gives no weight to the moral obligation clause. Consequently it rates New York's Battery Park bonds Ba, while Standard & Poor's rates them A.

Insured bonds are also rated differently by Standard & Poor's and Moody's. Two companies—MBIA and AMBAC—insure investors' municipal bond portfolios for payment of principal and interest. (Premiums are based on size of portfolio, bonds held, etc.) Standard & Poor's automatically rates MBIA-insured bonds AAA and AMBAC-insured bonds AA. Moody's gives no weight to insurance as a source of security. Thus it is theoretically possible for a bond to be in default, but be insured by MBIA, and thereby be rated AAA by Standard & Poor's and C by Moody's.

Following is a listing and explanation of Standard & Poor's and Moody's ratings:

Standard & Poor's	Moody's	Interpretation
AAA*	Aaa	Highest rating—extremely strong capacity to pay interest and repay principal
AA†	Aa	Very strong capacity—little difference from AAA or Aaa
A	A‡	Strong capacity to pay interest and repay principal
BBB	Baa	Adequate capacity—more susceptible to economic and market conditions
BB	Ba	Speculative—but lowest degree of speculation
B	B	More speculative
CCC	Caa	Increasingly speculative
CC	Ca	Most speculative
C	C	No interest being paid
D		Bond in default and payment of interest and/or payment of principal is in arrears

* Under present commercial bank regulations issued by the Comptroller of the Currency, bonds in the top four categories (generally called "investment grade") are usually considered suitable for bank investment.

† Standard & Poor's further refines its ratings from AA to BB with plus and minus signs to indicate relative standing within these major rating categories.

‡ Moody's further refines its ratings in the A and Baa groups by using the symbols A-1 and Baa-1 to indicate the strongest bonds in these groups.

Bond yields are of major importance to the investor, but the term "yield" itself is an oversimplification. Investors must concern themselves with two types of yields: current yield and the yield to maturity.

A bond's *current yield* is its annual income (as calculated by using its coupon—the interest rate stated on the face of the bond) divided by its current market price:

Coupon	Price	Current Yield
7.00%	80	8.75%
7.00	90	7.78
7.00	100	7.00
7.00	110	6.36

The lower the price, the higher the current yield, and vice versa.

But current yield is only part of the picture. Whether that bond was bought at 80 or 110, the investor will receive 100 if the bond is redeemed at par. The 20-point profit or the 10-point loss have to be factored into the yield over the number of years until the bond's maturity date to arrive at a more accurate picture of the yield, called the *yield to maturity*. As a rough calculation:

Yield to maturity = Current yield
$$+ \frac{\text{Difference between bond price and 100 (+ or -)}}{\text{Number of years to maturity}}$$

Thus the bond bought at 80 has a yield to maturity higher than its current yield of 8.75%; if the bond matured in 10 years, for example, its yield to maturity would be roughly 10.75%. The bond bought at 110 has a yield to maturity lower than its current yield of 6.36%; if it matured in 10 years, its yield to maturity would be roughly 5.36%. Yields to maturity can be looked up quickly in a manual called a basis book, which has several hundred pages of tables combining variables of current yields and years to maturity. Basis books can be found in most brokerage houses and financial libraries.

To further complicate matters, an investor who buys the bond at 80 and redeems it at 100 must pay a capital gains tax on the 20-point gain (so that her actual—net— yield is really less than the stated yield to maturity), but the investor who buys the bond at 110 and redeems it at 100 can't take the 10-point loss.

Because income from municipal bonds is exempt from taxes, it has a far higher value than income that is subject to taxes. This concept, known as a *tax-equivalent yield,* is shown in Table 5.1. A taxpayer in the 50% bracket would need to earn 12% pretax on a taxable investment to equal a tax-exempt yield of 6%. If she were in the 40% bracket, she would need to earn 10% pretax on her investment to equal that 6% yield. At the highest end of the scale, a taxpayer in the 67% bracket would need to earn 24% pretax on an investment to equal a tax-exempt yield of 8%. The risk inherent in such investments—assuming they could be found—is far greater than the risk presented by municipal bonds as a class. Compare, for example, the AA or A rating of a 6% municipal bond with a 12% corporate bond rated BB or B.

Table 5.1
TAX-EQUIVALENT YIELDS ON TAX-EXEMPT SECURITIES

Total tax bracket		4%	5%	6%	7%	8%
				Coupon		
25%		5.33%	6.67%	8.00%	9.33%	10.67%
33		6.00	7.50	9.00	10.50	12.00
40	Tax-	6.67	8.33	10.00	11.67	13.33
50	equivalent	8.00	10.00	12.00	14.00	16.00
60	yield	10.00	12.50	15.00	17.50	20.00
67		12.00	15.00	18.00	21.00	24.00

Table 5.2
FEDERAL, STATE, AND CITY TAXES
FOR NEW YORK RESIDENTS*

Marital status	Net taxable income	Federal income tax	State income tax	City income tax	Total
	$10,800	24%	7%	2.5%	33.5%
Single	18,200	34	11	3.3	48.3
taxpayers	23,500	39	14	4.0	57.0
	34,100	49	15	4.3	68.3
	16,000	24	10	3.1	37.1
Married taxpayers—	24,600	32	14	4.0	50.0
one income	35,200†	40†	15	4.3	59.3
	45,800	49	15	4.3	68.3
Married taxpayers—	16,000	24	6	2.3	32.3
assuming net income	24,600	32	8	2.7	42.7
earned equally by	35,200†	40†	11	3.3	54.3
both	45,800	49	13	3.8	65.8

* Federal tax rates are for 1979. New York State and City tax rates are for 1978. Whether they will be reduced for 1979 or remain the same has not yet been voted on.

† These figures are approximate because the actual adjacent tax brackets are 37% and 43%.

How applicable are these calculations to most of us? Table 5.2, "Federal, State, and City Taxes for New York

Residents," has the dismaying answer. In the lowest brackets shown, where net taxable income is only $10,800 for single taxpayers and $16,000 for married couples filing jointly, federal income tax alone is 24%. New York State and New York City income taxes, chosen as an example, raise the total tax bite to 33.5% for the single taxpayer, 37.1% for the married couple if one partner worked, and 32.3% for the married couple if both partners worked, assuming that the income was earned equally by both. Obviously, even at this level, which in terms of today's purchasing power is hardly middle class, tax-exempt bonds are a valid investment decision and can make a substantial difference in disposable income.

And New York residents, while hardest hit, are not the only victims. Table 5.3, "States and Cities That Impose Income Taxes," shows that most states and many cities now impose an income tax.

Table 5.3
STATES AND CITIES THAT IMPOSE
INCOME TAXES

State	Cities
Alabama	Birmingham
	Montgomery
Alaska	
Arizona	
Arkansas	
California	Oakland
Colorado	
Connecticut	Residents who work in New York pay taxes on New York income
Delaware	Wilmington
District of Columbia	
Georgia	
Hawaii	
Idaho	
Illinois	
Indiana	
Iowa	
Kansas	
Kentucky	Louisville and approximately 50 localities
Louisiana	
Maine	

State	Cities
Maryland	
Massachusetts	
Michigan	Detroit
	Flint
	Grand Rapids
	Hudson
	Lansing
Minnesota	
Mississippi	
Missouri	Kansas City
	St. Louis
Montana	
Nebraska	
New Hampshire	
New Jersey	Residents who work in New York pay taxes on New York income
New Mexico	
New York	New York
North Carolina	
North Dakota	
Ohio	Akron
	Canton
	Cincinnati
	Cleveland
	Columbus
	Dayton
	Parma
	Toledo
	Youngstown
Oklahoma	
Oregon	Portland
Pennsylvania	Philadelphia
	Pittsburgh
Rhode Island	
South Carolina	
Tennessee	
Utah	
Vermont	
Virginia	
West Virginia	
Wisconsin	

Municipal bonds are traded on an over-the-counter basis. As a result, commissions on purchases and sales are flexible and can vary depending on size of the order, whether bonds purchased are part of a new issue or part of the dealer's inventory, and other factors. Most bonds are sold in $5,000 denominations, which investors refer to as a *five-bond block.* Although the bonds are sold in $5,000 denominations, they are quoted as a percent of $1,000 (called *par*), and investors should think in terms of five-bond blocks for greatest ease in buying and selling. (Investors who buy one $1,000 bond at a time will find purchase price, selling price, and commissions punitive; they'd be far better off buying a bond fund, as described later in this chapter.)

Low-Coupon Discount Bonds Versus High-Coupon Bonds at a Premium

In the discussion of yield to maturity earlier in this chapter, low-coupon discount bonds seemed to have it all over high-coupon bonds selling at a premium. After all, the discount bonds offer not only a good current yield but also capital gains opportunities. And even though the capital gain and therefore the yield to maturity is reduced by tax, the Revenue Act of 1978 has reduced the maximum capital gains tax to 28%, so that capital gains are even more desirable now than in the past.

Nevertheless, for some investors, the high-coupon premium bonds are a better choice. All other variables (like ratings and maturities) being equal, these bonds offer the highest current yield; and for highest-bracket investors and/or investors who need maximum current income, high-coupon premium bonds may be a better investment. (A good example is the 10 to 11% Municipal Assistance Corporation ["MAC"] bonds issued during the 1975 New York City fiscal crisis.) With these bonds, the investor pays a premium, which he loses, but he enjoys a current stream of maximum tax-free income.

Municipal bond funds are designed for investors who cannot afford to buy a large, diversified portfolio but still wish to spread their investment risk. In effect, these funds are mutual funds comprised solely of municipal bonds. They are sold in $1,000 units and, since the IRS has recently ruled that the actual owners of the municipal bonds in the fund are the holders of the fund units, the pass-through feature of the fund's tax-free income is assured. This means that tax-free income that is distributed (passed through) by the fund to the unit owners is treated as tax-free income to the unit owners.

There are two basic types of municipal bond funds. *Local funds* are invested solely in state, county, and city issues to provide complete exemption from federal, state, and city income taxes. *National funds* are completely exempt from federal income taxes; the amount of exemption from state and local income taxes depends on the makeup of the particular fund and the residence of the fund buyer. National funds provide more safety and stability than local funds because they are diversified with respect to geographical area.

Perhaps more important, municipal bond funds are also classified by whether or not they are managed. *Managed funds* are open-ended and can buy and sell bonds in their portfolios. Therefore the income from the fund will fluctuate. *Nonmanaged funds* cannot trade their holdings; income from the fund is fixed.

Municipal-bond-fund investors should look for liquidity—the fund's sponsor should be willing to repurchase the units from the investor—and the option to reinvest interest payments, which will compound the growth of their investment.

6 Life Insurance Tax Shelters

There are two major types of life insurance tax shelters: straight life insurance and deferred annuities.

Straight life insurance offers a tax shelter because dividends (if reinvested) are completely free from income and capital gains taxes since they are considered to be a return of premium. Dividends that are taken in cash will be taxed as ordinary income at some distant point in the future, when total cash dividends exceed total gross premiums paid. For example, on one $17,000 whole life policy issued to a man age 45, total premiums at age 65 would be $11,500, and total cash dividends would be $3,600. It would still be many years before the dividends exceeded the premiums. Thus, as a general rule, all dividends credited before the maturity or surrender of a life insurance contract are tax-exempt.

Increases in cash value are completely free from income and capital gains taxes until a policy is surrendered for its cash value. At that point, there may be taxable ordinary income if the surrender value exceeds the cost of the contract.

Many companies offer straight-life policies paid for by

one lump-sum premium (single-premium life) for people up to age 75 if they can pass a physical examination. This in itself is an important benefit, since insurance for older people may be difficult or expensive to obtain.

Tax-free dividends, cash values, and death benefits increase each year. For example:

$10,000 SINGLE-PREMIUM POLICY
FOR 54-YEAR-OLD MAN

Year	Annual tax-free dividend	Cash value	Death benefit
2	$395	$ 9,875	$13,580
5	425	10,630	13,690
10	481	12,033	14,250

However, if a periodic-premium policy is available for the same age group, it may be a more advantageous method of purchasing life insurance. For example, if death were to occur after 3 years, a person might have been better off paying approximately $2,700 in annual premiums than $10,000 in a lump sum at the onset of the policy.

Deferred annuities offer a tax shelter by providing a tax-free compounding of interest (often called "inside build-up"), a factor which is extremely significant over the 20- or 25-year life of the annuity. Because the investor pays no taxes while the funds accumulate, a quoted 8% return is equivalent to a 16% taxable yield for a taxpayer in the 50% bracket.

The best way to buy a deferred annuity is with a single payment. While most insurance companies have a $5,000 minimum, it's possible to buy deferred annuities with regular monthly payments—but it's more expensive.

The "8% annuity" needs some clarification: it does not mean that the annuity funds are compounded at 8% for the 20 or 25 years of its life. Instead, the annuity will be compounded at 8% for a stated period of time: 2 and 3 years are common, 5 is less so, and 10 is unusually generous. Then the *guaranteed rate* drops sharply—often to only 3 or 4%. However, the *actual rate* paid, which depends upon the money market, is considerably higher. It might conceivably remain 8% for the life of the annuity, but it would be composed of the guaranteed portion of 4% (in this example) and a portion that would fluctuate with money-market rates. The variable portion is called *excess interest* if the annuity is issued by a stock company or a *dividend* if the annuity is issued by a mutual company.

Buyers should find out whether the excess interest rate is based on the insurance company's investment earnings on *money invested the year the annuity was purchased* or on its *overall portfolio investment* performance. The difference is enormous. Insurance companies are earning 10 to 11% on investments made in 1979. But since their portfolios also include investments made earlier at 5 or 6%, their calculations based on *overall rate of return* might be only 8 to 8 1/2%.

Sales charges can also make a significant difference. Some insurance companies charge commissions. Others may call their annuities "no-load," but their administrative and other fees may be high. Investors should look at the bottom line to make comparisons, rather than relying on the "load/no-load" designations.

There may also be significant differences in the penalties assessed for early withdrawal of funds and conditions under which they are imposed. The charges might run anywhere from 1 to 6% and might apply only to the first 5 years, the first 10 years, or until the annuity matures.

Similarly, some insurance companies may penalize policyholders as much as 6% for taking the matured annuity as a lump sum; other companies offer the lump-sum payment as an option. (Although the 6% charge seems small, remember that on a base of $50,000 or $100,000, that's $3,000 or $6,000 for what is probably less than one day's clerical and administrative work!)

Investors should be alerted that after several years the IRS will permit them to make a few random withdrawals that will be treated as a return of principal. If the withdrawals are frequent and regular, either in terms of timing or amount, the IRS may hold that the withdrawals are *interest* as well as principal, and will tax them accordingly.

In comparing annuity policies, rather than looking at the number of charges or what they're called, investors should ask these questions:

1. How much will I get out for what I put in?
2. If I make an early withdrawal, will there be any penalty? How much is it? Under what circumstances is it charged?
3. What guarantee is there on the maximum rate quoted?
4. What is the minimum rate?
5. What is the monthly income payable when I want to retire?

A reliable policy should have all these answers—and in a comprehensible format. Furthermore, an investor should be able to receive answers to these questions *before* buying the annuity.

A typical annuity might be bought by a 30-year-old man who wants to begin drawing on it at the age of 55. If he deposits $10,000, in 25 years at only 6% his $10,000 will have grown to approximately $42,500. At age 55, he can collect $5,000 a year for as long as he lives. For the first 10 years or so, he's drawing on his own fund; after that, he's being paid with the insurance company's money.

When it comes to taxes on the income payments, the first $10,000 is considered a return of capital and is untaxed; the remainder is taxed as ordinary income. Some investors, considering inflation and the future value of money, prefer to take a lump-sum payment when the annuity matures. Then the first $10,000 they receive will be considered their return of capital.

Others, who are more concerned about spreading their tax liability, prefer to spread their investment over the entire payment period in equal amounts, so that each annuity payment is part taxable and part nontaxable. Annuity payments which are made over the lifetime of the policyholder are taxed according to the rules outlined in Section 72 of the Internal Revenue Code. Essentially, there are two basic elements involved: how much an individual puts into the annuity contract (the "investment in the contract") and how much an individual can be expected to receive over his or her expected lifetime (the "expected return"). The expected return is calculated by using IRS life-expectancy tables. For example, the IRS figures say that a man aged 65 will live for 15 years. If he receives annuity payments of $1,000 per year, the expected return for that particular contract will be $15,000. The amount *excluded* from federal income taxation is, *in general,* a percentage ("exclusion ratio") equal to the expected return divided by the investment in the contract. Once the exclusion ratio is calculated, it remains applicable as long as payments are made.

A financial planner's advice is valuable here. In both cases, when the policyholder retires, if he's in a lower tax bracket, his taxes on the taxable portion of the annuity should be relatively low.

Following are some representative annuities for men and women at different ages. One insurance company currently offers a guaranteed rate of 9.31% for 120 days, 7.77% for 1 year, and 3% for the remaining life of the annuity—with the provision that if the current rate drops more than 1/2% (i.e., from 7.77% to less than 7.27% at the end of that year), policyholders are allowed to withdraw the entire value of the annuity without penalty.

$10,000 TWENTY-YEAR DEFERRED ANNUITY PROJECTED
AT 9.31% FOR 120 DAYS AND 7.77% FOR REMAINDER

Value of annuity	Age at withdrawal	Monthly payment Men	Women	Amount of Difference	Percent Difference
$44,871	50	$314.39	$292.48	$21.91	7.0%
44,871	60	364.93	333.17	31.76	8.7
44,871	70	461.08	412.78	48.30	10.5

Note that the payout for women is lower than the payout for men because of women's greater longevity, and that the difference is greater as the age at which annuity payments begin increases.

NOTE: Although annuities are a nice, safe investment and a conservative tax shelter, they are not without risk. As always, there is the risk of inflation: what will that $5,000 a year buy 25 years from now? And there is always the secondary political risk: in today's complex world situation, should any investment be tied up for 20 or 25 years?

Variable annuities provide some protection against inflation because they are backed by a portfolio of investment-grade common stocks. If the portfolio performs well, its value should rise even faster than the Consumer Price Index and, unlike straight annuity policyholders' fixed payments, policyholders should receive larger annuity payments each year.

The old "investment annuities" investors bought from stockbrokers that were so popular in the 1960s and 1970s were quashed by the IRS two years ago. Because investors could choose their investment vehicle (common or preferred stocks, bonds, etc.) and would receive a "wraparound" annuity guarantee on their portfolios from an insurance company, the IRS held that for tax purposes the investment annuities were not annuities because they were not designed to serve as retirement-income vehicles. Thus they were no longer permitted to take advantage of the tax-free compounding of interest which made them a tax shelter.

As an alternative to a deferred annuity as a tax shelter, a portfolio of *heavily discounted convertible bonds* may offer deferred taxes and safe return—plus a kicker: long-term capital gains.

Investors can create a portfolio of heavily discounted convertible bonds, choosing staggered maturity dates to begin around retirement. If the bonds are purchased on 50% margin, the interest received from the bonds will be offset by the interest paid on the margin account. Therefore there will be little or no current tax liability.

When the bonds are redeemed at maturity, there will

be long-term capital gains. Furthermore, if the market rises, long-term gains can be taken if the bonds are held for only a year.

The following table makes the comparisons clear:

Feature	Convertible bond portfolio	Deferred annuity
Rate of return	Varies—possible to match deferred annuity's return	Fixed—usually 7½% to 8%
Tax treatment	Capital gains if held at least one year	Ordinary income—after principal is returned
Commission costs	1 to 2% for round-trip trade. Increased portfolio turnover will increase total commissions.	Varies—7% is average
Safety	Not as safe as deferred annuity—but can be increased with careful selection and diversification	Very great

In addition, convertible bonds may yield a much higher rate of return if the stock market rises, since convertible bonds generally move up along with the underlying common stock.

Investors with $50,000 or so who like both of these approaches and can't decide between them might do well to hedge and invest $25,000 in a straight or variable deferred annuity and $25,000 in a portfolio of deep-discount convertible bonds.

7 Clifford Trusts

People who earn substantial income from stocks, real estate, or other property can shelter most of that income from taxes by placing the assets in a 10-year living trust—also called a reversionary, short-term, inter vivos, or Clifford trust— which dissolves at the end of 10 years and 1 day and reverts the property to the original owner.

While the usual tax rule states that an owner can avoid being taxed on income produced by a property only by selling it or giving it away irrevocably, the Clifford trust is a valuable exception to that rule. Under the stipulations of the Clifford trust (named for George B. Clifford, Jr., a key figure in the Supreme Court ruling that spelled out the guidelines on this tax-shelter trust), if the property is given to a trust that is irrevocable for at least 10 years and 1 day, the income will be taxed to the trust or its beneficiaries who are in a lower bracket even though the property reverts to the original owner at that time.

Because of its reversionary and income-transferring features, a Clifford trust is perfect for accumulating funds for a child's education or for supporting an aged parent or relative.

High-tax-bracket parents who own $100,000 worth of common stocks that pay $6,000 a year in dividends are taxed at the 70% level. This means that they pay $4,200 tax on the dividends on the federal level alone and keep only $1,800. If they give the stock to a living trust for the benefit of a 12-year-old daughter, they can direct the trustee (and the parents themselves can be the trustees) to accumulate and reinvest the dividend income until their daughter starts college, and then pay her college expenses with it. After 10 years and 1 day (or whenever she graduates—whichever is later), any remaining income is distributed to the daughter, the trust is automatically dissolved, and the stock reverts to her parents.

If the daughter should die before the expiration date of the trust, the trust ends immediately. Any accumulated income becomes part of her estate. The stock reverts to her parents.

Because the daughter is in a lower tax bracket than her parents, the tax savings on the dividends are enormous. Assuming that the $6,000 annual dividends are her sole income, she would pay only $444 in federal income taxes and could keep $5,556—roughly $3,700 more per year than her parents could if they held the stocks. And, since the trust lasts 10 years, the cumulative difference—compounded—works out to over $40,000 over the life of the trust.

If the trustee sells assets of the trust at either a capital gain or loss, the gain or loss is reported on the parents' tax return in the year of the transaction. The IRS reasons that the asset is basically their property (since it will revert to them when the trust expires) even though they've given up the income for the life of the trust. (The Trust agreement must stipulate that capital gains will be taxed to the parent.)

The $100,000 gift of stock to set up the trust is a taxable gift (in the year the trust is set up) of about $44,000—the estimated current value of the right to receive income for 10 years. This gift doesn't qualify for the $3,000 annual gift-tax exclusion ($6,000 for a couple) *unless* the trust stipulates that the income is to be distributed to the beneficiary as it is received.

If the parents are the trustees, the trust shouldn't give them too much leeway in withholding or distributing the income. Otherwise the IRS might claim that the trust is a tax-avoidance scheme in which the donors didn't really relinquish control. And, of course, there are times when parents have second thoughts about distributing income or relinquishing control of the assets to their children, whose behavior may be less than desirable. (Fortunately, this problem usually doesn't occur when children have set up a Clifford trust to support their aging parents.)

Unlike a trust set up by a will, Clifford trusts are not subject to court supervision. However, because these trusts must be drawn carefully to qualify for favorable tax treatment, good professional advice is necessary.

There is a more sophisticated use of the Clifford trust, too. A recent Tax Court decision lost by the IRS should make owners of closely held businesses and professional corporations look at Clifford trusts more closely. While usually, as discussed above, trust assets have been securities and real estate, the Tax Court decision (*Lerner* v. *Commissioner* 71 No. 24, 11/27/78) seems to indicate that assets also include business machinery—like medical and dental equipment, or a car fleet.

The IRS case concerned an ophthalmologist who simultaneously incorporated his practice and transferred his medical equipment to a Clifford trust which benefited his children. Because there was a loan outstanding on the equipment, shifting it into the trust reduced its tax base and enabled the ophthalmologist to avoid the gift taxes usually inherent in transferring property to a Clifford trust.

The trust then leased the equipment to the ophthalmologist's professional corporation; thus he could get a rental deduction at the corporate level to balance income from his practice and simultaneously transfer income to his children, who were in a lower tax bracket.

There was an additional kicker. Out of its rental income, the trust intended to buy new equipment which would revert to the doctor when the trust expired. In effect, he was buying equipment with tax-deductible dollars.

Although the IRS attacked the strategy on the ground that the professional corporation was an extension of the ophthalmologist's personal pocketbook and therefore hadn't entered into an arm's-length transaction, the Tax Court disagreed. According to the Tax Court, the ophthalmologist had created a foolproof package that satisfied the court that the equipment rental rate was reasonable, that it had been fairly appraised by an independent trustee, and that it was leased to a separate taxable entity—the ophthalmologist's professional corporation—not to the ophthalmologist himself.

Such an equipment-leasing Clifford trust makes sense for doctors, dentists—in fact, almost any professional corporation or closely held business. Instead of looking outside to oil and gas or real estate tax shelters, these professionals and executives should first examine the tax-shelter potential within their own businesses.

⑧ Conservative Real Estate Tax Shelters

There are four major benefits in investing in real estate:

1. Cash flow—the extent to which the real estate is leveraged, the quality of the tenant(s) occupying the property, and the operating expenses are the overriding factors affecting the level of cash flow. Cash flow varies inversely with the risk of the investment.
2. Tax losses from depreciation—varies with the extent to which the real estate is leveraged and on the stage of construction at the time it was purchased (to be built, under construction, existing). Usually there will be enough tax losses to shelter the cash flow. In some cases, investors may be eligible to use an accelerated method of depreciation which will give them losses in excess of those used to shelter their cash flow. In some cases it may even be equal to or greater than the amount of their investment.
3. Equity buildup—the existing mortgage balance is reduced monthly with each mortgage payment. Thus, at the end of a certain number of years, the property may be sold for the same price for which it was purchased, and an investor whose cost is essentially the same as his equity will still make a profit. (Of course, the extent to which his profit is

real depends on the purchasing power of those dollars and other factors.)

4. Appreciation potential—real property is one of the best hedges against inflation.

The extent to which investors derive all or none of these benefits is usually tied to the risks they assume. A very speculative property has much more appreciation potential— *and more downside risk*—than a more conservative property.

Some brokerage houses are zeroing in on middle-income investors and are offering real estate tax shelters marketed like mutual funds. These tax shelters estimate a payout of 6% or more tax-sheltered income a year; the income is tax sheltered because the investors or limited partners are eligible to take a depreciation deduction, which is a loss in terms of reporting to the IRS, but actually results in no cash loss at all. The partnership, consisting of thousands of limited partners, each investing as little as $5,000, typically may buy 5 to 10 apartment buildings in the United States with the intent of selling them in 5 to 15 years—with, it is hoped, substantial capital gains. Investors expect to get back not only their $5,000 investment, which is a return of capital, but also 6% (or more) tax sheltered on an annual basis and perhaps sizable capital gains. In this type of conservative real estate tax shelter, income and future capital gains are emphasized, rather than large write-offs.

As an example, with a $5,000 investment in this type of real estate tax shelter, an investor might receive tax-sheltered payments of $300 (6%) for the first 2 years. Because these payments are treated by the IRS as a return of capital (because of the depreciation taken), her basis in the investment is reduced by the $300 each year, so that at the end of the 2 years her basis is $4,400. If the depreciation exceeded the earned income, as it might do if accelerated depreciation were used, the investor might receive a note saying, "Congratulations! We enclose your partnership's income check for $300, but you'll be able to deduct $500 this year because of accelerated depreciation." If this happened, the investor would reduce her investment basis by $500, rather than by the $300 she actually received. In this case, her basis after 2 years would be $4,200 ($5,000 − [$300 + $500]).

At the beginning of the third year, the investor might receive a check for $3,000 with the statement: "This check represents a $2,000 return of your original capital and a $1,000 capital gain because your partnership has sold one of the pieces of property in its investment portfolio."

Now the investor's cost basis is reduced to $2,200, and she reports a capital gain of $1,000 on her income tax. Her estimated 6% tax-sheltered return will be based on the adjusted portfolio and will be less than the original $300, since one of the properties has been sold. Let's assume that she receives $150 tax-sheltered income in the third and fourth years. Now her basis is $1,900 ($2,200 − [$150 + $150]).

In the fifth year, if the partnership sends her a check for $5,000, she reports a $3,100 capital gain because $1,900 of the payment represents a return of her capital. In subsequent years, because all her capital has been returned and her adjusted cost basis is zero, any additional future profits from sales of the partnership's property are capital gains for her.

The most conservative real estate tax shelter is a building that is already built. Buildings planned or not yet completed can be vulnerable to construction risk: cost overruns which can dramatically increase the cost of the building. Existing buildings, of course, do not suffer from this problem.

A second feature that is crucial to conservative real estate tax shelters is tenant quality: the higher the tenant's credit rating, the lower the investment risk of the tax shelter.

The most conservative real estate tax shelter, then, consists of an entire existing building leased to a single tenant with an excellent credit rating on what is known as a net-net-net basis, or *triple-net lease*. Under a triple-net lease, a tenant agrees to pay rent at a specified rate no matter what happens—often for a period as long as 30 years. (In a sense, this promise to pay a stated amount of rent every year is analogous to a bond's indenture, which guarantees to pay a stated amount of interest every year.) In addition to the rent, the tenant—and not the owner—is responsible for all of the variable costs associated with owning the building—for instance, insurance, maintenance, repairs, taxes, utilities. Because the only cost the owners have is the mortgage, they are protected from rising costs to a certain extent, and their cash flow is fairly predictable.

Of course, the locked-in feature of a long lease poses its problems. Owners of these properties give up the potential for increased cash flow; as long as the lease is in effect, they are unable to increase rents and will suffer from eroded purchasing power on their constant-dollar rent base.

(As a contrast, at the opposite end of the risk spectrum is an apartment building whose tenants sign 2-year leases. These tenants, whose credit rating does not begin to approach that of prime corporate tenants, can break leases and move out very quickly, leaving the owners with reduced cash flow. Sometimes, if vacancies are high, the owners may have to dip into their own funds to pay the mortgage.)

There are three major real estate funds which specialize in triple-net investments:

1. American Property Investors series, which started around 1971
2. Century Properties Fund, originated on the West Coast four or five years ago
3. Corporate Property Associates, a new fund started recently by E. F. Hutton

All these funds are public offerings registered with the SEC. As specifically outlined in the "objectives" portion of their prospectuses, they purchase real estate leased for long periods of time to what is defined as "major credit corporate tenants." Most major brokerage houses carry one or all of these funds, and investors who are interested in this tax-sheltered investment vehicle can simply call a broker and say, "I'm interested in a $5,000 investment in real estate leased to major corporations for long periods of time"—or, to use the buzz-word, "I'm interested in triple-net-lease real estate."

With few exceptions, the yields on triple-net-lease real estate funds will not vary by more than 1/2% because buyers of this type of real estate—as well as the funds themselves—are very competitive with each other. The properties in the various portfolios are similar, too. Sales charges and commissions are essentially the same. (These run between 8 and 10%, with no breakpoint for larger orders.)

Slightly more risky—but with more upside potential, and still conservative—are real estate tax shelters with several high-rated commercial/industrial tenants. There may be a major tenant who occupies more than half the space and a few smaller tenants in each building. These leases are shorter—typically 5 to 10 years—and investors own the land and building on what is called a *fee-simple basis*. Under fee-simple ownership, the owner is responsible for insurance, utilities, taxes, and other variable costs. However, the upside potential is that after 5 or 10 years—whenever the lease expires—owners can raise the rent when a new lease is signed. If a triple-net-lease tax shelter resembles a bond, a fee-simple tax shelter is like a riskier bond with a kicker: the interest payments can go up every 5 years.

In the triple-net-lease tax shelter, investors generally receive 7% to 8%, of which 70% to 100% is tax-sheltered. They are giving up some appreciation potential in return for safety and high cash flow. This type of investment might be suitable for retirees looking for partially sheltered generous income with some protection against inflation and some appreciation potential. These people might consider investing 20% to 30% of their portfolios in the safest of real estate tax shelters, rather than in straight bonds, which offer no protection of purchasing power.

Income-oriented real estate tax shelters owned under

the fee-simple method offer a little less current income with a little more risk and considerably more appreciation potential because leases are renegotiated more frequently than triple-net leases, and buildings are bought with an eye to selling them in 7 to 15 years. Income is typically 6% to 7%, but is usually 100% tax-sheltered. Because of its slightly more aggressive investment posture, existing real estate tax-sheltered investments with fee-simple ownership are suitable for retirees who can afford more risk and for all people who want moderate, completely sheltered income combined with moderate appreciation potential and a reasonable hedge against inflation.

⑨ Charitable Gifts as Tax Shelters

Several years ago, an advertising executive donated the 138-carat star ruby which bears his name to the National Museum of Natural History at the Smithsonian Institution. His generosity to the Smithsonian was exceeded only by the generosity of the IRS to him. The ruby, which he bought at auction for $140,000, was appraised by the Smithsonian for $950,000. The executive was able to write off the entire $950,000 as a charitable contribution. At the time, his tax bracket was 70%, which meant that his donation was worth $665,000 in after-tax dollars—in effect, nearly a 5-to-1 write-off!

The rules are a little different now, but they're still generous—if taxpayers know how to take advantage of them.

Perhaps most important is the beneficiary of the gift and the use to which the gift is put. If Mrs. Connoisseur donates a Renoir drawing she bought for $5,000 to the Metropolitan Museum of Art, she can deduct its entire fair market value—let's say it's been appraised at $25,000—because she's giving a tangible piece of property to a charity which will use it for its own charitable and educational purposes.

If, however, she donates the Renoir to the Metropolitan Opera for a fundraising auction, her donation is limited because the Metropolitan Opera is not going to use the drawing itself. In this case, the deduction for her donation is limited to her cost plus half her gain:

$25,000	Fair market value
− 5,000	Cost
20,000	Gain
$10,000	Half of gain
+ 5,000	Cost
$15,000	Value of donation (deduction)

If the Metropolitan Museum of Art de-acquisitions the drawing at some time in the future, to raise cash for other purposes, the tax treatment of Mrs. Connoisseur's gift is not affected because she donated the drawing to the museum, not for a specific fundraising event.

Stamps and coins are valuable charitable donations, too—if they are given away properly. In order to take their fair market value as a deduction, it is best to donate them to philatelic or numismatic museums or societies.

Precious and semiprecious stones make an interesting charitable donation because they have appreciated so rapidly in the past few years. According to Internal Revenue Code Section 170(e), if the stones have been held for a year and would qualify for long-term capital gain treatment if they were sold, if they are given to a museum or university (qualifying as "public" because it receives its principal support from the general public or from the government) *for use in a manner related to its exempt purpose* (e.g., for display by a museum or for study by university students), the donor may take a charitable deduction equal to the full fair market value of the stones, regardless of their original cost. When making the gift, the donor should obtain a declaration from the museum or university regarding the purpose for which the stones will be used. If the stones are given to a private foundation or to a public charity for a use which is unrelated to the exempt functions of the charity, however, the value of the stones will be subject to special rules which reduce the amount of the charitable gift and can modify the amount of the deduction.

One diamond dealer claims that it is possible to take a 3-to-1 write-off on gifts of precious stones to charities because diamonds and precious stones have appreciated so rapidly. According to his figures, if a diamond is bought at 5% over wholesale through a diamond broker or a diamond investment firm, is held for at least a year, and is then donated at retail value, the overall appreciation amounts to a 3-to-1 write-off.

Similarly, it may be possible to buy posters or lithographs in quantity at a discount ("wholesale"), give them to a museum to hold for a year, then get a retail appraisal, and give them to the museum as a charitable donation.

There are two basic problems with gifts of this nature. First and easier to circumvent, in order to deduct the full retail fair market value *the donor must be a collector, not a dealer who is contributing inventory, which will be appraised only at cost by the IRS.* The easiest way to deal with this problem is to make gifts that have nothing to do with the donor's business. Thus, an art dealer should donate diamonds; a gem dealer should donate paintings. An eclectic collector should donate different types of valuables, in rotating sequence, rather than a piece of sculpture every year for 10 years, followed by a painting every year for 10 years. Because this strategy hinges on buying wholesale and donating at the retail price that the IRS recognizes for valuation purposes, it is imperative that the donor not give too many similar objects, in order to prevent an IRS claim that the donor is giving away inventory.

Second and potentially more serious is the problem of appraisal. A one-carat diamond can be worth anything from $1,000 to $20,000. A Degas can be worth $25,000 or $250,-000. How good is an appraisal, and will it stand up with the

IRS? There's no hard answer. A museum's curators are likely to make a generous appraisal if they think their museum will be the recipient of the donor's gift. Depending on the appraisal value and the donor's actual cost, a gift can provide a sizable deduction and can substantially reduce taxes.

What does the IRS have to say about the fact that the same museum that appraises the objects is likely to receive them as gifts, so that their appraisal is not an arm's-length transaction? The IRS maintains its own panel of appraisers who may dispute the donor's valuation if it seems unusually high. Essentially, it depends on whether the donor's proof is stronger than that of the IRS's appraisers.

Real estate makes an interesting gift because it is often divisible, in a way that works of art are not. Because there are limitations to the value of gifts made—the most frequent limitation is 50% of adjusted gross income, with a 5-year carryover, but there are others—it may make sense to subdivide a 50-acre property to be donated to, say, the World Wildlife Fund, and to give a 5-acre piece of the property every so many years to maximize tax benefits.

Another possibility in donating real estate involves selling the entire property to the charity, taking back a mortgage, and forgiving the appropriate portion of the mortgage every year. This strategy may create a problem if the IRS holds that this is then a bargain sale to a charity, and that therefore the donor must pick up a certain portion of the gain every year. This is very tricky and requires expert advice; depending on the donor's tax situation, it may be wiser to give all the property in one year and use the 5-year carryover.

All in all, charitable donations are still a viable tax shelter—especially for taxpayers whose unearned income is taxed at 70%. They can take the largest write-offs in terms of adjusted gross income, and they can offset the most heavily taxed dollars.

10 Your Own Corporation as Tax Shelter

For the self-employed executive or professional, incorporation is an excellent tax shelter. Some of the benefits incorporation offers are:

1. "Free" life and disability insurance (the premiums are fully deductible by the corporation and reduce its pretax income, but are not treated as taxable income to the insured stockholder/employee).
2. "Free" medical insurance and payment of drugs and medical expenses for the stockholder/employee and his or her family.
3. More generous and more flexible retirement plans than the Keogh Plan—including one option, Employees' Stock Ownership Plan, that doesn't require any actual cash investment.
4. Tax-free dividend income.

"Free" Life and Disability Insurance

"Free" life insurance (also called Section 79 insurance) consists of one-year renewable term policies of up to $50,000 face value as group insurance in groups of 10 people or more. But smaller groups—including a "group" of one—can also qualify for these policies and get similar tax treatment from the IRS. A corporation can discriminate among classes of employees in setting the face value of these policies; $50,000 policies for officer/employees and $10,000 for other employees is a frequent option.

If more than $50,000 coverage is desired, the employee must pay taxes on "imputed income": an amount per $1,000 of coverage over $50,000 based solely on the age of the employee—it is not a percentage of the monthly premium. The following table shows monthly premiums and imputed income at various age levels:

Age	Approximate monthly premium per $10,000	Approximate monthly imputed income per $10,000
30–34	$ 2.00	$ 1.00
35–39	2.30	1.40
40–44	3.00	2.30
45–49	4.40	4.00
50–54	7.10	6.80
55–59	11.10	11.10
60–64	18.80	16.30

Since at all ages the imputed income is equal to or less than the premium for the additional insurance, it is advisable for the corporation to pay for the additional insurance and for the shareholder/employee to accept the imputed income.

Many entrepreneurs and professionals don't want or need life insurance, but they do need disability insurance—income protection if they are unable to work because of illness or injury. One of the advantages of incorporation is workmen's compensation, one type of disability insurance which is available *only* to employees, not to sole proprietors. Disability insurance premiums are fully deductible by the corporation but are not considered income to the insured. Disability coverage is an area for individual treatment, frequent examination and revision, and professional advice. As a general rule, generous—if not maximum—coverage is probably the best idea for the one-person corporation, especially now, during periods of escalating medical costs and living expenses. What little extra the corporation pays for the executive's being overinsured against possible disability is certainly worth the price in terms of peace of mind. Also, because the premiums are paid out of pretax dollars, they're less expensive than they appear—especially if they are able to pull the corporation down from the 30% bracket into the 20% bracket.

Medical Benefits

Corporate employees can benefit from "free" medical insurance and payment of drugs and medical expenses for themselves and their families. Like the "free" life and disability insurance, the corporation can deduct these payments as a business expense, but the IRS does not treat them as income to the individuals receiving them.

Although the IRS terms them "medical reimbursement plans," a corporation can actually pay medical bills directly rather than reimbursing medical expenses. While legally this plan can be informal and unwritten (especially in the case of a sole employee and stockholder) and can consist of the understanding that the corporation will pay all medical bills, in actual practice, where the IRS is concerned, a formal written corporate resolution of the type shown below carries much more weight.

In a one-person corporation, that one officer/stockholder/employee unquestionably provides significant services as an employee and can be covered, along with his or her family. In larger corporations, the IRS has ruled that medical reimbursement plans must benefit employees, rather than stockholders as such. The basis of the plan must be the employer-employee relationship, and not the stockholder relationship. Of course, covered employees can also be stockholders, and, in fact, many closely held corporations limit participation in their medical reimbursement plans to officers who are also stockholders. If these officers

contribute substantial services as employees, the medical reimbursement plan will resist any challenge by the IRS.

In a one-person corporation, the corporation can—and
should—arrange to reimburse 100% of medical expenses. In
a larger corporation, thought must be given to the total
medical expenses among the plan's participants; it may be
wise to set a limit on the amount of reimbursement per eligible employee. It may also be advisable to set up a medical
care reimbursement plan for stockholder/employees and to
provide a more limited plan—or just Blue Cross/Blue
Shield—for ordinary employees.

Following is a sample medical care reimbursement
plan and minutes of a meeting of the board of directors ap-
proving the plan. Like other areas of corporate life, a plan
can be amended as situations change; as the corporation
covers an increasing number of employees, it may be wise to
lower the reimbursement limit per employee.

(NAME OF CORPORATION)
MEDICAL REIMBURSEMENT PLAN

ARTICLE I—Benefits

The Corporation shall reimburse all eligible employees for expenses incurred by themselves and their
dependents, as defined in Internal Revenue Code Section 152, as amended, for medical care, as defined in
IRC Section 213(e), as amended, subject to the conditions and limitations hereinafter set forth. It is the in-
tention of the Corporation that the benefits payable to
eligible employees hereunder shall be excluded from
their gross income pursuant to IRC Section 105, as
amended.

ARTICLE II—Eligibility

All corporate officers employed on a full-time basis
at the date of inception of this Plan, including those who
may be absent due to illness or injury on said date, are
eligible employees under the Plan. A corporate officer

shall be considered employed on a full-time basis if said officer customarily works at least seven months in each year and twenty hours in each week. Any person hereafter becoming an officer of the Corporation, employed on a full-time basis, shall be eligible under this Plan.

ARTICLE III—Limitations

1. The Corporation shall reimburse any eligible employee (without limitation)/(no more than $_____) in any fiscal year for medical care expenses.

2. Reimbursement or payment provided under this Plan shall be made by the Corporation only in the event and to the extent that such reimbursement or payment is not provided under any insurance policy(ies), whether owned by the Corporation or the employee, or under any other health and accident or wage-continuation plan. In the event that there is such an insurance policy or plan in effect, providing for reimbursement in whole or in part, then to the extent of the coverage under such policy or plan, the Corporation shall be relieved of any and all liability hereunder.

ARTICLE IV—Submission of Proof

Any eligible employee applying for reimbursement under this Plan shall submit to the Corporation, at least quarterly, all bills for medical care, including premium notices for accident or health insurance, for verification by the Corporation prior to payment. Failure to comply herewith may, at the discretion of the Corporation, terminate such eligible employee's right to said reimbursement.

ARTICLE V—Discontinuation

The Plan shall be subject to termination at any time by vote of the board of directors of the Corporation; provided, however, that medical care expenses incurred prior to such termination shall be reimbursed or paid in accordance with the terms of this Plan.

Article VI—Determination

The president shall determine all questions arising from the administration and interpretation of the Plan except where reimbursement is claimed by the president. In such case, determination shall be made by the board of directors.

MINUTES OF SPECIAL MEETING OF DIRECTORS OF (NAME OF CORPORATION)

A special meeting of the board of directors of (name of corporation) was held on (date) at (time) at (address where meeting was held).

All of the directors being present, the meeting was called to order by the chairman. The chairman advised that the meeting was called to approve and adopt a medical care expense reimbursement plan. A copy of the plan was presented to those present and upon motion duly made, seconded, and unanimously carried, it was

RESOLVED, that the "Medical Care Reimbursement Plan" presented to the meeting is hereby approved and adopted, that a copy of the Plan shall be appended to these minutes, and that the proper officers of the corporation are hereby authorized to take whatever action is necessary to implement the Plan, and it is further

RESOLVED, that the signing of these minutes by the directors shall constitute full ratification thereof and waiver of notice of the meeting by the signatories.

There being no further business to come before the meeting, upon motion duly made, seconded, and unanimously carried, the meeting was adjourned.

_____
Secretary

_____   _____
Chairman   Director

_____   _____
Director   Director

The advantages of a corporation's paying medical expenses are tremendous because a corporation, unlike an individual, is not subject to the 1% and 3% reductions illustrated below.

As concrete proof, let's take Mr. Entrepreneur, whose adjusted gross income is $25,000 and Ms. Successful, whose adjusted gross income is $50,000. Both have identical medical expenses:

Medical insurance	$1,000.00
Medicine and drugs	300.00
Doctors, dentists, etc.	400.00
Other (contact lenses)	250.00
	$1,950.00

Mr. Entrepreneur's medical deductions have been chopped in half: from $1,950 to $950. If he is in the 30% bracket, his medical deductions are now worth only $285 in after-tax dollars.

Ms. Successful has come out even worse. Her medical deductions have shrunk to 7 1/2% of her actual cost—from $1,950 to $150—and she gets the $150 write-off only because of line 1's exclusion for medical insurance. Even if she is in the 50% bracket, her medical deductions are worth only $75 in after-tax dollars.

Since a corporation is not subject to the 1% and 3% reductions, its bottom-line total medical expenditures are $1,950, rather than Mr. Entrepreneur's $950 or Ms. Successful's $150. Consequently, their value in after-tax dollars is much greater:

Corporate income	Tax bracket as percentage	Dollar value of $1,950 deduction
$ 0–$ 25,000	17%	$331.50
$ 25,000–$ 50,000	20	390.00
$ 50,000–$ 75,000	30	585.00
$ 75,000–$100,000	40	780.00
$100,000+	46	897.00

146

Name(s) as shown on Form 1040

M_R. E_NTREPRENEUR

Medical and Dental Expenses (not paid by insurance or otherwise) (See page 15 of Instructions.)

1 One-half (but not more than $150) of insurance premiums you paid for medical care. (Be sure to include in line 10 below.) . ▶	150 —
2 Medicine and drugs	300 —
3 Enter 1% of Form 1040, line 31 . . .	250 —
4 Subtract line 3 from line 2. If line 3 is more than line 2, enter zero	50 —
5 Balance of insurance premiums for medical care not entered on line 1	850 —
6 Other medical and dental expenses:	
a Doctors, dentists, nurses, etc. . . .	400 —
b Hospitals	
c Other (itemize—include hearing aids, dentures, eyeglasses, transportation, etc.) ▶ CONTACT LENSES	250 —
7 Total (add lines 4 through 6c)	1550 —
8 Enter 3% of Form 1040, line 31 . . .	750 —
9 Subtract line 8 from line 7. If line 8 is more than line 7, enter zero	800 —
10 Total medical and dental expenses (add lines 1 and 9). Enter here and on line 33 . ▶	950 —

Name(s) as shown on Form 1040

Ms. Successful

Medical and Dental Expenses (not paid by insurance or otherwise) (See page 15 of Instructions.)

1 One-half (but not more than $150) of insurance premiums you paid for medical care. (Be sure to include in line 10 below.) . ▶	150	—
2 Medicine and drugs	300	—
3 Enter 1% of Form 1040, line 31 . . .	500	—
4 Subtract line 3 from line 2. If line 3 is more than line 2, enter zero	0	
5 Balance of insurance premiums for medical care not entered on line 1	850	—
6 Other medical and dental expenses:		
a Doctors, dentists, nurses, etc. . . .	400	—
b Hospitals		
c Other (itemize—include hearing aids, dentures, eyeglasses, transportation, etc.) ▶ CONTACT LENSES	250	—
7 Total (add lines 4 through 6c)	1500	—
8 Enter 3% of Form 1040, line 31 . . .	1500	—
9 Subtract line 8 from line 7. If line 8 is more than line 7, enter zero	0	
10 Total medical and dental expenses (add lines 1 and 9). Enter here and on line 33 . ▶	150	—

More Generous and More Flexible
Retirement Plans

Retirement planning needs and deserves a book to itself. Nevertheless, the advantages of corporate retirement plans over Keogh Plans can be summarized briefly:

1. Corporations can contribute *more money* to defined-contribution retirement plans—25% of annual compensation, including bonuses, if desired, with a limit upwards of $25,000, versus 15% under a Keogh Plan, with a limit of $7,500. (Defined-benefit plans and Subchapter S corporations are too complex to be discussed here.)
2. Corporations have a *greater choice of investment vehicles*—especially one-person corporations. While a Keogh Plan is limited to stocks and bonds (only if a custodian agrees to handle the account), mutual funds, savings certificates, and similar investments, corporations can invest not only in these, but also in any valuable objects so long as they come under the "prudent man" rule—gold bullion, coins, stamps, art, antiques.
3. Corporations can *create tax deductions with a retirement plan that does not require any cash outlay.* This profit-sharing plan, called ESOP (Employees' Stock Ownership Plan) generates legitimate "cashless" deductions at the corporate level and is recommended by many major accounting firms for one-person general business and professional corporations.

Tax-free Dividend Income

People who receive dividend income from common or preferred stocks must pay taxes on all but $100 of the income. But corporations that receive dividend income from common or preferred stocks can exclude 85% of the dividend income; they pay taxes on only 15% of that income.

The issues in the sample portfolio below are not to be construed as recommendations; they are simply illustrative of high-quality, high-yielding stocks appropriate as corporate investments. The preferred stocks are all AAA rated by Standard & Poor's Corporation; the common stocks possess low price/earnings ratios, high yields, and moderate growth.

REPRESENTATIVE CORPORATE PORTFOLIO

Standard & Poor's rating	Preferred stocks	Price 7/3/79	Dividend	Yield	Income from 100 shares
AAA	duPont $3.50	44	$3.50	7.95%	$ 350
AAA	duPont $4.50	54⅜	4.50	8.28	450
AAA	General Motors $3.75	45⅞	3.75	8.17	375
AAA	General Motors $5.00	60⅝	5.00	8.25	500
					$1,675
	Common stocks				
*	Chemical New York	40¼	3.16	7.85	316
A−	Gulf Oil	27¼	2.05	7.52	205
A+	Reynolds Industries	57¼	3.80	6.64	380
A−	Southern Pacific	30⅝	2.40	7.84	240
A	Texaco	27⅝	2.16	7.82	216
					$1,357
					$3,032

* Standard and Poor's does not rate financial corporations.

The function of this high-yield portfolio is the compounding of dividends, 85% of which are totally excluded from taxes; and 15% of which are taxed at 17% if net corporate income is under $25,000, at 20% if net corporate income is between $25,000 and $50,000, and at 30% if net corporate income is between $50,000 and $75,000. (Over $75,000, the advantage declines, but is still worth pursuing; although the corporate tax rate rises to 40%, personal income tax at this level is much higher.)

Consider a portfolio consisting of 100 shares of each security. The annual income from the portfolio would be $3,001.

A sole proprietor in the 40% bracket would pay $1,-160.40 in taxes on his dividend income and would be able to keep only $1,840.60:

Dividend income	$3,032.00
Less $100 exclusion	− 100.00
	$2,932.00
Tax rate	× .40
Tax	$1,172.80
Net dividend income	$1,859.20

However, if his corporation owned the portfolio, the taxes are *only one-tenth as high:*

	Assuming 17% Bracket Net Corporation Taxable Income Under $25,000
Dividend income	$3,032.00
Less 85% exclusion	−2,577.20
Taxable portion of dividends	$ 454.80
Tax rate	× .17
Tax	$ 77.32
Net dividend income	$2,954.68
Amount saved from individual tax	1,095.48
Percent saved from individual tax	93%

	Assuming 20% Bracket Net Corporation Taxable Income $25,000–$50,000
Dividend income	$3,032.00
Less 85% exclusion	−2,577.20
Taxable portion of dividends	$ 454.80
Tax rate	× .20
Tax	$ 90.96
Net dividend income	$2,941.04
Amount saved from individual tax	1,081.84
Percent saved from individual tax	92%

	Assuming 30% Bracket Net Corporation Taxable Income $50,000–$75,000
Dividend income	$3,032.00
Less 85% exclusion	−2,577.20
Taxable portion of dividends	$ 454.80
Tax rate	× .30
Tax	$ 136.44
Net dividend income	$2,895.56
Amount saved from individual tax	1,036.36
Percent saved from individual tax	88%

Extrapolating this unchanged portfolio over a period of time results in compounding the more than $1,000 saved each year on the corporate stock portfolio alone into more than $5,000 in 5 years and approximately $11,000 in 10 years. Carrying this extrapolation further, if the portfolio is treated as a unit, and an additional unit is purchased each year, so that at the end of 10 years there are 1,000 shares each, providing substantial dividends that are 85% tax-free, the savings are enormous.

The only concern a successful corporation head has in this area is that portfolio income not exceed 60% of total corporate income in any year. If it did, the corporation would be construed as a personal holding corporation by the IRS and would forfeit its 85% dividend exclusion for the year.

With these major tax benefits which substantially increase disposable personal income, it's easy to see why most lawyers and accountants recommend incorporation for businessmen and professionals.

(Additional information on incorporation can be found in Appendix B, "State Requirements for General Business and Professional Corporations," and Appendix C, "Sample Minutes and Bylaws for a Small Corporation" and in the author's book, *Inc. Yourself: How to Profit by Setting Up Your Own Corporation.*)

Part
THREE: **HIGH-RISK**
TAX SHELTERS

11 Municipal Bonds as Speculations

Although "municipal bonds" and "speculation" sound like a contradiction in terms, many high-bracket taxpayers looking for above-average rates of tax-free income have invested profitably in this area by purchasing bonds that have a greater element of risk. Risk refers here not only to the probability of default, but also to the probability of a significant price decline in periods of bear markets.

Investors who are happy with a modest amount of speculation might consider buying the weakest investment-grade bonds (rated BBB-) or bonds that for a variety of reasons are unpopular in the market or which have some negative connotation. Bonds issued by Puerto Rico and Guam are prime examples. Although they are not U.S. municipalities, their bonds are exempt from federal, state, and city income taxes. Nevertheless, because they are not part of the United States, their bonds trade at a very strong concession to the general municipal bond market. If an A-rated bond issued by a state agency offered a current yield of 6.50%, an A-rated bond issued by its opposite number in Puerto Rico would probably offer a current yield of 7.00% to 7.50%.

Tax-free bonds issued by hospitals also fall into this category. Because of their dependence on a third-party source of income such as Medicaid or Medicare, any change in the reimbursement policies of these programs could have a deleterious effect on the hospitals' ability to pay debt service. For this reason, many hospital issues offer yields close to 8%.

Other investors who are willing to assume larger risks for a commensurately large return can do so in a variety of ways. One such opportunity occurred during the New York City fiscal crisis. At the peak of the crunch, investors could have bought New York City bonds that yielded 12% to maturity. If the investors believed that fundamentally New York City would turn around (as actually happened in late 1978 and early 1979 when the city returned to the credit markets after a four-year absence and received upgraded ratings on its notes from the financial services) and be able to repay its debt, they would enjoy very high yields and, in some cases, substantial capital gains. For example, investors were able to buy New York City general obligation bonds for as little as 40 to 60 cents on the dollar, depending upon the maturity, with the longest maturities going most cheaply. (The market always rewards individuals who are willing to risk their money for the longest period of time.) When New York City's financial situation improved gradually, prices on its outstanding debt rose; even prior to maturity, investors holding these bonds earned significant capital gains.

Another way to speculate in the municipal market is to buy bonds that are rated less than investment grade (B or Ba) but that appear to be able to continue paying debt service. This class of bonds includes industrial development bonds where the corporation paying debt service has had its credit rating lowered but remains a viable concern. These bonds can generally be purchased at a substantial discount from par.

Also in this category are new-issue bonds that are rated less than investment grade. The bonds sold to finance the

Meadowlands Sports Complex (Giants Stadium) in New Jersey are a prime example. Because the bond proceeds were used to build a new project that had no previous operating history, they were rated Ba by Moody's. The bonds also had a 7.50% coupon ($75 per year tax-free income) which made them very attractive to State of New Jersey residents. After the project was completed and became profitable, Moody's reviewed and upgraded the rating, which caused the bonds to rise in price. The bonds ultimately sold at a substantial premium over par.

The recent fiscal crisis in Cleveland is another example of purchasing bonds with a less-than-an investment-grade rating that still appear to be viable. Cleveland is now rated Caa by Moody's because it defaulted on $15.5 million privately placed bank loans. (This default has nothing to do with Cleveland's public debt.) Aggressive investors could buy general obligation bonds at substantial discounts, which yield as much as 11% to 12%. Since Cleveland, unlike New York, suffers more from political than from financial problems, many investors feel that the city will eventually turn itself around and solve its problems. These investors are encouraged by the fact that Cleveland has yet to miss an interest payment on its public debt. Also, because both Ohio and Cleveland impose income taxes, Cleveland bonds are double-tax-exempt for Ohio taxpayers and triple-tax-exempt for Clevelanders; a factor which makes them especially attractive.

Many high-bracket outright speculators habitually buy high-risk industrial development bonds or municipal bonds yielding 9.00% or 9.50%; in their brackets, these bonds offer a tax-equivalent yield anywhere from 11.97% to 12.64% (25% tax bracket) to 27.00% to 28.50% (67% tax bracket). They argue that in 4 to 8 years they've recaptured their principal, and that subsequent payments are tax-free gravy. For example, an investor in the 50% bracket who bought $10,000 of 9.00% bonds would receive $900 a year in tax-free income, or an equivalent pretax income of $1,800. Using this logic, the investor would recapture the cost of his bond in about 5½ years. An investor in the 67% bracket who made the same investment would receive the same $900 a year in tax-free income, but his equivalent pretax income would be $2,700. This investor would recapture the cost of his bond in about 4 years.

These speculators regard their high-coupon high-risk bonds as an annuity and are completely unconcerned about whether the bonds will be paid off when they mature (usually sometime in the twenty-first century) or whether the borrower will default. In fact, they're much more concerned about whether the bond might be called before that time and whether they'd then have to invest their money at far lower interest rates.

Investors who are outright speculators might also choose unrated bonds or bonds that are in default but which might eventually pay off. These bonds generally offer yields in the range of 8% to 10%. Some of these bonds in default include highway or bridge bonds where new traffic patterns have developed after the construction of a shorter toll-free highway. The loss of vehicular traffic to the original road results in a decrease in revenue so that the issuer can no longer pay debt service. In some instances, such as with the Chesapeake Bay Bridge and Tunnel Authority bonds, which defaulted, the old traffic patterns have resumed again, and the issuer has resumed payment of debt service from the point in time when it was suspended. These bonds generally offer investors exceptional returns to match their risks.

Nevertheless, at least one municipal bond analyst suggests that investors in very high tax brackets look for yield and security, not risk. If a 7% tax-free yield is equivalent to a 14% taxable yield in the 50% bracket, investors might be wise to accept that yield with grace, thereby protecting their capital. Greedy investors who reach for tax-equivalent yields of 25% or more are risking too much and are really just plain crap shooting.

12 High-Risk Real Estate Tax Shelters

Perhaps, as one real estate tax-shelter specialist suggested, this chapter should be called "Higher-Risk . . ." rather than "High-Risk." While the real estate tax shelters discussed in this chapter are all higher risk than the ones discussed in Chapter Eight, they represent a risk spectrum ranging from ventures offering moderate appreciation with some income to projects which offer so much tax risk and investment risk that most experts advise against them.

Conventional (to-be-constructed) real estate tax shelters are the most conservative of the higher-risk real estate tax shelters. Because these projects have not yet been built, it takes a greater degree of management competence to monitor construction: cost overruns can be deadly.

A typical project is a residential garden-apartment complex of 200 to 300 units, located in a suburb—very likely in the Sunbelt—offering all the amenities: swimming pool, recreation and laundry rooms, ultramodern kitchens, and so on, which takes about a year to build. An investor who puts up $10,000 will generally be matched by a bank's lending $30,000 on the project, so that he has really bought

$40,000 worth of real estate with his money—leverage which will work to his benefit. For his investment, he receives a series of moderate tax losses that look like this:

Year	Tax loss	Amount of write-off
1	40%–50%	$ 4,000–$ 5,000
2	30%–35%	3,000– 3,500
3	18%–25%	1,800– 2,500
4	15%–18%	1,500– 1,800
		$10,300–$12,800

Ultimately, the tax losses total between 100 and 120% of his investment, with the largest part of the write-offs occurring in the first 4 years. The tax losses are so large because they're based on a $40,000 investment: the investor's share plus the bank's share, represented by the $30,000 portion of the mortgage. Since this is a real estate venture, the $30,000 portion of the mortgage is nonrecourse to the investor; this is the leverage advantage that only real estate ventures still offer: the ability to take write-offs where nonrecourse loans are utilized.

In addition to the large write-offs, once the building is occupied, there will be 100% tax-sheltered cash-flow income, ranging between 5½% and 6½%, even after payments for taxes, mortgage, maintenance, insurance, and other expenses—except for utilities, because the apartment units are usually individually metered and paid for by the tenants. This is an important point for investors to look for when they are signing up a potential real estate investment. The cash flow will probably fluctuate because tenants are likely to be moving in and out of the buiding. Cash flow may also rise periodically because management can raise rents when tenants' leases are renewed—generally at the end of 1 to 3 years.

While the write-offs and tax-shelter cash flow are certainly advantageous, what makes a conventional (to-be-constructed) real estate tax shelter an equity builder is the project's appreciation potential. Management usually plans to sell the building in about 8 to 10 years. In the past, similar buildings have appreciated at anywhere from 3% to 5% compounded annually; like the write-offs, this figure is calculated on the leveraged $40,000 base. A portion of these profits will be taxed as capital gains, depending on the method of depreciation used.

A higher-risk—and not generally recommended—version of this tax shelter involves much higher leverage, which means a much higher risk/reward ratio, with an emphasis on the risk. Here an investor who puts down $10,000 will acquire $60,000 to $80,000 worth of real estate. Since there is a very low equity-to-debt ratio, tax losses will be magnified—and so will the risk. In this form of real estate tax shelter, the bank still lends only $30,000—since the bank is certainly not going to assume an unusually high degree of risk with its own money. The additional $20,000 or $40,000 is provided by the seller, in terms of a second mortgage—or, in some cases, what is known as a wraparound mortgage.

This tax shelter is risky on two grounds: First, the IRS may question the value of the property and hence the write-offs because it feels the seller has artificially inflated the value of the property by adding a second mortgage. If the IRS disallows the write-offs, the investor will lose his tax deductions and will also have to undergo the trouble, annoyance, and expense of refiling his tax returns.

Second is the investment risk. Because the investor paid more than he should have, and because the property is so highly leveraged, there's a chance that he may lose his entire investment. As broad advice, investors who see conventional real estate offered at 5-to-1 or 7-to-1 debt-to-equity ratios should be extremely wary of the deal.

Still more risky—and to be avoided by all except the most intrepid and knowledgeable investors—are *distressed-property deals*. Typically, these are existing apartment or commercial buildings that for some reason are unoccupied or only partially occupied, and are unable to meet mortgage payments. Very often a promoter will approach the bank that holds the mortgage and offer to get some investors together and bail out the bank or whoever owns the building. That's why these deals are referred to as "bailouts." The bank is usually more than willing to accept—it may not have collected on the mortgage for as long as several years and may not have been able to sell the property.

What usually happens, though, is that the promoter will raise money from investors—but it will all be spent in promoter's and management fees. What's in it for the investors? The advantage of not having to put up much cash, and the usual tax deductions of up to 300% of the investment in the year the investment was made.

Like the preceding example, bailout tax shelters have two major flaws: First, the deductions probably won't hold up if audited by the IRS, since this may be another case of artificially inflating the value of the property in order to take large deductions, and there is also some highly questionable tax accounting involved. And the IRS knows it.

Second, and more serious, this tax shelter is not much of an investment. Very rarely has anyone selling "distressed properties" performed any service or turned them around to make them "undistressed." Most of the so-called shelters of this type seem to be an excuse for promoters to generate fees and disappear, leaving little—if any—qualified management to do something to improve the property and safeguard the investors' interests. Investors should be very suspicious about these deals and ask: "If the building hasn't been successful over the past 3 or 4 years, what makes the promoter think he can do something to reverse the trend?" There is always the remote possibility that the promoter will bring in innovative management with a track record and a plan; then this could be an interesting high-risk investment. Generally, though, the wisest course is to avoid these deals: why buy something that's already a problem?

Subsidized-housing real estate tax shelters belong in a different framework. They're not more risky than any of the tax shelters discussed so far, but they are different, and they serve a different function. Unlike the preceding tax shelters, which are—or which claim to be—equity builders, subsidized-housing tax shelters are what are known as "deep shelters," whose primary purpose is to give investors substantial write-offs (300% to 350%) over a long period of time. Because these tax shelters are for high-bracket investors, nearly all of them are private placements. The one exception to date is Real Estate Associates Limited, a public program which expects to raise $15 million through $5,000 minimum investments.

To the uninitiated, government-subsidized housing has a bad sound; people think of the South Bronx, Harlem, Bedford-Stuyvesant, Watts. However, the overwhelming majority of government-subsidized housing has not been built in inner cities since 1974. Today most government-subsidized housing—a $100 billion market in 1978—is suburban and is indistinguishable from—and in many cases superior to—conventionally financed housing; some of the buildings even have swimming pools and other amenities. Government-subsidized housing is no longer for the hardcore unemployed poor; it is for the elderly and for people who can't afford to buy their own homes—a large segment of the population. A typical tenant might earn $15,000 and be unable to save the $5,000 to $10,000 necessary for the down payment on a house.

Essentially, Section 8 of the U.S. Housing Act of 1937, which was incorporated into the Housing and Urban Development Act of 1968, provides that a developer whose plans are approved by HUD (Department of Housing and Urban Development) can receive a "Section 8" contract on some or all of the apartment units in his building. For the developer to receive a Section 8 subsidy, tenants occupying the apartments must earn 80% or less of the median income in the area where the building is located. (In some neighborhoods, the median might be $15,000 to $20,000.) The Section 8 contract generally stipulates that for periods of 20 to 40 years, the owner of the building (in this case, the investors) will receive a subsidy equal to the difference between the apartment's market-rate rent and 25% of the tenant's income. Thus, if an apartment rents for $400 a month and the tenant earns $800 a month, the tenant pays $200 a month rent and the government pays the owners $200 a month rent.

Because the government guarantees the rents as long as the owner fills the building with qualified tenants, risks of bank foreclosure are minimal. In fact, there has never been a foreclosure under the Section 8 program, which has been successful in its goal of providing good housing for people who cannot afford it.

Investors can also benefit from another subsidy: very often, state agencies provide mortgage money for these buildings from municipal bond underwritings, which means that mortgage money is cheaper than it would be through other sources. Now, when private mortgages cost 10½% to 12%, state-subsidized mortgages may cost only 7½% to 8½%.

Government-subsidized housing is highly leveraged; usually a $10,000 investment will buy as much as $80,000 worth of real estate. Tax losses for the first few years look like this, compared with conventional (to-be-constructed) real estate:

Year	Government-subsidized housing tax loss	Conventional real estate tax loss
1	45%–50%	40%–50%
2	40%–45%	30%–35%
3	38%–40%	18%–25%
4	35%	15%–18%

After 6 years, approximately 200% of the investment will have been written off; at this point, a 50% taxpayer will have gotten all his money back.

Cash flow is minimal: 2% to 3%, at most. There are two reasons for this. First, the investment is leveraged so highly that mortgage payments eat up most of the cash flow. Second, in return for granting all these subsidies, the government puts a lid on what investors may receive in cash flow, generally not more than 6%, making what is known as a "limited-dividend corporation."

But government-subsidized-housing investors don't buy these tax shelters for the cash flow; they buy them for the large tax losses each year. Taxpayers in the 60% bracket who can take a $5,000 loss on a $10,000 investment the first year save $3,000 in taxes. The next year, taking a $4,500 loss saves them $2,700 in taxes. In a sense, it's like having a stock or bond that yields 30% tax-free.

But no investment is perfect. Government-subsidized-housing tax shelters have some disadvantages.

First, this tax shelter has very limited marketability. Investors should plan on being locked in for 15 to 20 years.

Second, government-subsidized housing creates a negative tax basis. If an investor pays $10,000 and writes off $35,000, he has a negative tax basis of $25,000. When the property is sold, he will pick up the −$25,000 as taxable income (not necessarily cash). Because accelerated depreciation is used, the difference between straight-line and accelerated depreciation is potentially recapturable at ordinary-income rates. The difference decreases each year, so investors must look at each year separately. Roughly, after about the seventh or eighth year, approximately 50% of the gain would be recapturable as ordinary income, and approximately 50% as capital gain.

Although the building—as distinguished from the investment unit, with its limited liquidity—can be sold at virtually any time, most buildings aren't sold for 14 to 18 years. When they are sold, though, there could be a tax bonus in addition to any appreciation: the law allows a tax-free rollover. If the building is sold to a tenant group (like co-oping), the sale is treated exactly like the sale of a private home. An investor who reinvests the proceeds in another subsidized-housing property does not have to pay taxes on any gains. This creates the opportunity to pyramid any potential profits.

Portfolio Strategies Using
Subsidized-Housing Tax Shelters

Government-subsidized housing also provides portfolio-building strategies in combination with other tax shelters. Because a government-subsidized-housing tax shelter bought in one year creates current and future losses with one payment, an oil and gas program can be bought the second year with tax savings from this real estate shelter, and this, in turn, can be pyramided:

> $20,000 subsidized-housing tax shelter in Year 1 creates a $10,000 write-off in Year 1, which generates $5,000 cash in the 50% bracket and purchases $5,000 oil and gas tax shelter. In Year 2 there is a subsidized-housing write-off of $9,000 plus a $4,500 oil and gas write-off which equals $13,500, generating $6,750 in cash in the 50% bracket to purchase another half of a $10,000 unit of a subsidized-housing tax shelter or another $5,000 unit of an oil and gas tax shelter, et cetera.

Another strategy combines subsidized-housing and conventional real estate (to be constructed) tax shelters. The $5,000 write-off on a $10,000 subsidized-housing tax-shelter unit the first year buys a $2,500 unit of a conventional real estate tax shelter, which will provide a 40% to 50% write-off in its first year at the same time that the subsidized-housing tax shelter provides a tax deduction of 40% to 45% (its second year). In addition, the conventional real estate tax shelter offers a yield of 5% to 6%, which compensates for the minimal—if any—yield on the subsidized-housing tax shelter.

A third strategy combines subsidized-housing tax shelters with cattle feeding, which is a deferral tax shelter. Ordinary income from the sale of cattle in the second and subsequent years of the program is offset by deductions from the subsidized-housing tax shelter.

"Rehab" housing—often cynically called "five-year slums"—is the riskiest form of real estate tax shelter. These

old buildings, typically located in inner cities, are attractive to investors because they can deduct the costs of rehabilitation in 5 years on a straight-line basis, rather than waiting 16 to 18 years to get most of their deductions. Most rehabs are done as private placements and are suitable for taxpayers earning $80,000 to $100,000 a year, who can benefit most from the substantial write-offs—which average 200% to 250% of the investment every year for the first 2 or 3 years.

As in any risk/reward situation, though, investors must remember that rewards are generous because the risks are so high. Rehabilitation neighborhoods are dangerous, and the odds that the property will have any residual value are slim. Investors may lose their investment, but they are buying enormous write-offs and are providing housing for people who otherwise wouldn't have it.

13 Oil, Gas, and Mineral Tax Shelters

What do Liza Minnelli and Fred J. Borch, former chairman of General Electric, have in common?

Barbra Streisand and William S. Lasdon, former executive committee chairman of Warner-Lambert?

Jack Benny and Walter Wriston, chairman of Citicorp?

Candice Bergen, Buddy Hackett, Andy Williams, and Russell McFall, chairman of Western Union?

This isn't a trivia quiz, and the answer is far from trivial: together they lost $3,136,287 in the biggest Ponzi* scheme in U.S. history. The Home-Stake Production Company, ostensibly an oil and gas tax shelter, promised investors 400% profits on their investments plus big tax write-offs—and took the rich and famous, sophisticated financial managers, and top corporation executives and politicians for over $140 million.†

* Charles Ponzi was a swindler who flourished in Boston in 1919–20. He promised investors huge returns from dealing in international postal-reply coupons but actually paid them off with money from newer investors. Eventually his pyramid scheme collapsed and he was imprisoned.

† For the full story, read David McClintick, *Stealing from the Rich: The Home-Stake Oil Swindle* (New York: M. Evans, 1977).

Why did the Home-Stake scam work so beautifully? Other than such motivations as human greed and the joy and delight in diverting money from the IRS, perhaps it has something to do with former IRS Commissioner Mortimer M. Caplin's characterization of oil and gas drilling as "the kingpin of tax shelters."

Indeed, for many investors, oil and gas is the perfect tax shelter; it offers a large first-year write-off, tax-favored treatment of income, the possibility of long-term capital gains treatment upon liquidation, and liquidity of investment.

The most valuable feature of oil and gas tax shelters is that, with a very small investment, an investor buys the possibility of increasing his assets many times over. While this potential is also true of the stock market, commodities market, options market, and venture-capital opportunities, these investment media usually require a great deal more money than oil and gas program units (and in some cases much more knowledge), and these investments are more expensive because there are no offsetting write-offs, as there are with oil and gas tax shelters.

In an oil and gas program, investors typically participate in an undivided pool of money drilling for oil and gas. There are two basic types of oil and gas tax shelters: exploratory programs and development programs. *Exploratory programs* are the highest risk/reward ventures. They involve drilling in areas where oil and gas have not yet been found. If an exploratory well is successful, the program drills several additional nearby wells (sometimes called "sister wells") to fully exploit the reservoir.

Development programs are less risky because they begin where exploratory programs end: with drilling near known finds. Leases are more expensive and returns per well are lower; however, the probability of finding oil and gas is higher, too.

Both types of program offer investors approximately the same write-off; the difference is in the possible return. A successful exploratory oil and gas program could return as much as 10-to-1, although the odds against a payoff of this size are very high. Developmental wells succeed 65% to 85% of the time, but the odds against a program's paying off substantially more than 2-to-1 are quite small.

Oil and gas shelters are especially good as shelters for large one-year chunks of income, bonuses, and capital gains because intangible drilling costs (IDCs), which are the major source of deductions, are incurred primarily in the first 12 months of the program. In fact, the largest write-offs (usually 85% to 100% of the total investment) occur in the first drilling year, a characteristic which best benefits the investor who realizes that he needs a tax shelter early in the year.

The 12-month figure is important because it's 12 months regardless of when the counting starts. If an investor buys a drilling program in July, the 12 months will encompass two calendar years, not one. The drilling company and the broker can report quite accurately: "You will get a 90% deduction in the first year." But because they mean July to June and the investor is thinking January to December, many investors wake up the following year when they receive their K-1 forms for the IRS and discover that their deductions for the prior year were only half of what they expected. (They'll pick up the other half this year, but that's cold comfort now.) While it is the broker's responsibility to point out any difference between the drilling year and the calendar year, it's also the investor's responsibility to ask about this point.

Many people start looking for a tax shelter in October and November. Or even December. This is a mistake. First, fraudulent tax shelters come out of the woodwork during the late fall. Their promoters know very well that as the end of the year approaches, people lose all common sense in their "gimme shelter" syndrome and will more readily buy deductions than quality. The odds on getting stung escalate as December 31 approaches.

Second, as mentioned before, an investor's deduction is going to be lower because the program will not be able to complete as much drilling by year-end as if the investor had participated in a program started earlier that year. An investor who starts a drilling program early can usually take a 90% or sometimes a 92% deduction; an investor who starts in October or November will usually be able to write off no more than 60% or 70% that year and the remainder the following year.

If a large write-off in one calendar year is necessary and the investor knows he will receive a bonus in October, he should probably begin a drilling program as early as February or March and borrow the money, if necessary. Even at today's high interest rates, this makes sense because he is permitted to write off up to $10,000 net investment interest, after offsetting investment income. Thus, a taxpayer in the 50% bracket who borrows money at 10% to invest in a tax shelter is really borrowing the money at a net effective rate of 5%.

If a drilling program is successful, cash will eventually flow to the investor; some of this is considered tax-free income. The *depletion allowance* is now 22% of gross revenues, up to 50% of taxable income from the property before depletion allowance, and is tax-free. (It will decrease to 20% in 1981 and eventually to 15% in 1984.) If oil and gas wells produce $200 worth of income during the year, the depletion allowance is 22% of the gross, or $44, which is tax-free. *Lifting charges* (the cost of getting oil out of the ground and moving it to where it is sold) might be $100. In this case, then, the investor's net check and net taxable income before the depletion allowance is $100, of which $44 (22% of the gross) is tax-free. The investor pays taxes on only $56, which is classified as unearned income, which may be taxed at the 70% level.

The $44 depletion allowance is an item of tax preference; it, too, may be subjected to a 15% tax.

Still, despite possible high taxes on a part of the return, oil and gas tax shelters are attractive because of their large write-offs and capital gains potential.

For example, one unusually successful drilling program has estimated that future net revenues on a $10,000 exploratory investment will be in the area of $110,000. Approximately $44,000 of that $110,000 will be totally tax-free because it represents depletion (REMEMBER: up to 50% of net). The remaining $66,000 will be taxed at 70%, for a tax bite of $46,200. The investor will end up with approximately $63,800 net on a $10,000 pretax (or $5,000 after tax, if he is in the 50% bracket) investment. Of course, this is an unusually successful drilling program. Our investor could have lost his investment, too.

Investment Strategy

Because of the low probability of success in oil and gas ventures, most experts strongly advise against a one-time oil and gas investment. Oil and gas companies don't invest that way, and the investor shouldn't either. If possible, an investor should choose two—or, better yet, three—investments: if he has $15,000 to invest, he should buy three $5,000 units. He may want to put all of them with the same company or divide them among three different management companies; but he should diversify. Putting the $15,000 in just one program is really weighting the odds against himself, and oil and gas drilling is risky enough already!

The key strategy in drilling for oil and gas is to see to the bottom of as many holes as possible that have been originated by intelligent professionals. If an investor splits a $15,000 investment among Can-Am, Apache, and McCormick, he will see to the bottom of approximately 150 wells, and his chances of success will be greatly enhanced.

If an investor has only $5,000 to invest, he can still hedge his bets and limit his risk by buying a developmental program. It's probably always better to invest than not to—especially from a tax standpoint—and these drilling companies have a good track record: they typically return a significant portion of the investment and sometimes multiples of the investment. If an investor is in the 50% tax bracket, invests $5,000, and is able to take a $5,000 deduction, he has

only $2,500 at risk because his $5,000 deduction saved him
$2,500 in taxes he otherwise would have paid. His risk is
further decreased because there are few programs offered by
responsible brokerage houses that have not returned at least
$2,500 per $5,000 program, which would cover his investment cost.

Risk Gradients

While all oil and gas programs are classified as high-risk tax
shelters, there is a recognizable and definable risk gradient
in both developmental and exploratory oil and gas programs. The risk gradient is understood most clearly at the
highest tax-shelter adviser levels, but the average tax-shelter
broker, who is not as knowledgeable about these subtleties
as his supervisors, should still be able to provide useful answers to the right questions. For example, there are extremely high-risk, moderately high-risk, and lower-risk
exploratory programs, based on their investment potential.
All of these are higher-risk than development programs,
which can also be classified into three or four risk
categories.

Performance of Oil and Gas Tax Shelters

As examples of outstandingly successful oil and gas programs, here are three oil companies whose exploratory programs drilled with great success in three different
geographical areas:

1. McCormick's 1973 program covered southern Louisiana
   and made one major discovery and several minor ones.
   An investment of $12,500 (including assessments) has re-
   turned $36,000 after approximately 4 years. The $36,000
   was treated primarily as capital gains; and since the
   $12,500 investment was deducted from income, an inves-
   tor in the 50% bracket really had only $6,250 at risk.
2. Apache, the oldest drilling company, explored the
   Springer Trend in Oklahoma in its late 1973 and early
   1974 programs. The 1973-II program has already re-

turned $65,000 to its limited partners on an investment of
$17,250 ($15,000 + $2,250 assessment). The 1974-I pro-
gram has returned $50,000 on an investment of $15,000.

3. Can-Am made a major discovery at its Pineview Prospect,
a major Rocky Mountain Overthrust play in the Uinta
Mountains outside Salt Lake City. Its 1973 programs will
probably ultimately return approximately 5½- or 6-to-1,
and increase in the price of oil and gas may send the
payout even higher.

Of course, these and other drilling companies have had fail-
ures, too.

Assessments

Many exploratory and development programs have a kicker
that most investors aren't aware of. And brokers usually
don't mention it because generally there's no further commission involved for them. The majority of drilling programs provide for some kind of future assessments—with
exploratory investors more likely to be called on than developmental investors—which are invested in drilling "sister wells" adjacent to promising existing wells. The odds on
drilling successful sister wells are far more favorable than
exploratory drilling—3 chances in 4, as opposed to 1 in 8, so
they're often called "gravy wells." One tax-shelter expert
says bluntly, "In 90% to 95% of the cases, assessment calls
aren't made unless something good has happened."

But many investors have a peculiar attitude toward
these requests for additional money, which usually amounts
to 20% to 30% of their original investment: "Damn it! I gave
them my $10,000, and now they want to come back and nick
me for another $3,000—and I really haven't seen that much
payoff yet—and to hell with them!"

The drilling company writes to the investor once,
twice—then puts up the money itself. When the company
receives as much as three times its investment on the particular wells which were drilled with the assessment money, it
may, depending on the terms of the deal, reinstate the investor's percentage.

Thus the investor who doesn't contribute the additional assessment has acted as the company's stalking horse. He has done all the company's dirty work by assuming all the risk and letting the company benefit from its subsequent investment in much more certain drilling locations.

Selling Out

Unlike many forms of tax shelters, oil and gas programs provide liquidity without complete sacrifice of capital gains.

Liquidations are voluntary. Investors can leave their limited partnership units to their spouses, children, or other beneficiaries. But assume that after 3 or 4 years an investor wants to sell his partnership unit. Perhaps he will be retiring soon. Maybe interest rates are at very low levels, which means that his oil and gas program is worth more than when interest rates are at high levels.

After drilling is completed and reserves are measured, the drilling company establishes a liquidating value for each investment unit. The liquidating value is based on a double-discounted formula: a portion of the ultimate return is deducted for risk, and a portion is deducted because the company calculates that the future value of the oil and gas in the ground is a function of the money market and interest rates. Therefore, during a time of low interest rates, cash liquidating values will rise.

For the same program, with no production to alter the variables, if an engineering review said, "There is $110,000 of oil and gas per investment unit in the ground," in May 1977, when interest rates were low, that $110,000 might have been worth $25,000. By early 1979, because of rising interest rates, that same $110,000 in the ground may be worth only $20,000 to the company because of the increased cost of removing the oil. (This, of course, is an oversimplification. Projections based on the rising price of oil and gas must also be factored into the liquidating-value calculations, but that gets complicated for the scope of this book and is unnecessary to the basic explanation of liquidating values.)

If the investor wishes to liquidate his investment, a large portion of the cash liquidating value receives capital gains treatment. Although the Tax Reform Act of 1976 materially changed the method of calculating the gain, the investor still receives capital gains treatment, which is even more favorable now that capital gains rates have been lowered.

Public drilling programs usually write their investors once a year, offering to repurchase units at a stated price for the next 90 days. Smaller or private programs generally have to be contacted by the investor. Companies are eager to buy back limited partners' units because the discount is so large. (REMEMBER: $110,000 of oil and gas in the ground is worth only $25,000 or less today, depending on money markets.) Companies are willing and able to wait; individual investors may not be.

Discounts are not as deep in private programs or in developmental programs, which stress a more rapid payout of cash. Because the time-frame is shorter in developmental programs, there is no long debt exposure, which is a major factor in discounting calculations to determine liquidating values.

NOTE: If a program is very unsuccessful, the company may attempt to persuade limited partners to liquidate their units so that the company can stop paying for expensive accounting and reporting. The sweeteners the company offers are similar to the premium in a bond's call provision.

Used Units

There is a very active aftermarket for limited partnership units within the major brokerage houses. These "used units," as they are called, are bad for the seller, who takes a loss compared to what he would receive if he held onto his investment. (He may be taking a gain compared to his purchase price.) But the used units are very good for the purchaser, who is, in effect, buying a large stream of income at a bargain price. Let's say the buyer has purchased the $110,-000 tax shelter for $28,000. Because he has bought a tax shelter that has no more tax-shelter benefits except the depletion allowance, the entire first $28,000 the buyer receives is considered to be a return of capital and is tax-free.

Not all used units sell so high. A less productive unit that was expected to return $5,500 on a $5,000 investment recently sold for $2,000. And it was still considered a good investment.

Investors should remember that buying a discounted program is like buying a discount bond: it's an investment, not a tax shelter.

Oil and Gas Programs as Gifts

Oil and gas tax shelters are an ideal gift because of their large write-offs. An investor can put $10,000 into an oil and gas tax shelter and get deductions as high as 92%, which bring his cost basis down to $800. Even on an outstandingly successful program, the first liquidating value offered by the company will probably be around 30%, or $3,000. He can therefore give a $10,000 asset with a cost basis of $800 to his children or grandchildren tax-free because it comes under the $3,000 annual gift limitation.

Many older investors use this method to transfer assets to their children and grandchildren. They can buy ten $10,-000 units this way, take approximately $90,000 in write-offs the first year, and give a unit to each of ten children and grandchildren—all under the $3,000 annual gift limitation. Or they can give one unit each year to each child and grandchild.

Oil and gas tax shelter units can also be accumulated in Clifford trusts, after the parents take the write-off themselves, as described in Chapter Seven.

Coal

The Tax Reform Act of 1976, as amended by the Revenue Act of 1978 and the "Halloween pronouncements" of 1977, has virtually killed the most popular mining tax shelter: coal. Before the bloodbaths, an investor or investor group would lease a coal property, get an engineer to take core samples to determine how much coal was there, make arrangements to sell the coal in advance on a schedule basis, and pay an advance royalty to the owner of the property, using an interpretation of the Revenue Codes made in the early 1970s. On October 31, 1977, the IRS reinterpreted the old ruling, saying that investors could no longer pay 4 or 5 years' royalties in advance, but could write off the royalties for only one year at a time. Unfortunately, the royalties for that one year would never cover the deductions the investors were looking for, so the investors backed off. The new coal shelter became like the oil and gas shelter: developmental expenses were deductible items, but investors could no longer take 4-to-1 or 5-to-1 write-offs.

But coal promoters are undeterred and are attempting to get around the Revenue rulings and borrowing money on a nonrecourse basis, which is no longer permitted in the limited-partnership form, by asking investors to become joint venturers. *Any investor who is not in the coal business should avoid this ploy.* Coal mining is a capital- and labor-intensive business that is extremely dangerous. Mining can cause explosions and forest fires. Mines can collapse and kill people. Mining can pollute a water supply. Joint venturers, unlike limited partners, can become *personally liable* for the debts and suits incurred by their activities. With so many other, safer tax shelters available, choosing a coal joint venture is risky to the point of downright stupidity.

14 Be an Angel: Theatrical Investing

In one sense, theatrical investing is not a tax shelter; there are only 1-to-1 write-offs. In another sense, however, because a successful theatrical investment can create a stream of deferred income over a period of years, much like an annuity, theatrical investing does possess some of the characteristics of a tax shelter.

Buying a piece of a Broadway show is a high-risk investment. One recent prospectus states:

> The General Partners of _____ wish to emphasize that no one should consider the purchase of the interests being offered without recognizing the nature of and the risks of loss involved in the purchase of an interest in an enterprise devoted to a particular theatrical production. There can be no assurance as to income or as to return of the investment. An investor purchasing a limited-partnership interest should understand that he may lose his entire investment or may not receive any return thereon. Additional risk factors are discussed in this prospectus, which should be studied carefully prior to purchasing the limited-partnership interests offered hereunder.

The prospectus makes its point by listing over a dozen risk factors, the most significant of which are

- the necessity of a minimum Broadway run to return the initial contribution to the limited partners, and the low probability of that event on a historical basis.
- the possibility that the general partners (producers) might abandon production of the play before it opened and liquidate the partnership.
- the illiquidity of the limited partners' investment and restrictions on the assignment of limited-partnership interests.
- the responsibility to bear all the losses up to the amount contributed.

Nevertheless, an investment in a Broadway show is exciting and in recent months even affordable. Although 1% limited partnerships can sell for anywhere from $5,000 to $20,000, one recent production company which offered 1% units for $12,000 also offered one-tenth limited partnerships for only $1,200, a sum most investors could afford to lose.

Hit shows, while not numerous, have paid investors spectacularly. *Oklahoma!, South Pacific,* and *My Fair Lady* are classic examples. More recently, *You're a Good Man, Charlie Brown* has paid investors more than $25 for every dollar invested, and is still paying off. *Annie* is still paying investors, too; a major contribution to the high return on investment is the $9.5 million movie sale.

Where does the money come from? In addition to the Broadway run, which usually starts being profitable after 4 or 5 months, there are road companies, foreign companies, television sales—now enhanced by sale possibilities to cable TV stations and to video-cassette and video-disk producers—and record sales. Depending on the terms of the prospectus, the limited partners receive a certain percentage of income from each of these areas. Musicals have more of these subsidiary rights to sell than straight dramatic plays.

To balance the picture, a musical costs more money to

produce and generally takes longer to break even and then return a profit. Most fledgling angels are flabbergasted to discover that just one item in a musical—shoes—can easily cost $35,000 if the cast is large and there are frequent changes. Adding a new musical number to a show can cost between $25,000 and $50,000 divided among the orchestrations, costumes, choreography, lighting, sets, and props. At that rate, an investment of $500,000 to $1,000,000 can evaporate very quickly.

Producers who wish to broaden the base of potential support for a new play may advertise for new backers in the theatrical section of Sunday's *New York Times* or *The New Yorker*. The producers feel that even though it costs more money to sell fractional units at $1,000 to $2,000, the extra expense is more than compensated for by the number of new investors who are certain to buy tickets and urge everyone they know to see "their" show. In addition, these new investors will provide a much larger pool of capital for future productions if this production is even a modest success. And the solicitation costs for this future capital will be virtually nil.

Potential investors should be given a prospectus and a limited-partnership agreement for their accountants and lawyers to examine. In most cases, the limited partners provide all the money for the play but share the net profits equally with the producers, who are the general partners and who make no cash contribution. For example, if a production company sold 50 units at $12,000 to raise $600,000, a limited partner who owned 1 unit would be entitled to 1% of the profits. The prospectus should spell out the legal and financial rights and obligations of both the general and limited partners and should provide a prospective budget showing an estimated breakdown for scenery, props, costumes, lighting, fees to director, choreographer, set, costume, and lighting designers, casting director, hair stylist, orchestration, rehearsal salaries and expenses, publicity and advertising, administration and general expenses, and similar costs.

Using the $600,000 production as an example, following is an estimated allocation of proceeds:

TOTAL CAPITALIZATION $600,000

Physical production

Scenery	$43,545
Props	2,819
Costumes	13,025
Electric and sound	10,000
	$69,389

Fees

Director	5,300
Choreographer	8,000
Set, lighting, and costume designers	16,500
General manager	5,000
Dance arranger	2,500
Casting director	1,000
Hair stylist	500
Orchestration and copying	15,000
	53,800

Rehearsal salaries

Principals, chorus, understudies	31,748
Stage managers	5,778
General and company manager	7,340
Company crew	5,650
Wardrobe	850
Rehearsal pianist	3,500
Musical director	3,200
Musicians	4,320
Press agent	3,125
Production secretary	900
	66,411

Rehearsal expenses

Rehearsal halls	5,250
Scripts	250
Stage manager and departmental expenses	1,500
Theater expenses	3,000
	10,000

Publicity and advertising

Newspaper and TV	50,000
TV commercial	5,000
Photos and signs, etc.	10,000
Press expenses	500
	65,500

Administration and general

Office	3,900
Legal and legal advertising	13,000
Auditing	4,000
Insurance	4,000
Payroll taxes	9,917
Pension and welfare	3,481
Preliminary box office	2,500
Take-in*	25,000
Hauling	4,000
Opening-night expenses	2,500
Telephone and telegraph	1,000
	73,298

Operating losses

Previous production out-of-town	99,319

Bonds and deposits

Actors Equity	35,907
International Alliance of Theatrical Stage Employees	4,200
Association of Theatrical Press Agents and Managers	2,520
American Federation of Musicians, Local 802	9,278
	51,905

Total	$489,622
Reserve	110,378
Capitalization	$600,000

* This term refers to physically bringing the production into the theater and includes moving and placing sets, props, lights, marking the stage, stagehands' salaries, trucking and hauling expenses, and so on.

Prospective investors should have an accountant—preferably one who is experienced in theatrical accounting—review the budget. A number of questions may arise: Precisely what does each fee cover? Is it reasonable? Should there be more detailed breakdowns of some of the larger figures? And the prospective investors themselves can use the budget as a guide to ask questions, too: Who is being hired for these jobs? Have they been hired yet, and do they have contracts? What are their credentials? Of course, if the investors ask too many questions, they may be treated as nuisances and asked not to invest in the play. Still, investors should use common sense and not let themselves be completely dazzled by the glamour of the theater. A good rule of thumb is to ask questions in direct proportion to the amount of the proposed investment.

In most cases, only people who are considering an investment of a full unit (1%) or more, which can range from $5,000 to $20,000, are invited to backers' auditions. These events are held to raise money and consist of actors performing scenes and singing songs from the play. If dancing is a major part of the play, dance numbers will be performed, too. The backers' auditions are lots of fun. They are also deadly serious and nerve-racking, with producers, actors, and investors praying for a hit—and producers worrying even more about whether they'll be able to raise the money they need and be able to begin rehearsals on schedule. (In retrospect, it seems unbelievable, but *Oklahoma!* took more than a dozen backers' auditions and nearly a year to raise the required funds.)

The small investors miss some of this glamour. But they, too, can buy tickets for opening night, rush to Sardi's to wait for the notices, and brag to their friends. Most important, large and small investors alike, in return for the chance to lose their entire investment or see it returned at higher odds than most racetrack long shots, have the opportunity to participate in the American theater.

15 Movie Tax Shelters

For some people, the golden age of movie tax shelters was more exciting and more profitable than the golden age of movies. Movie tax shelters were—and still are—very high-risk investments because public taste and receptivity is involved; and public taste is fickle and unpredictable. Unlike a piece of real estate that can be sold later, if not now, and meanwhile acts as a hedge against inflation, a film that is badly received has limited or no value.

Still, before the Tax Reform Act of 1976, it hardly mattered whether a film was good or bad if it was a good tax shelter, because investors could wind up with cash equivalents of over $200,000 for a $50,000 investment. Here's how it worked:

Limited partners would buy a film for $1,000,000 by putting up $100,000 cash and giving the owner of the film a nonrecourse note for $900,000, maturing in 10 or 15 years, with principal and interest payable solely out of the proceeds of the film rentals. The investors often obtained even greater leverage by putting up only half their investment the first year ($50,000) and signing a recourse note for the second half, to be paid the second year. Thus, for the first year, the limited partners invested only $50,000 to acquire a $1,- 000,000 film.

But why would the owner of the film agree to such a deal? What was in it for him?

To begin with, the value of the film certainly was nowhere near the $1,000,000 agreed on; most probably it was only about $200,000 or $300,000. Nevertheless, because the sale was considered an arm's-length transaction between the buyer and the seller, the sale price was unquestioned—at least, for a while. Eventually, of course, the IRS put an end to the abuses of excessive depreciation arising from grossly inflated purchase prices. What took them so long? The aesthetics of each film are unique. The IRS couldn't really make artistic—and from there, financial—value judgments.

Meanwhile, the seller had received a down payment of $100,000 on an installment sale of $1,000,000. By the time the note had been paid off or the buyers had defaulted on the note, the film owner might well have collected the $200,- 000 or $300,000 the film had actually cost him to produce. He might have received even more. Or he might have suffered a loss if the payments were less than his cost. In any case, unless he collected the entire $1,000,000, he got to repossess the film—at which point he could sell it to a new group of investors as a tax shelter! (Of course, he might have trouble finding buyers, since this film would now be 10 years old and would not have an outstanding track record. Also, since the film was "used," it would not have been eligible for the investment tax credit.)

Two kinds of write-offs were available to the investors: the investment tax credit and depreciation. Both were based on the $1,000,000 purchase price.

At the time of the Tax Reform Act of 1976, the investment tax credit was 7% if the asset had a useful life greater than 7 years. Most films, however, were considered to have a life expectancy of 3 to 5 years and took the one-third pro-rata investment tax credit of 2.33%. Based on the $1,000,000 purchase price, the film would give the limited partners an investment tax credit of $23,300. This was a *tax credit,* and not a deduction, so it reduced income tax dollar for dollar. Thus, with the investment credit alone, the limited partners' investment exposure was cut nearly in half; they actually had only $26,700 ($50,000 − $23,300) at risk in the first year.

Meanwhile, using income-forecasting techniques, the investors might estimate the life expectancy of their film to be 4 years, with 40% of the total revenues to be received in the first year. Under the accounting concepts of matching deductions with income, they could write off 40% of the cost of the film in the first year. With a film cost of $1,000,000, the investors could take a depreciation deduction of $400,-000 the first year if revenues were minimal. If they were in the 50% bracket, this deduction was equivalent to $200,000 in after-tax dollars. Thus, for an investment of only $50,000 the first year, they could realize cash equivalents of $223,-300. It was certainly an elegant 4½-to-1 tax shelter.

This example is only slightly exaggerated; 3-to-1 and 4-to-1 film tax shelters were quite common.

What happened 10 or 15 years later, when the $900,000 nonrecourse note came due? Usually it could not be paid, and the original owner repossessed the film. At that point the investors incurred a large tax liability resulting from the difference between their investment and their deductions. Many investors attempted to protect themselves from the enormous amount of taxes due ... by going into a new tax shelter, if necessary, to cover any exposure from the closing-out of the first deal. If they were able to consummate this pyramid scheme before the Tax Reform Act of 1976 was passed, they were home free—at least until the second tax shelter's nonrecourse note fell due (not until 1985 or 1990).

But those were the glorious days of yesteryear. What's available to investors now?

At first there were attempts to get around the nonrecourse rules which affected only partnerships and Sub-chapter S corporations, but did not affect individuals, by creating tax shelters wherein each investor—as an individual—would own one episode of a 13-episode or 26-episode television series. As an individual, the investor would still be able to take substantial write-offs based on a nonrecourse purchase price, not on the smaller, actual at-risk investment. The series would be sold as a package, but the accounting and allocation of income would be made on an individual-episode basis. Unfortunately for the investors and the pro-moters, the IRS saw through this ploy, and recent IRS rul-ings have declared this procedure to be a fiction and a sham.

Although the leverage feature of nonrecourse financing has been destroyed, the Tax Reform Act of 1976 provided a bonus by liberalizing the investment tax credit. Not only was the credit increased from 7% to 10%, but also its terms were made more advantageous. The owner of a motion pic-ture had the option of ignoring the length of its life and tak-ing two-thirds of the investment tax credit's effective rate (which presently is 6.67%) or of taking a life expectancy of 7 years and qualifying for the full tax credit (suitable for wildlife films, classics, documentaries, etc.). Most movie tax-shelter partners chose the former route. In effect, this meant that a film could bomb out completely, last through only one distribution cycle, and still receive two-thirds of the current investment tax credit—no questions asked. That's the good news. The bad news is that the investment tax credit is now based only on the at-risk investment. So is depreciation.

Returning to the original example, the investment tax credit and depreciation base would be only $100,000—a far cry from the original $1,000,000. The investment tax credit would be $6,667 (versus $23,300 in the good old days) and the first year's depreciation would be $40,000 (versus $400,000)—equivalent to $20,000 in after-tax dollars for in-vestors in the 50% bracket. The investment of $50,000 would produce cash equivalents of $26,667 (versus $223,300). Thus movie tax shelters are now really only a speculative investment; their tax-shelter features have largely been destroyed.

As an investment, rather than a pure tax shelter, a movie deal's prospectus assumes a new importance. The prospectus should thoroughly discuss the screenplay, budget, producer and director, cast, and, most important, the distribution agreements (since a film must be distributed properly to maximize its profitability). A good distribution agreement should say something like: "The production group has arranged to book the film into 500 theaters this year" or "Colossal Pictures has guaranteed an advance of $250,000 against rental income." Key personnel—especially the stars and leading actors—should be insured so that the abandonment of the film in the event of their illness or death would not cause the partners to lose their investment.

Besides a detailed budget, the prospectus should discuss completion bonds, which provide for additional funds if the production exceeds its budget—as most do. Usually the limited partners will not be required to come up with the additional funds; but the lender who does will have to be repaid first and may also get a piece of the gross, too, as a "sweetener." If the prospectus states that there will be an overcall on the limited partners, who will have to supply any additional funds themselves, the deal should be reviewed very carefully to determine the investors' maximum exposure.

For the undeterred star-struck, there are other problems. Unlike other forms of tax-sheltered investment, where the usual minimum contribution is $5,000, movie deals may require minimum investments of up to $25,000 per unit. This can be a considerable sum to risk in one venture.

More major problems are geography and contacts. Movies are primarily an East Coast/West Coast industry; it's very difficult for an executive in Dubuque to find out about movie deals. Still, there are ways for the indefatigable.

The easiest way is to be a client of the right accounting

or law firm. Second best—especially for out-of-towners—is for investors to ask their lawyers or accountants to contact the right people in California or New York. There is an informal network operating, and contacts will eventually be made.

High-bracket professionals like doctors and dentists have it relatively easy. Since they're frequently contacted by stockbrokers and tax-shelter salesmen, all they have to do is mention their preference for movie deals. Their interest will be spread along the grapevine, and sooner or later, salesmen being salesmen, they'll probably be deluged with deals. A few of them may even be attractive. Because there's a grapevine at work, with many salesmen to share the spoils, commissions and fees may be very high. As always, investors should obtain solid advice from their lawyers and accountants.

16 Book, Record, and Cable Television Tax Shelters

Were it not for investors expecting to read about the glamorous book and record deals they've heard of so often at cocktail parties, this chapter would not appear in the book. Since the Tax Reform Act of 1976 and the Revenue Act of 1978 closed the door on nonrecourse deductions except for real estate, very few book and record deals have been made. With the advantage of large write-offs no longer available, investors have lost interest in this area. At least one major New York promoter has closed his offices and disconnected his phone.

Nonetheless, it is useful to examine book and record tax shelters, if only from a *caveat emptor* standpoint, to protect the investing public.

When nonrecourse financing was still legal, a promoter would sell the rights to receive a share of future royalties on a book or a record in a private placement. The percentage might vary, with the investors generally receiving from 25% to 50% of the author's or singer's royalties; sometimes, instead, the investors would receive a portion of or all royalties in excess of a certain figure. Since the authors and singers were usually unknown, the probability of the investors making a good profit on their investment was virtually nil; but the investors didn't care, they were buying tax deductions.

Typically, the investors would make a payment of $5,-000 or $10,000, sign a nonrecourse note for a much higher figure (e.g., $20,000 to $50,000), and deduct the entire amount ($25,000 to $60,000) as a tax loss. And who was to say what the artificially inflated property was worth? After all, these were financial judgments about "aesthetic" and "artistic" subjects.

Now the scenario is a little different, but the caveats remain. Book and record tax shelters may still offer 300% to 600% write-offs, but investors must now sign recourse notes, which may fall due in 10, 12, or 15 years. Sometimes a promoter will organize a ring of investors to hold each other's notes to prevent anyone's calling the notes, since the first note called would trigger all the others. Because the IRS views this technique as a sham and takes the position that these notes aren't really recourse notes, these write-offs will be disallowed if the arrangement is discovered.

Because the investment risk (how likely are the investors to make a profit? to lose their investment?) and the tax risk (how likely is the IRS to question the deduction, and then to disallow it?) are so high—to say nothing of the promoter's fees—there seems little reason for investors to consider book and record tax shelters.

A recent entry in the field of tax shelters is cable television systems. Cable systems, too, are marketed as private placements, which means that regulation is virtually nonexistent. Probably the largest danger in cable television deals is the promoter's projection of future revenue, based on saturation rates for basic cable service. One recent proposal for metropolitan Kansas City used figures of 20% of homes with cable television in 1978, 40% in 1979, 60% in 1980, 65% in 1981, and 70% in 1982 and subsequent years. Unfortunately, these projections are extremely unrealistic. Except for very mountainous areas where cable television is necessary to provide good reception, average saturation figures are much lower than the ones created by the promoter. In most of the United States, 40% to 50% saturation is considered very good.

Here, too, promoters' fees are large, and return on investment—if any—will be small. Because of these factors, cable television systems do not appear to be good tax shelters.

17 Equipment-Leasing Tax Shelters

Because equipment-leasing transactions are deferral tax shelters designed for wealthy investors who can afford to commit a minimum of $25,000 to $30,000, approximately 99% of the deals are private placements. These deals are not designed for investors earning $40,000 to $60,000 a year; they are designed for people with incomes well over $100,-000, preferably with a substantial portion coming from unearned income which is taxed at 70%. If all income is earned and therefore taxed at 50%, equipment leasing is generally an unsuitable tax shelter. Ideally, these investors should be close to retirement, or in some other situation where income is expected to decline in 4 or 5 years. At that point, when income will be reported, if the investors are in a lower tax bracket, the tax bite won't be as heavy.

Most equipment-leasing deals are triple-net-lease transactions, similar to the triple-net-lease concept in real estate discussed in Chapter Eight. The corporations leasing the equipment—usually computers, aircraft, barges, railroad cars—will be responsible for maintenance, insurance, and taxes; the owners will be responsible only for loan payments. Because the corporations leasing equipment like computers are major corporations with very high credit ratings, banks will usually lend 90% to 95% of the purchase price; $30,000 will therefore usually buy almost $300,000 worth of computers.

Table 17.1 is a good example of an equipment-leasing transaction. This particular deal involves leasing the central processing unit (CPU) of a used IBM 370 mainframe computer. The $32,000 investment is made in two installments: $20,000 in 1979 and $12,000 in 1980. In the first year, the $20,000 investment generates a $38,200 loss. The loss is so large because the Asset Depreciation Range (ADR) guidelines of the IRS allow owners of data-processing equipment to write off their cost down to salvage value in approximately 5 to 7 years, depending upon the type of equipment purchased. In addition, the transaction is leveraged very heavily; this, too, magnifies the tax loss. In this example, $32,000 buys about $200,000 of computer equipment. For an investor in the 60% bracket, the $38,200 loss is equivalent to a tax saving of $22,920. Thus, in the first year, the investor has made an after-tax profit of $2,920 on his investment. (For a 70% taxpayer, the tax saving is an even higher $26,640.)

In 1980 the second and final payment is made. There is minimal flow of tax-sheltered income because it's all going to retire debt. The second-year write-off of $23,600 produces $14,260 in tax savings for taxpayers in the 60% bracket. Based on the cash investment of $12,000, the taxpayer is ahead $2,260 for the year, $5,180 to date, and, with assumed 5% interest on the savings, is ahead $5,339.

Without any further investment, the third year the taxpayer deducts $10,300, which is worth $6,280 in after-tax dollars in the 60% bracket, and so on through the fifth year, with depreciation decreasing each year.

Table 17.1
EQUIPMENT LEASING EXAMPLE—COMPUTERS

Form of investment: Limited Partnership (nonassessable)
Cash investment: $20,000 on subscription
                           $12,000 second year
Equipment: Used IBM 370 mainframe computer central processing unit (CPU)
Term of leases: 5 to 7 years (full payout of debt over lease term)   *EVALUATING THE*
Investment tax credit: (unavailable on used equipment)   *TIME VALUE OF*
Analysis of economics: *MONEY*

Year	Cash invested	In-come	Profit (loss)	Tax savings (cost) 60% bracket plus income	Earnings on tax savings at 5% (after tax)	Cumulative out of pocket
1979	$20,000	-0-	(38,200)	22,920	-0-	+ 2,920
1980	$12,000	100	(23,600)	14,260	159	+ 5,339
1981	-0-	100	(10,300)	6,280	481	+12,100
1982		100	(5,800)	3,580	684	+16,364
1983		100	(4,100)	2,560	846	+19,770
1984		100	6,000	(3,500)	713	+16,983
1985		100	22,500	(13,400)	79	+ 3,662
1986		-0-	20,600	(12,360)	-0-	(8,698)
1987		7,500	11,700	480	-0-	(8,218)
	$32,000	8,100	(21,200)	20,820	2,962	

Estimates	Residual cash Gross	Net
10%	$19,900	7,960
16	26,600	10,640
22	35,300	14,120

Tax preference (per unit)		Investment interest (per unit)	
1979	17,100	1979	2,200
1980	10,500	1980	11,900
		1981	10,300
		1982	8,800
		1983	7,000
		1984	5,300
		1985	3,400
		1986	1,500
		1987	200

Suddenly there's a change in the sixth year, and the transaction "turns around" on the investor, who must start reporting taxable income because the decreasing depreciation is no longer greater than the income from the level-payment lease, and thus can no longer shelter all of it—or, at that point, the investor may buy another shelter to shelter his gain or begin to pay back some of the tax savings gained in prior years. As the years go on and the depreciation decreases further, the net income increases each year. (NOTE: The investor doesn't see the income—it's paying off the loan at the bank—but he still must report it.)

Since this is unearned income, it may be taxed at a maximum rate of 70%; that is why it is so important that investors shelter 70% unearned-income dollars earlier in the program. It makes no sense to write off 50% earned-income dollars and to pay back 70% unearned-income dollars. On the other hand, sheltering 70% dollars and paying for them with 30% retirement-bracket dollars makes very good sense indeed.

Equipment leasing is a very illiquid investment; it can't be sold, say, in the year before turnaround because of its very high negative tax basis ($82,000 less $32,000 investment, or $50,000). If the equipment were sold for whatever salvage value was obtainable, the investor would have to report all that negative tax basis as taxable income in that year—and incur an enormous tax burden. Or, again, he would have to buy a shelter to shelter his shelter. Virtually the same tax consequence would apply if he made a charitable donation of the equipment. If the investor died before the end of 1980, under current law his heirs would benefit by inheriting a stepped-up carryover basis on the tax shelter. But it's a terrible way to get out of a tax shelter! In short, the investor should plan to stay with the transaction to the end. Of course, if he should have to get out and incur a tax burden, he can always buy a shelter to shelter his shelter, although most responsible tax advisers don't recommend this strategy.

Let's jump to 1987, when the transaction is closed out and the computer is sold. This transaction is unique because the loan is retired in 1986 (almost a full year before the lease expires), so the investor gets to keep $7,500 in income during 1987 that would otherwise have gone to the bank.

To see how the investor has fared, we must go to the column labeled "Tax savings (cost) 60% bracket plus income." This column is the annual stream of the net benefits (and the negative benefits when they are paid back) of the transaction. When the pluses (tax savings) and minuses (taxes due) are netted out, the investor will be left with $20,-820 (as well as any interest earned on his tax savings).

Now let's separate the good deals from the bad ones. How much can this equipment be sold for? Under the heading "Residual cash," there are three different assumptions: that the equipment is sold for 10%, 16%, and 22% of its cost.

Let's look at the 16% assumption. If the IBM 370 central processing unit is sold for 16% of its cost, the investor will receive $26,600 in cash, which must be reported as unearned taxable income. If the investor is still in the 60% bracket, the sale will leave him with net cash of $10,640 ($26,600 − [60% × $26,600]). It is this figure added to the "Tax savings plus income" that should equal the cost of the investment ($20,820 + $10,640 = $31,460 versus the investment of $32,000).

This 16% figure is extremely important since it is the residual value that the equipment must be sold at for the investor to break even. And this is what separates a good equipment-leasing tax shelter from a bad one. If the computer can be sold at a higher price than the breakeven point, that's gravy.

The higher the breakeven point, the lower the chances that the equipment can indeed be sold at the breakeven price, and the riskier the deal. Proposals with breakeven points of 30% and 40% for computers are considered risky; investors should look for breakeven points of 20% or so for computer and data-processing equipment. In other types of equipment, the breakeven point can be higher. For example, aircraft has retained its value quite well, and in many instances has been sold for much more than its cost at the end of the lease period.

What has the investor actually achieved with all these complicated moves?

- He has transformed a $32,000 investment into an $82,000 tax loss over 5 years.
- He has—or should have—earned money on the funds he had use of during that period. The 5% rate of return assumed in Table 17.1 is rather conservative, although it represents an after-tax rate of return. The investor could have bought municipal bonds and gotten a tax-free yield of 7½ or 8% without too much risk.
- Depending upon the value of the equipment, he may make a profit, which would be taxed at the capital-gains rate maximum of 28%.

Equipment-leasing transactions have two unfavorable tax aspects: they generate sizable amounts of both tax-preference income and investment interest. Accelerated depreciation creates tax-preference income, which is calculated as the difference between accelerated depreciation and straight-line depreciation each year. Equipment leasing probably generates more tax-preference income than any other type of tax shelter.

Investment interest is the interest paid on a loan made to carry investments and the amount deductible is limited by the IRS to an excess of $10,000 over investment income (interest, dividends, rents, royalties, short-term gains, etc.). Thus, if an investor has investment income of $5,000, he may deduct investment interest of $15,000; if his investment interest is $16,000, he'll have to forfeit deducting $1,000 that year, but he can carry the $1,000 forward to a year in which he can use it.

In Table 17.1, $2,200 of the first year's $38,200 tax loss is generated by investment interest. However, in the second year, $11,900 of the $23,600 tax loss is generated by investment interest. Assuming there is no other investment interest, the investor will need approximately $2,000 in investment income to offset the investment interest in excess of $10,000 or will have to forfeit $1,900 of his $23,600 deduction that year—although he can carry it forward until it can be used. (NOTE: This investment-interest problem occurs only on full-payout triple-net equipment leases, which are the most conservative leases because they are designed to last as long as the loans.)

There is only a minor at-risk issue here, but it must nevertheless be mentioned. Because the investor is deducting more than his investment, he must be at risk to do so. Therefore the investor must sign a recourse note for the amount by which his losses exceed his investment. Thus, the investor is at risk for the difference between $20,000 and $38,200 in the first year, between $12,000 and $23,600 in the second year, and for $10,300 in the third year, and so on. The brokerage house arranging the placement will ask the investor to sign a note which states that in the event of default, he is personally liable to the bank.

Bul how risky is this transaction, really? First, since the equipment is leased to major corporations, their creditworthiness determines the risk of the transaction, which should be minimal. Second, the bank's willingness to lend anywhere from 9 to 19 times the investor's commitment on a nonrecourse basis—the only recourse the bank has is repossessing the equipment—should say something about the bank's assessment of the risk involved. All in all, the investment risk seems quite low.

In contrast to computers, which lose some of their value over a number of years, aircraft (10- to 12-year leases), barges (up to 18 years), and railroad cars (up to 18 years) have appreciated, and people investing in leasing transactions involving these types of equipment often find that they have a very valuable asset at the end of the lease and may sell it at a capital gain. For example, one DC-9 that was bought used in 1975 and was leased to Hawaiian Airlines is now worth approximately 20% more than the investors paid for it. Inflation is a major factor which makes old equipment look more attractive—especially compared to prices of replacement equipment.

18 Do-It-Yourself: Urban Reclamation Tax Shelters

Up until now, most of the tax shelters discussed have been types that required the assistance of investment brokers or advisers. And, up until now, with the exception of municipal bonds, the tax shelters discussed have come under the scrutiny of the IRS—and have often been modified, to the detriment of their investors.

But here's a tax shelter that doesn't need investment brokers and that actually has the blessing of the IRS: preservation and rehabilitation of historic commercial and income-producing structures. Examples of preservation can be found across the country—from The Cannery in San Francisco and Pioneer Square in Seattle to Old Town in Chicago and the old "cast-iron" districts of most major cities and many smaller ones.

"Income-producing" is the crucial concept: an investor can't buy an old house, restore it, and live in it herself alone, but she can buy the same house, convert it into duplex apartments, a boutique, or a restaurant, and either rent out the entire building or occupy part of it herself and rent part of it.

There are three ways a structure can be designated a "certified historic structure." Generally, a certified historic structure is any structure, subject to depreciation as defined by Section 167 of the Internal Revenue Code of 1954, which is either (1) listed individually in the National Register of Historic Places; or (2) located within and certified by the Secretary of the Interior as being of historic significance to a district listed in the National Register of Historic Places; or (3) located within a historic district designated under a state or local statute that has been certified by the Secretary of the Interior. Of these, the last classification is the most common.

Both the National Park Service and the IRS are involved in historic preservation. The National Park Service, on behalf of the Secretary of the Interior, evaluates, for the purposes of certification, the historical significance of certain historic properties, the effectiveness of the preservation provisions of state and local statutes designating historic districts, and the quality and appropriateness of rehabilitations.

The IRS, on behalf of the Secretary of the Treasury, administers and develops regulations on the tax aspects of the historic-preservation incentives in the Tax Reform Act of 1976.

There's a carrot-and-stick approach to historical preservation. The carrot is favorable tax treatment: the investor can choose between taking 200% depreciation or 60-month amortization of rehabilitation costs and 125% straight-line depreciation on the actual structure. Depreciation must exceed either the adjusted cost or $5,000; an investor can't qualify with a building purchased for $1,000 into which he's put $1,000 in rehabilitation.

The stick is tax "disincentives" for demolishing buildings rather than preserving them. Briefly, the demolition provisions (Section 2124[b] of the Tax Reform Act of 1976) provide that demolition costs or losses sustained as a result of demolition of a certified historic structure must be capitalized (added to the cost of the land) rather than being currently deductible along with the remaining undepreciated basis of the demolished building or, in some cases, added to the cost of the replacement structure for depreciation purposes.

The Tax Reform Act also prohibits accelerated depreciation for any property in whole or in part constructed, reconstructed, erected, or used on a site that was occupied by a certified historic structure.

To qualify as a certified rehabilitation, rehab projects are evaluated by the National Park Service, using the Secretary of the Interior's "Standards for Rehabilitation," which are 10 broadly worded criteria for rehabilitating all historic buildings—for example, houses, schools, factories, warehouses. The goal is to prevent the destruction of the historical and architectural integrity of the building being rehabilitated.

Following are the Secretary of the Interior's standards for rehabilitation:

SECRETARY OF THE INTERIOR'S STANDARDS FOR REHABILITATION

The following "Standards for Rehabilitation" shall be used by the Secretary of the Interior when determining if a rehabilitation project qualifies as "certified rehabilitation" pursuant to the Tax Reform Act of 1976. These standards appear in Section 36 of the Code of Federal Regulations, Part 67.

1. Every reasonable effort shall be made to provide a compatible use for a property which requires minimal alteration of the building structure, or site and its environment, or to use a property for its originally intended purpose.

2. The distinguishing original qualities or character of a building, structure or site and its environment shall not be destroyed. The removal or alteration of any historic material or distinctive architectural features should be avoided when possible.

3. All buildings, structures and sites shall be recognized as products of their own time. Alterations that have no historical basis and which seek to create an earlier appearance shall be discouraged.

4. Changes which may have taken place in the course of time are evidence of the history and development of a building, structure or site and its environment. These changes may have acquired significance in their own right, and this significance shall be recognized and respected.

5. Distinctive stylistic features or examples of skilled craftsmanship which characterize a building, structure or site shall be treated with sensitivity.

6. Deteriorated architectural features shall be repaired rather than replaced, wherever possible. In the event replacement is necessary, the new material should match the material being replaced in composition, design, color, texture and other visual qualities. Repair or replacement of missing architectural features should be based on accurate duplications of features, substantiated by historic, physical or pictorial evidence rather than on conjectural designs or the availability of different architectural elements from other buildings or structures.

7. The surface cleaning of structures shall be undertaken with the gentlest means possible. Sandblasting and other cleaning methods that will damage the historic building materials shall not be undertaken.

8. Every reasonable effort shall be made to protect and preserve archeological resources affected by, or adjacent to, any rehabilitation project.

9. Contemporary design for alterations and additions to existing properties shall not be discouraged when such alterations and additions do not destroy significant historical, architectural or cultural material, and such design is compatible with the size, scale, color, material and character of the property, neighborhood or environment.

10. Wherever possible, new additions or alterations to structures shall be done in such a manner that if such additions or alterations were to be removed in the future, the essential form and integrity of the structure would be unimpaired.

Guidelines for Applying the Secretary of the Interior's Standards for Rehabilitation

The following guidelines are designed to help individual property owners formulate plans for the rehabilitation, preservation and continued use of old buildings consistent with the intent of the Secretary of the Interior's "Standards for Rehabilitation." The guidelines pertain to buildings of all occupancy and construction types, sizes and materials. They apply to permanent and temporary construction on the exterior and interior of historic buildings as well as new attached or adjacent construction, although not all work implied in the standards and guidelines is required for each rehabilitation project.

Techniques, treatments and methods consistent with the Secretary's "Standards for Rehabilitation" are listed in the "recommended" column on the left. Those techniques, treatments and methods which may adversely affect a building's architectural and historic qualities are listed in the "not recommended" column on the right. Every effort will be made to update and expand the guidelines as additional techniques and treatments become known.

Specific information on rehabilitation and preservation technology may be obtained by writing to the Technical Preservation Services Division, National Park Service, U.S. Department of the Interior, Washington, D.C. 20240, or the appropriate State Historic Preservation Officer. Advice should also be sought from qualified professionals, including architects, architectural historians and archeologists, skilled in the preservation, restoration and rehabilitation of old buildings.

THE ENVIRONMENT

Recommended	*Not Recommended*
Retaining distinctive features such as the size, scale, mass, color and materials of buildings, including roofs, porches, and stairways that give a neighborhood its distinguishing character.	Introducing new construction into neighborhoods which is incompatible with the character of the district because of size, scale, color and materials.
Retaining landscape features such as parks, gardens, streetlights, signs, benches, walkways, streets, alleys and building setbacks which have traditionally linked buildings to their environment.	Destroying the relationship of buildings and their environment by widening existing streets, changing paving material or by introducing inappropriately located new streets and parking lots incompatible with the character of the neighborhood.
Using new plant materials, fencing, walkways, streetlights, signs and benches which are compatible with the character of the neighborhood in size, scale, material and color.	Introducing signs, street lighting, benches, new plant materials, fencing, walkways, and paving materials which are out of scale or inappropriate to the neighborhood.

BUILDING SITE

Recommended	*Not Recommended*
Identifying plants, trees, fencing, walkways, outbuildings and other elements which might be an important part of the property's history and development.	Making changes to the appearance of the site by removing old plants, trees, fencing, walkways, outbuildings and other elements before evaluating their importance in the property's history and development.
Retaining plants, trees, fencing, walkways, streetlights, signs and benches which reflect the property's history and development.	Leaving plant materials and trees in close proximity to the building that may be causing deterioration of the historic fabric.
Basing decisions for new site work on actual knowledge of the past appearance of the property found in photographs, drawings, newspapers and tax records.	Providing site and roof drainage that causes water to splash against building or foundation walls or drain toward the building.
If changes are made they should be carefully evaluated in light of the past appearance of the site.	

ARCHEOLOGICAL FEATURES

Recommended	*Not Recommended*
Leaving known archeological resources intact.	Installing underground utilities, pavements and other modern features that disturb archeological resources.
Minimizing disturbance of terrain around the structure, thus reducing the possibility of destroying unknown archeological resources.	Introducing heavy machinery or equipment into areas where their presence may disturb archeological resources.
Arranging for archeological survey by a professional archeologist of all terrain that must be disturbed during the rehabilitation program.	

BUILDING: STRUCTURAL SYSTEMS

Recommended	*Not Recommended*
Recognizing the special problems inherent in the structural systems	Disturbing existing foundations with new excavations that under-

Recommended

of historic buildings, especially where there are visible signs of cracking, deflection or failure.

Undertaking stabilization and repair of weakened structural members and systems.

Replacing historically important structural members only when necessary. Supplementing existing structural systems when damaged or inadequate.

Not Recommended

mine the structural stability of the building.

Leaving known structural problems untreated which will cause continuing deterioration and will shorten the life of the structure.

BUILDING: EXTERIOR FEATURES
EXTERIOR FINISHES

Recommended

Discovering the historic paint colors and finishes of the structure and repainting with these colors to illustrate the distinctive character of the property.

Not Recommended

Removing paint and finishes down to the bare surface; strong paint strippers whether chemical or mechanical can permanently damage the surface. Also, stripping obliterates evidence of the historical paint finishes.

Repainting with colors that cannot be documented through research and investigation to be appropriate to the building and neighborhood.

ENTRANCES, PORCHES AND STEPS

Recommended

Retaining porches and steps which are appropriate to the building and its development. Porches or additions reflecting later architectural styles are often important to the building's historical integrity and, wherever possible, should be retained.

Repairing or replacing, where

Not Recommended

Removing or altering porches and steps which are appropriate to the building and its development and the style it represents.

Stripping porches and steps of original material and architectural features, such as hand rails, balusters, columns, brackets and roof decoration of wood, iron,

212

Recommended	Not Recommended
necessary, deteriorated architectural features of wood, iron, cast iron, terra-cotta, tile and brick.	cast iron, terra-cotta, tile and brick. Enclosing porches and steps in a manner that destroys their intended appearance.

MASONRY: ADOBE, BRICK, STONE, TERRA COTTA, CONCRETE, STUCCO AND MORTAR

Recommended*	Not Recommended
Retaining original masonry and mortar, whenever possible, without the application of any surface treatment.	Applying waterproof of water-repellent coatings or surface consolidation treatments unless required to solve a specific technical problem that has been studied and identified. Coatings are frequently unnecessary, expensive and can accelerate deterioration of the masonry.
Repointing only those mortar joints where there is evidence of moisture problems or when sufficient mortar is missing to allow water to stand in the mortar joint.	
Duplicating old mortar in composition, color and texture.	Repointing mortar joints that do not need repointing. Using electric saws and hammers to remove mortar can seriously damage the adjacent brick.
Duplicating old mortar in joint size, method of application and joint profile.	
Repairing stucco with a stucco mixture duplicating the original as closely as possible in appearance and texture.	Repointing with mortar of high portland cement content can create a bond that is often stronger than the building material. This can cause deterioration as a result of the differing coefficient of expansion and the differing porosity of the material and the mortar.
Cleaning masonry only when necessary to halt deterioration or to remove graffiti and stains and always with the gentlest method possible, such as low pressure water and soft natural bristle brushes.	Repointing with mortar joints of a differing size or joint profile, texture or color.
Repairing or replacing, where necessary, deteriorated material with new material that duplicates	Sandblasting, including dry and wet grit and other abrasives, brick or stone surfaces; this method of

* For more information consult Preservation Briefs: 1: The Cleaning and Waterproof Coating of Masonry Buildings and Preservation Briefs: 2: Repointing Mortar Joints in Historic Brick Buildings. Both are available from Technical Preservation Services Division, National Park Service, Washington, D.C. 20240.

Recommended

the old as closely as possible.

Replacing missing significant architectural features, such as cornices, brackets, railings and shutters.

Retaining the original or early color and texture of masonry surfaces, including early signage, wherever possible. Brick or stone surfaces may have been painted or whitewashed for practical and aesthetic reasons.

Not Recommended

cleaning erodes the surface of the material and accelerates deterioration. Using chemical cleaning products which would have an adverse chemical reaction with the masonry materials, i.e., acid on limestone or marble.

Applying new material which is inappropriate or was unavailable when the building was constructed, such as artificial brick siding, artificial cast stone or brick veneer.

Removing architectural features, such as cornices, brackets, railings, shutters, window architraves and doorway pediments.

Indiscriminate removal of paint from masonry surfaces. This may subject the building to harmful damage and may give it an appearance it never had.

ARCHITECTURAL METALS: CAST IRON, STEEL, PRESSED TIN, ALUMINUM, ZINC

Recommended

Retaining original material, whenever possible.

Cleaning when necessary with the appropriate method. Metals should be cleaned by methods that do not abrade the surface.

Not Recommended

Removing architectural features that are an essential part of the building's character and appearance, illustrating the continuity of growth and change.

Exposing metals which were intended to be protected from the environment. Do not use cleaning methods which alter the color, texture and tone of the metal.

ROOFS AND ROOFING

Recommended

Preserving the original roof shape.

Not Recommended

Changing the essential character of the roof by adding inappro-

Recommended

Retaining the original roofing material, whenever possible.

Providing adequate roof drainage and insuring that the roofing materials are providing a weathertight covering for the structure.

Replacing deteriorated roof coverings with new material that matches the old in composition, size, shape, color and texture.

Preserving or replacing, where necessary, all architectural features which give the roof its essential character, such as dormer windows, cupolas, cornices, brackets, chimneys, cresting and weather vanes.

Not Recommended

priate features such as dormer windows, vents or skylights.

Applying new roofing material that is inappropriate to the style and period of the building and neighborhood.

Replacing deteriorated roof coverings with new materials which differ to such an extent from the old in composition, size, shape, color and texture that the appearance of the building is altered.

Stripping the roof of architectural features important to its character.

WINDOWS AND DOORS

Recommended

Retaining and repairing existing window and door openings including window sash, glass, lintels, sills, architraves, shutters, doors, pediments, hoods, steps and all hardware.

Duplicating the material, design and the hardware of the older window sash and doors if new sash and doors are used.

When needed, installing visually unobtrusive storm windows and doors that do not damage existing frames and that can be removed in the future.

Using original doors and door hardware when they can be repaired and reused in place.

Not Recommended

Introducing new window and door openings into the principal elevations or enlarging or reducing window or door openings to fit new stock window sash or new stock door sizes.

Altering the size of window panes or sash. Such changes destroy the scale and proportion of the building.

Installing inappropriate new window or door features such as aluminum storm and screen windows or insulating glass combinations that require the removal of original windows and doors or the installation of plastic, canvas or metal strip awnings or fake shutters that detract from the character and appearance of the building.

WOOD: CLAPBOARD, WEATHERBOARD, SHINGLES AND OTHER WOODEN SIDING

Recommended	Not Recommended
Retaining and preserving significant architectural features, whenever possible.	Removing architectural features such as siding, cornices, brackets, window architraves and doorway pediments. These are, in most cases, an essential part of a building's character and appearance, illustrating the continuity of growth and change.
Repairing or replacing, where necessary, deteriorated material with new material that duplicates in size, shape and texture the old as closely as possible.	Resurfacing frame buildings with new material which is inappropriate or was unavailable when the building was constructed such as artificial stone, brick veneer, asbestos or asphalt shingles, plastic or aluminum siding. Such material also can contribute to the deterioration of the structure from moisture and insect attack.

BUILDING: INTERIOR FEATURES

Recommended	Not Recommended
Retaining original material, architectural features and hardware, whenever possible, such as: stairs, elevators, hand rails, balusters, ornamental columns, cornices, baseboards, doors, doorways, windows, mantlepieces, paneling, lighting fixtures, parquet or mosaic flooring.	Removing original material, architectural features and hardware, except where essential for safety or efficiency.
Repairing or replacing, where necessary, deteriorated material with new material that duplicates the old as closely as possible.	Replacing interior doors and transoms without investigating alternative fire protection measures or possible code variances. Installing new decorative material and paneling which destroys significant architectural features or was unavailable when the building was constructed, such as

Recommended	*Not Recommended*
Retaining original plaster, whenever possible.	vinyl, plastic or imitation wood wall and floor coverings, except in utility areas such as bathrooms and kitchens.
Discovering and retaining original paint colors, wallpapers and other decorative motifs or, where necessary, replacing them with colors, wallpapers or decorative motifs based on the original.	Removing plaster to expose brick to give the wall an appearance it never had.
Where required by code, enclosing an important interior stairway in such a way as to retain its character. In many cases glazed fire rated walls may be used.	Removing paint from wooden architectural features by sandblasting and other abrasive techniques.
	Removing paint from wooden architectural features that were never intended to be exposed.
Retaining the basic plan of a building, the relationship and size of rooms, corridors and other spaces.	Enclosing important stairways with ordinary fire rated construction which destroys the architectural character of the stairway and the space.

NEW CONSTRUCTION

Recommended	*Not Recommended*
Keeping new additions and adjacent new construction to a minimum, making them compatible in scale, building materials and texture.	Designing new work which is incompatible with the earlier building and the neighborhood in materials, size, scale and texture.
Designing new work to be compatible in materials, size, scale, color and texture with the earlier building and the neighborhood.	Imitating an earlier style or period of architecture in new additions, except in rare cases where a contemporary design would detract from the architectural unity of an ensemble or group. Especially avoid imitating an earlier style of architecture in new additions that have a completely contemporary function such as a drive-in bank or garage.
Using contemporary designs compatible with the character and mood of the building or the neighborhood.	
Protecting architectural details and features contributing to the character of the building.	
Placing television antennae and mechanical equipment, such as	Adding new height to the building which changes the scale and character of the building. Addi-

Recommended
air conditioners, in an inconspicuous location.

Not Recommended
tions in height should not be visible when viewing the principal facades.

Adding new floors or removing existing floors which destroy important architectural details, features and spaces of the building.

MECHANICAL SERVICES

Recommended
Installing necessary mechanical services in areas and spaces that will require the least possible alteration to the structural integrity and physical appearance of the building.

Utilizing early mechanical systems, including plumbing and early lighting fixtures, where possible.

Installing the vertical runs of ducts, pipe and cables in closets, service rooms and wall cavities.

Insuring adequate ventilation of attics, crawl spaces and cellars to prevent moisture problems.

Installing thermal insulation in attics and in unheated cellars and crawl spaces to conserve energy.

Not Recommended
Causing unnecessary damage to the plan, materials and appearance of the building when installing mechanical services.

Having exterior electrical and telephone cables attached to the principal elevations of the building.

Concealing or "making invisible" mechanical equipment in historic walls or ceilings. Frequently this concealment requires the removal of historic fabric.

Installing "dropped" acoustical ceilings to hide mechanical systems. This destroys the proportions and character of the rooms.

Installing foam, glass fiber or cellulose insulation into wall cavities of either wooden or masonry construction. This has been found to cause moisture problems when there is no adequate moisture barrier.

SAFETY AND CODE REQUIREMENTS

Recommended
Complying with code requirements in such a manner that the

Not Recommended
Adding new stairways and elevators which alter existing exit fa-

Recommended	*Not Recommended*

Recommended

essential character of a building is preserved intact.

Working with local code officials to investigate alternative life safety measures which preserve the architectural integrity of the building.

Investigating variances for historic properties afforded under some local codes.

Installing adequate fire prevention equipment in a manner which does minimal damage to the appearance or fabric of a property.

Providing access for the handicapped without damaging the essential character of a property.

Not Recommended

cilities or important architectural features and spaces of the building.

Let's look at one example of a rehab project to see how an investor benefits from favorable depreciation and amortization treatment. An investor buys an old factory in Lowell, Massachusetts, for $60,000 and puts $100,000 of rehabilitation into it. The land is worth $10,000 and the useful life of the renovated factory is 25 years. The investor is in the 40% bracket.

Using the 200% depreciation:	
Purchase price	$60,000
Land	−10,000
Building	50,000
Rehabilitation	100,000
Total	150,000
	×.04
Ordinary depreciation	6,000
200% depreciation	12,000
Investor's tax bracket	×.40
Value of deduction each year	$ 4,800

Using 60-month amortization and 125% straight-line depreciation:	
Rehabilitation	$100,000
	×.20
Annual share	20,000
Investor's tax bracket	×.40
Value of deduction each year	$ 8,000
Building	$ 50,000
Depreciation rate	×.04
	2,000
	×1.25
	2,500
Investor's tax bracket	×.40
Value of deduction each year	1,000
Total deductions	$ 9,000

Without favorable tax-shelter treatment:	
Building	$ 50,000
Rehabilitation	100,000
	150,000
Depreciation rate	×.04
	6,000
	×1.25
Annual share	7,500
Investor's tax bracket	×.40
Value of deduction each year	$ 3,000

There is a hitch to the 60-month 125% method: If the building is sold within 5 years, the investor must recapture all the amortization and depreciation as ordinary income. Thus, unless the circumstances are extraordinary, it pays to hold on to the building for at least 5 years.

"Sweat Equity"

In this era of do-it-yourself-ism, are there any advantages to the investor's doing some or all of the rehab work himself? A great deal of money can be saved on rehabilitation through "sweat equity," but then the investor doesn't get the advantage of a large write-off. To get around this, one accountant suggests hiring members of your family as independent contractors. That way, the investor will have high rehabilitation costs on which to calculate his write-off, but will keep the money in the family. The family will have to pay taxes on these salaries, but it may still pay for him to adopt this approach.

Why This Tax Shelter?

At some point, the reader may well ask, "What's the point in laying out $160,000 here, plus interest on the mortgage, for around $50,000 worth of write-offs, when for that same $160,000 I can buy eight successive years of $20,000 oil and gas tax shelters and get over $140,000 worth of write-offs?"

From the strictly financial aspect, the argument is valid; but there are other advantages to rehabilitation. On the side of rehabilitation, depending on mortgage terms, the investor may not have to invest $20,000 each year. The property is virtually certain to produce income and to appreciate in value over the years. Then there's the aesthetic and civic-minded argument: many investors consider rehabilitating old buildings a labor of love as much as an investment. And the "Big Brother" argument: that this type of tax shelter is not likely to be questioned by the IRS.

And for corporate investors, rehabilitating old buildings is free advertising—it provides goodwill and publicity that money could never buy. People do remember—and are strongly affected by—a sign on a beautiful old building: "This building is being preserved by the ABC Corporation."

For people who don't live in major financial centers and aren't connected with high-powered investment advisers, for people who love old buildings, for corporations that can benefit from goodwill and free publicity, rehabilitating old buildings is a marvelous tax shelter. It makes investors happy, it makes citizens' groups happy, and it even makes the government happy.

A Reading List of Rehabilitation Information

Anderson Notter Associates, Inc., and City of Lowell. *Lowell: The Building Book.* Lowell, Mass.: City of Lowell, Division of Planning and Development, 1977.

Anderson Notter Associates, Inc., and Historic Salem, Inc. *The Salem Handbook: A Renovation Guide for Homeowners.* Salem, Mass.: Historic Salem Inc., 1977.

Boston Redevelopment Authority. *Recycled Boston.* Boston, Mass.: Boston Redevelopment Authority, 1976.

Bunnell, Gene; Massachusetts Department of Community Affairs, *Built to Last: A Handbook on Recycling Old Buildings.* Washington, D.C.: Preservation Press, National Trust, 1977.

Cantacuzino, Sherban. *New Uses for Old Buildings.* New York: Watson-Guptill Publications, 1975.

Educational Facilities Laboratories. *The Arts in Found Places.* New York: Educational Facilities Laboratories, 1976.

———. *Reusing Railroad Stations: A Report.* New York: Educational Facilities Laboratories, 1974.

———. *Reusing Railroad Stations: Book 2.* New York: Educational Facilities Laboratories, 1975.

Getzels, Judith N. *Recycling Public Buildings.* Planning Advisory Service Report No. 319. Chicago: American Society of Planning Officials, 1976.

Information series. Reports specializing in funding sources, adaptive use and a number of successful rehabilitation projects including *Rehabilitating Old Houses, Public Funds for Historic Preservation, Trolley Square, Long Wharf, Guernsey Hall* and *Stanford Court.* Washington, D.C.: Preservation Press, National Trust, 1976–77.

Kidney, Walter C. *Working Places: The Adaptive Use of Industrial Buildings.* Pittsburgh: Ober Park Associates, 1976.

Mintz, Norman M. "A Practical Guide to Storefront Rehabilitation." *Technical Series/2.* Albany, N.Y., Preservation League of New York State, 1977.

National Trust for Historic Preservation. *Economic Benefits of Preserving Old Buildings.* Washington, D.C.: Preservation Press, National Trust, 1976.

Phillips, Morgan. "The 8 Most Common Mistakes in Restoring Historic Houses (. . . and How to Avoid Them)." *Yankee Magazine,* December 1975.

Stephens, George. *Remodelling Old Houses Without Destroying Their Character.* New York: Alfred A. Knopf, 1972.

Technical Preservation Services

Division. *A Selected Bibliography on Adaptive Use of Historic Buildings.* Washington, D.C.: Office of Archeology and Historic Preservation, National Park Service, 1976.

Ware, Merrill. *Federal Architectture: Adaptive Use Facilities.* Washington, D.C.: Federal Architecture Project, National Endowment for the Arts, 1975.

19 Farming and Agricultural Tax Shelters

Let's face it: farming and agricultural tax shelters sound romantic. They carry the aura—especially cattle breeding and feeding shelters—of the Great American West we all grew up with, courtesy of Saturday matinees at the Bijou.

Unfortunately, reality is harsh. For most city dwellers—and I rather suspect that this covers most readers of this book—farming and agricultural tax shelters simply aren't very attractive; except, perhaps, for private placements, which are too individualistic to be covered in a book of this type.

The three most common types of farming and agricultural tax shelters are raw land—with or without crops, cattle feeding, and cattle breeding.

Farmland

Acreage prices have risen almost geometrically over the past 10 years. On the surface, then, farmland would seem like a great investment: make a small down payment, get a big mortgage, and take big write-offs.

This sounds like a great idea—until the investor discovers that prime farmland is presently going for $5,000 to $10,-000 per acre. A 10-acre plot (and few properties are this small) would cost $50,000 to $100,000. More realistically, 100 acres would cost $500,000 to $1,000,000. Where does the investor expect to get a mortgage? And can he—or his investment group—assume such a large mortgage?

If the land remains fallow, it won't produce any income to offset the expense until the day it is sold—and that day may be years away. If the land is to be farmed to produce income, who will farm it? And how much will professional management cost?

In addition, what about all the things that can go wrong with crops: weather, insects and disease, shifts in commodity prices, and so forth. Agriculture is really big business—it's no place for amateurs. There are better, safer, more profitable tax shelters.

Orchards

To bring the lesson home, let's look at a typical example of an agricultural tax shelter: fruit orchards. Orchards require huge capital investments in land and trees. Daily costs are high; agriculture is very labor-intensive. The rate of return on investment is often quite low. In the "good old days" of tax shelters, investors were able to expense these costs, to write them all off in one year. Now, however, investors must capitalize these heavy costs over the useful life of the orchard. Thus investors can no longer take all their expenses up front in one year and defer income—one of the primary goals of tax shelters.

Cattle Feeding

Cattle feeding is a deferral tax shelter. Typically, cattle are fattened up in feedlots for 4 to 8 months before they are sold and slaughtered. Thus investors can write off expenses in one year and receive ordinary income the following year—or can "roll over" the shelter the second year by buying another cattle-feeding shelter so that the new shelter's write-offs will offset the income from the first year's shelter.

But even though beef prices are escalating as this is written, there are too many uncontrollable variables for most city-dwelling investors and many professional advisers to be enthusiastic about cattle-feeding tax shelters. As one tax-shelter accountant said, "It's a funny thing—whenever my clients bought feed for the cattle, feed prices were sky-high; but somehow, when they sold the cattle, beef prices were at an all-time low! That's why my clients are in real estate now." He brings home the point which can never be reiterated too often: A tax shelter is an *investment* with favorable tax consequences.

Cattle Breeding

Cattle breeding sounds like a really exciting shelter—the Old West brought up to date with investment tax credits. In the March 27, 1979, edition of *Esquire,* Andrew Tobias nails this shelter "wherein you buy a bull and three cows now, which upon consumption of much feed and by means of much fornication, will someday multiply your tax-deductible investment into boxcars of hamburger at $1.89 a pound."

Still, an intrepid investor might look at Hereford (dairy) cows, with an eye toward privately placing a herd—at $50,000 to $60,000 per cow. Herefords are so desirable and so expensive because they are reported to produce 30,-000 pounds of milk a year while most other breeds produce only 15,000 to 18,000 pounds.

An investor buying a Hereford cow normally puts up 20% of the cost of the animal and assumes a nonrecourse note for the balance. He can commit himself to any portion of the balance to be designated as a recourse note at any time, or he can actually buy the cow on the installment plan. If the buyer does not pay a certain amount by a certain date, the seller can attach the collateral (the cow). Since, if we can extrapolate the trend, the fair market value of these animals is rising, the seller would easily get enough money to cover the note. And the note is so limited that the lender can't go after the buyer's assets—just after the collateral. Those are the terms of the recourse note.

All right, where is our urban investor going to house his Hereford tax shelter? Since Herefords are such spectacular producers, most farmers will be delighted to house them (after all, what's one more cow to take care of in a herd of 20 or 30) in return for their production, and may charge "room and board" only for the period when the cow goes dry (around 3 months). The investor's goal is to have the cow bred, in hopes of getting more female calves (called heifers), which will then also be bred at maturity. Heifers sold after 2 years get capital gain treatment. They generally sell for $20,-000 to $40,000 themselves because by that time they'll already have been bred and will be ready to calve. The new owner is really buying cow-plus-calf.

This tax shelter has some advantages: an investor can get a naturally multiplying investment, if he's lucky. There's also the investment tax credit and accelerated depreciation on the cow (but not on the calf, because it's "free"—the investor has no cost basis). In addition, the investor can take bonus depreciation. As its name implies, this is a sweetener: any person who owns property or depreciable assets can depreciate up to 20% of its value, limited to $10,000 worth of assets, for a $2,000 ceiling, in the first year. The remaining balance is amortized normally. Thus small investors can get twice the usual depreciation in the first year of ownership.

Nevertheless, for urban investors, the problems with a Herford herd of one or more outweigh the benefits. First, of course, the investor must find someone willing to sell the Hereford cow and to assume the note. Then he must find someone to house the cow. And here the IRS enters the picture: it may attack the shelter as a hobby. To counter the IRS's claim, the investor will have to show that he's serious about his Hereford shelter; the best way to do this is to have a professional manager (the farmer) who is willing to show the animal at county fairs and expositions, et cetera. The third problem is nature. There's no guarantee that the cow will produce a heifer, and male calves are worth very little.

Some problems can be avoided by buying a participation in a herd. But buying a participation creates still other problems. Although the investor no longer has to find someone to sell him a Hereford cow and a farmer to board her, he now has to worry about the honesty and competence of the management group. For some reason, cattle breeding has had a particularly bad record. Even veteran investors remember the Black Watch Farms/Berman Leasing debacle with a shudder.

Other Livestock

Other animals can be used as tax shelters, too. Horses—for breeding or racing—are one example.

Few people realize that breeding dogs or cats can also qualify as a tax shelter. And it's a lot easier for most people than breeding Herefords or Black Anguses! To use dogs and cats as a tax shelter, investors must demonstrate their seriousness—if they are attacked by the IRS as having a hobby, which does not qualify for tax-shelter treatment—by having taken their animals on show circuits, having professional training, winning ribbons, selling puppies and kittens at good prices, and so on. Like other animals, sale of the puppies and kittens is subject to capital gains treatment.

All in all, for most investors, real estate and oil and gas shelters seem better, safer, and more profitable than farming and agriculture tax shelters.

APPENDIX A

Internal Revenue Manual Supplement— Audit Procedures for Tax Shelters

TAX SHELTER PROGRAM

Section 1. Purpose

.01 This Supplement provides revised instructions, guidelines and procedures for handling cases under the Tax Shelter Program. Examinations and investigations in this Program will involve Oil and Gas Drilling Funds, Farm Operations, Real Estate, Motion Pictures, Coal, Records (Master Recordings), and other industry shelters used by promoters and investors.

.02 Program cases generally involve examinations of limited partnerships, small business corporations, syndicated investment units and other entities with a significant unresolved and abusive tax shelter issue, the resolution of which would have broad application with respect to the taxpayer public, or it must have a large number of taxpayers in varying districts and regions requiring coordination to ensure uniformity and consistency of treatment among taxpayers.

.03   The Program's objective is to identify and examine abusive tax shelter returns. The Program will ensure uniform treatment of all investors by consistent resolution of identified issues and the coordination with other IRS offices and functions for early solution of mutual problems and areas of concern.

Section 2. Background

.01   The National Office Coordinated Program for examination of the oil and gas drilling industry began in 1973. IRS and the Securities and Exchange Commission agreed to exchange information, to the extent allowed by law, in an effort to prevent fraud and sham transactions resulting in tax abuses. In 1974 and 1975 the Program was expanded to include shelters involved in real estate, farm operations and motion picture ventures.

.02   Tax shelter returns utilizing the partnership form generally involve large numbers of related entities located throughout the nation. The size and diversity of tax shelter returns create major administrative problems for the Internal Revenue Service. To alleviate this, the Service has instituted a program for obtaining early Service positions on new areas of tax shelter abuse and has developed computer programs to expedite the manual processing workflow in these examinations.

.03   This incorporates a teletype, dated June 23, 1977, to all Regional Commissioners, ARC's (Audit) and District Directors, from the Assistant Commissioner (Compliance).

.04   This also incorporates a memorandum, dated September 21, 1977, to all Regional Commissioners, ARC's (Audit) and District Directors.

Section 3. Organizational Responsibilities

.01   *Director, Audit Division*

1   The Director, Audit Division, is responsible for the overall planning, coordinating and monitoring of the Tax Shelter Program and for uniformity and nationwide coverage within the Program. This includes the development of guidelines and procedures, liaison with other National Office functions, as well as providing assistance in the establishment of an effective training program.

2   The Director, Audit Division, will submit information concerning new or novel schemes, obtained on abusive tax shelters by the districts, to Technical. Technical will use the information to establish a Service position that will be disseminated to the public in the form of a Revenue Ruling.

.02 *Regional Office*

1 Each ARC (Audit) will be responsible for designating an analyst who will be responsible for the Tax Shelter Program within his/her region. The analyst will coordinate his/her regional activities with representatives of National Office Audit Division, other regional functions and other regions, and with appropriate district Audit and service center personnel.

2 Each ARC (Audit) will be responsible for:

a orientating appropriate regional, district and service center personnel with Tax Shelter Program responsibilities; and

b ensuring that districts are taking affirmative action to implement the Program in connection with the examination of promoters of tax shelters as well as the tax shelter and investor returns.

3 Each ARC (Audit) will be responsible for screening and evaluating information furnished by the districts, as a result of the liaisons established with state securities agencies. The region will furnish to the Director, Audit Division, Attn: CP:A:G:E, only information which indicates new or novel abusive schemes or situations not previously identified and where corrective action should be taken. The Director, Audit Division, will submit information concerning new or novel schemes to Technical for use in the preparation of a Service position. The Service position will be published as a Revenue Ruling.

.03 *District Office and Office of International Operations*

1 Each District Director, in order to identify new areas of tax shelter abuse where the Internal Revenue Service has not established a position, will establish a liaison or contact with local state securities agencies, or similarly titled "blue sky" agencies to obtain information on potentially abusive tax shelter schemes. An information gathering project must be established in accordance with the requirements contained in IRM 4568. Information obtained will be forwarded to the appropriate ARC (Audit) for screening and evaluation.

2 Each Chief, Audit Division, will be responsible for:

a establishing an action plan containing methods of identifying and examining abusive tax shelter returns. The plan will be submitted to the appropriate ARC (Audit) for information and follow-up purposes. In addition, the program will be reviewed by the district each calendar quarter and quarterly status reports will be forwarded to the appropriate ARC (Audit).

b assigning a coordinator to be responsible for coordinating district activities with the assigned regional analyst and other district tax shelter coordinators.

3 Coordinating districts, districts having jurisdiction over the tax shelter entity or the first tier in a multitier tax shelter (unless otherwise agreed), will be responsible for:

a establishing and maintaining communication channels with other districts and regions, as appropriate, to facilitate monitoring the progress of cases.

b developing and disseminating, to the responsible regional analyst, novel examination techniques, unique issues, abusive tax schemes, and other information.

4 Audit Group or Case Managers will be responsible for:

a fully utilizing the procedures provided in IRM 4550 for requesting technical advice regarding unique or novel issues.

b assigning returns in the Tax Shelter Program to examiners who are in a position to commence, proceed with, and conclude the examination expeditiously.

c providing guidance to ensure that tax shelter examinations proceed timely and consistent with National Office, regional office and district office instructions.

d conferring with District Program Coordinator when additional guidance is needed.

e assuring that during the examination of program returns, examiners will be alert to indications of fraud. Where indications of fraud are found, ensure that referrals are made to the Intelligence Division in accordance with IRM 4565 or 42(11)9, as appropriate. All copies of Form 2797 (Referral Report for Potential Fraud Cases) will be stamped "Tax Shelter Program" in the upper left corner. Upon approval of the referral by the Chief, Audit Division, a copy will be given to the District Program Coordinator, who will advise the appropriate regional analyst of the fraud referral.

f closely coordinating, controlling and monitoring identified syndicated cases with District Program Coordinators.

g requesting legal advice from Regional Counsel, when needed, through established Audit organizational channels. Regional Counsel's advice and assistance is required on statutory notice and restricted consent language for all tax shelter cases. This is necessary to ensure uniformity and consistency.

h fully utilizing the technical coordination reporting procedures provided in Chapter (12)00 of IRM 4810, Audit Reports Handbook, Technical Coordination Reports (Forms 3558) will be used to report cases or practices which indicate tax abuses, inequities, or administrative problems in the interpretation and application of the tax laws that have not been previously identified. It is emphasized that this procedure is in addition to, not a replacement for, requests for Technical advice.

.04 *Review Function*

1 Tax shelter cases are to be selected for mandatory review. All cases should be thoroughly reviewed to assure proper development and explanation of adjustments.

2 If the tax shelter case warrants, the district should consider the use of on-site reviews.

3 Issues arising from tax shelter examinations, and the techniques used in their development, should be submitted to the appropriate regional office for inclusion in the Regional Review Digest, as appropriate.

.05 *Conference Function*

Tax shelter cases will receive the benefit of regular district conference procedures. District conferees should give priority handling to these cases.

.06 *Appellate Division*

1 To enable authorized representatives of tax shelter cases to secure Appellate consideration of partnership issues, at least one partner must request Appellate consideration. If no partner filed a return in the district where a partnership return is filed, advance approval is granted to transfer the case of a protesting partner to the Appellate Office servicing that district. Appellate Appeals Officers should give priority handling to these cases.

2 Appellate Appeals Officers should be particularly alert to potential abusive tax shelter schemes or devices which may not have been identified by Audit. These should be brought to the attention of the National Office Appellate Tax Shelter Coordinator.

.07 *Intelligence Division*

1 Intelligence Division National Office Project Number 23 has been assigned to track "Coordinated Tax Shelter Program Cases." Accordingly, each region and each district will establish a project number, using National Office Project Number 23 as the first two digits (see 330 of IRM 9570, Case Management and Time Reporting System Handbook). The designated project number will be entered in Item 17 of Form 4930 (Intelligence Case/Project Record) for each case in this project.

Section 4. Case Selection Procedures

.01 Returns Program Managers, classifiers and/or district examiners will make an analysis of returns with tax shelter features to determine if the return should be forwarded to the District Program Coordinator for consideration. The return will be forwarded if the following criteria are present:

1 first-year return of entity that was formed late in the year;

2 large net loss;

3 low gross income;

4 nonoperating entity;

5 negative capital account at year end; or reduction in capital assets by 50 percent or more;

6 capital contributions, other than cash, which are small relative to the total cost of assets;

7 mischaracterization of capital items such as management fees, covenants, large payments to partners, etc.;

8 IRM 4140 and Exhibit 4140-1 contain additional factors that may be considered.

.02 The following information will be submitted, through the Group Manager, to the District Program Coordinator:

1 taxpayer's name, address, identification number, and taxable year(s) under examination;

2 number and type of related returns;

3 taxpayer's principal business;

4 basic criteria identified and reason for referral; and

5 examiner's name, group number, and telephone number.

.03 After submitting the information to the District Program Coordinator, the examiner will continue the examination, but will not close the case.

.04 The District Program Coordinator will review the information for the basic criteria identified in .01 above.

.05 If the case is identified for inclusion in the Tax Shelter Program, the District Program Coordinator will:

1 notify the Group Manager that the case has been accepted in the Tax Shelter Program; and

2 send a copy of the referral to the appropriate regional analyst, who will forward the necessary information to the National Office.

.06 If the District Program Coordinator determines that the case is a tier in a multitier tax shelter, he/she will secure all returns (or copies of the returns) constituting a tier in order to properly evaluate the total impact of the case. Once all tiers have been obtained and evaluated, a determination can be made regarding the inclusion of the case into the Tax Shelter Program. If the case is selected for the Program, the District Program Coordinator will proceed in accordance with the provisions of .05 above. The district having the first tier of the tax shelter will serve as the Coordinating District, unless otherwise agreed, and will issue requests for collateral examinations, as appropriate.

.07 If the information submitted is based on an examination of a Form 1040 (Individual Income Tax Return) and the related partnership return is located in another district, the District Program Coordinator will forward the information to the district having jurisdiction over the partnership. The District Program Coordinator in the receiving district will obtain the partnership return and determine whether or not to include the case in the Tax Shelter Program, and notify the requesting district of the decision. The district having jurisdiction over the partnership return will serve as the Coordinating District.

.08 If the District Program Coordinator determines that the case will not be selected for inclusion in the Tax Shelter Program, the reasons for the nonacceptance will be discussed with the examiner. The examiner will be instructed to complete the examination and close the case. The examiner will give full consideration to the District Program Coordinator's comments concerning disposition of the case.

.09 If, after a case has been referred and not accepted for the Program, additional facts are developed that warrant reconsideration of the case by the District Program Coordinator, the case should be referred again.

Section 5. Management of Tax Shelter Cases

.01 To promote uniformity and consistency in the management of tax shelter cases involving partnerships, joint ventures, corporations, and syndicates, responsibility for controlling and monitoring the progression of all related and interrelated cases involved in the examination of the partnership or key entity is vested with the Coordinating District.

.02 Tax shelter cases that have a partnership as the controlling or key entity are to be controlled in accordance with the Form 918-A (Notice of Examination of Fiduciary, Partnership, or Small Business Corporation Returns) procedures provided in IRM 4220.

.03 Tax shelter cases that have a corporation or other agent as their key entity are more difficult to control. The investors are not related, as in the case of partnerships, by ownership in a common entity. An example of this type of relationship exists when a promoter (usually a regular corporation) sells a program to individual, partnership, and/or corporate investors who claim the deduction on Schedule C or F of Form 1040, or other schedule, as appropriate. In order to control this type of case, the following procedures will apply:

1 Procedures for Coordinating District

a The Coordinating District will obtain a list of investors from the promoter and notify the districts having investors of the examination by use of Form 918-A procedures as described in IRM 4220. To assist the receiving districts, each Form 918-A will be marked "Special Use–Agency Relationship" in a conspicuous place. The provisions of IRM 4220 will be followed by the receiving districts.

b Status updates and progress reports will be sent to the receiving districts in accordance with the provisions of IRM 422.1:(4).

c Upon completion of the promoter/corporation

examination, the Coordinating District will use Form 918-B (Status of Examination) as a transmittal to forward pertinent information regarding the transactions of the individual investors. The Revenue Agent's Report on the promoter/corporation is not to be furnished as information relating to the investments made by the investors. The information furnished should be complete enough to allow the receiving district to make a determination as to the correctness of the amounts claimed on the investors' returns. Information is to include, but is not limited to, the following:

(1) Information about the overall agency program, such as:

(a) A memorandum describing the agency/investor relationship, the manner in which the shelter program operates, the issues to be proposed at the investor level and the facts supporting these positions.

(b) A copy of the prospectus or other offering memoranda.

(2) Information specific as to each investor, such as:

(a) The local market prices for the item purchased at the time of the investor's purchase.

(b) Investor's invoice.

(c) Specific payments made by the investor.

(d) Financing documents, notes, and security agreement.

(e) Reports made to the investor, such as monthly reports, closeout statements or summaries, or significant correspondence.

2 Procedures for Receiving District

a Receipt of a Form 918-A that is identified as "Special Use–Agency Relationship" will be acknowledged in accordance with the provisions of IRM 4220.

b The returns will be requested immediately upon receipt of the Form 918-A.

c If an investor's return has been previously examined, the reopening procedures provided in IRM 4023 will apply and the return will be reopened, if appropriate. Unlike adjustments to partnership returns, changes made as a result of an examination of a promoter/syndicator (agency relationship) do not automatically flow through to the investors. Instead, the facts and documentation that are developed during the examination of the promoter/syndicator are used in proposing adjustments to the investor's returns. Adjustments cannot be proposed on previously examined returns until they have been formally reopened.

      d Cases involving 30 or more investors and/or entities may use computer assistance as described in Section 7.

Section 6. Development of Cases

      Examiners, through District Coordinators, are encouraged to seek guidance on complex technical issues from the district review staff. Examiners should consider requesting technical advice on controversial or technical issues from the National Office as they arise. Prior to requesting technical advice, care should be taken to ensure that the facts concerning the issue are fully documented. Such requests should be identified on the front of the Form 4463 (Request for Technical Advice) as a Tax Shelter Program case. The front of Form 4463 will be red-stamped "Tax Shelter Program." The district will send the technical advice to the region before mailing to the National Office. *The red stamp will ensure that the technical advice receives expeditious handling.*

Section 7. Computer Preparation of Forms 918-A

      .01 All tax shelter cases, regardless of the type of entity—i.e., a partnership, regular corporation or other agency relationship—selected for examination, having 30 or more investors and/or entities, will use computer assistance.

      .02 A Manual Supplement, Related Returns Notification System, is being prepared that will provide instructions for requesting computer assistance to prepare the Forms 918-A (Notice of Examination of Fiduciary, Partnership, or Small Business Corporation Return). Two phases of the program will be operational in the near future.

      1 Phase I provides for nationwide notification of the partnership examination and will automatically requisition and secure individual partners' returns. Form 918-A, Part 1, will be prepared to notify all receiving district offices that the partnership is under examination. Forms 918-B will be generated, at 90-day intervals, upon request of the Coordinating District, to notify all receiving district offices of the status of the partnership or key entity examination.

2 Phase II serves to prepare the report of partnership examination, Form 4605 (Audit Changes: Partnerships, Fiduciaries and Small Business Corporations) and distribute Form 918-A Part 2, to notify all receiving district offices of the newly adjusted partnership distributions.

3 It is anticipated that the program will be expanded to include a third phase, which will generate report Forms 4549 or 4549-A (Income Tax Audit Changes) for each partner or investor.

Section 8. Reporting Procedures

.01 Each Coordinating District making principal entity examinations under this Program must submit a report to the ARC (Audit) within five workdays after the end of each calendar quarter ending March, June, September, and December. The report, Form 5584 (Narrative Report on Tax Shelter Program) (Report Symbol NO–CP:A-389), Attachment 1, should indicate the type of shelter, name and address of principal entity, status of examination including the estimated completion date, identified issues, amount of adjustment, areas of concern, and examiner's name, location and telephone number. Once a case has been placed in suspense under IRM 4559 and Forms 1254 (Audit Suspense Report) have been sent to the National Office, Attention: CP:A:S:E, the status reports may be discontinued. The reports will recommence upon the release of the case from suspense.

.02 In the event of transfers, etc., the district offices will notify the ARC (Audit), through the use of a copy of the transfer control Form 3185 (Transfer of Returns—Transfer of Administrative File) when a case in the Tax Shelter Program leaves their jurisdiction.

.03 The ARC (Audit) will include, as part of the Quarterly Narrative Report required by Section (10)20 of IRM 4810, a section on the Tax Shelter Program. The report will include, but is not limited to, the following information:

1 Summary, by shelter area, of information furnished by the districts on Form 5584 (Report Symbol NO-CP:A-389).

2 Inventory report of tax shelter cases, containing the following information:

    a unassigned returns;

    b assigned returns, unstarted;

    c assigned returns, in process; and

d returns received during quarter (transfers in).

3 Current status of the Tax Shelter Program, identified issues, fraud referrals (number accepted and rejected) and areas of concern for each shelter area.

.04 Each ARC (Audit) will make necessary arrangements with the ARC (Intelligence) and ARC (Appellate) to assure that status information pertaining to cases under Intelligence or Appellate consideration is provided timely to the ARC (Audit).

.05 In instances where an investigation is being conducted by the Intelligence Division on the syndicator/promoter, consideration will be given to the balancing of civil and criminal aspects of the case in order to maximize civil enforcement without imperiling criminal prosecution in accordance with Policy Statement P-4-84 and Manual Supplement 51G-111, CR 45G-217, 5(11)G-51, and 93G-146 (renumbered 9G-14), dated January 6, 1975.

Section 9. Effect on Other Documents

.01 This supplements IRM 4200 and 330 of IRM 9570, Case Management and Time Reporting System Handbook.

.02 This also supplements IRM 8(24)00. This "effect" should be annotated in pen and ink on the text cited, with a reference to this Supplement.

.03 Manual Supplement 42G-350, CR 8(24)G-125, dated June 24, 1976, is superseded. Annotation made at IRM 4200 referring to MS 42G-350 is removed. Annotation made at IRM 8(24)00 referring to MS CR 8(24)G-125 should be removed.

/s/ William E. Williams
Deputy Commissioner
(11-23-77)

APPENDIX B:

State Requirements for General Business and Professional Corporations

State	Professions Covered by P. C. Act	Title and No. of P. C. Act
Alabama	All licensed professions	Professional Corp. Act No. 260
Alaska	All licensed professions	Alaska Statute 10.45
Arizona	Accountants, doctors, lawyers	Arizona Revised Statute 10-908
Arkansas	All licensed professions	Act 155 of 1963
California	Accountants, chiropractors, clinical social workers, dentists, doctors, lawyers, marriage, family & child counselors, optometrists, osteopaths, physical therapists, podiatrists, psychologists, shorthand reporters, speech pathologists	Part 4, Division 3, Title 1, California Corps. Code
Colorado	Accountants, architects, chiropractors, dentists, doctors, lawyers, optometrists, veterinarians	Title 12
Connecticut	All licensed professions	Professional Service Corps. Chap. 594a
Delaware	Accountants, architects, chiropodists, chiropractors, dentists, doctors, engineers, lawyers, optometrists, osteopaths, veterinarians	Chapter 6, General Corp. Law

Min. No. of Share- holders	Title of Form to Be Filed	Address	Filing Fee
1	Charter	Judge of Probate of County	N/A– Annual fee $10
1	Duplicate Originals of Articles of Incorporation	Dept. of Commerce & Economic Development Pouch D Juneau, Alaska 99811	$30
1	Articles of Incorporation	Sec'y of State 2222 West Encanto Blvd. Phoenix, Arizona 85009	$50
1	N/A	Sec'y of State Corporation Dept. State Capitol Bldg. Little Rock, Arkansas 72201	$15 min.
1	Articles of Incorporation*	Sec'y of State 111 Capitol Mall Sacramento, California 95814	$265
Not given	Articles of Incorporation	Sec'y of State 1575 Sherman Denver, Colorado 80203	$24.75 min.
1	Certificate of Incorpo- ration	Sec'y of State P. O. Box 846 30 Trinity St. Hartford, Connecticut 06115	$91 min.
1	Certificate of Incorpo- ration	**	N/A

N/A—not available

*After incorporation, application is made to the proper licensing board of the profession for a Certificate of Authority which, when granted, legally permits the corporation to practice the profession.

** Corporation must have registered office with registered agent in state. Certificate must be filed through registered agent.

State	Professions Covered by P. C. Act	Title and No. of P. C. Act
Florida	Accountants, architects, chiropodists, chiropractors, dentists, doctors, lawyers, life insurance agents, osteopaths, podiatrists, veterinarians	Professional Corp. Act Chap. 621
Georgia	Accountants, architects, chiropractors, dentists, doctors, engineers, land surveyors, lawyers, optometrists, osteopaths, podiatrists, psychologists (applied), veterinarians	Georgia Professional Corp. Act. No. 943
Hawaii	Accountants, chiropractors, dentists, doctors, lawyers and district court practitioners, naturopaths, opticians, optometrists, osteopaths, pharmacists, veterinarians	Part VIII of Chap. 416, Hawaii Revised Statutes
Idaho	All licensed professions	Title 30, Chap. 13
Illinois	All licensed professions	Professional Service Corp. Act
Indiana	All licensed professions	Professional Corp. Acts IC 23
Iowa	Accountants, architects, chiropractors, dentists, doctors, engineers, land surveyors, lawyers, optometrists, osteopaths, podiatrists, veterinarians	Professional Corp. Act 496C
Kansas	All licensed professions	Professional Corp. Law of Kansas Chap. 17
Kentucky	All licensed professions	Professional Service Corps., Kentucky Revised Statutes Chap. 274

Min. No. of Share-holders	Title of Form to Be Filed	Address	Filing Fee
1	Articles of Incorporation	Charter Section Sec'y of State Tallahassee, Florida 32304	$63
1	Articles of Incorporation	Sec'y of State 225 Peachtree St., N. E. Atlanta, Georgia 30303	$93
1	Articles of Incorporation and Affidavits of Officers	Dept. of Regulatory Agencies 1010 Richards St. Honolulu, Hawaii 96813	$50 min.
1	None	Division of Corporations Boise, Idaho	$20 min.
1	Articles of Incorporation	Sec'y of State Corporation Division Springfield, Illinois	$75 filing fee $25 min. initial franchise
1	Articles of Incorporation	Corporations Division #155 State House Indianapolis, Indiana 46204	$36 min.
1	Articles of Incorporation	Sec'y of State Corporation Division Des Moines, Iowa 50319	$20 min.
1	Articles of Incorporation	Sec'y of State Corporation Division Topeka, Kansas 66612	$50
1	No standard form for public use	Sec'y of State #150 Capitol Bldg. Frankfort, Kentucky 40601	$25 min.

State	Professions Covered by P. C. Act	Title and No. of P. C. Act
Louisiana	Accountants, chiropractors, dentists, doctors, lawyers	Louisiana Revised Statutes 12:8, 9, 11, 12, 14
Maine	Accountants, architects, chiropodists, chiropractors, dentists, doctors, lawyers, life insurance agents, osteopaths, podiatrists	Professional Service Corp. Act Chap. 22
Maryland	Accountants, doctors, lawyers, veterinarians. Architects and engineers can choose P. C.s or general business corporations.	Title 5, Maryland Code
Massachusetts	Accountants, chiropractors, dentists, doctors, electrologists, engineers, lawyers, optometrists, physical therapists, podiatrists, psychologists, veterinarians	Professional Corps., Chap. 156A
Michigan	All licensed professions	Act 192, P. A. of 1962, as amended
Minnesota	Accountants, chiropractors, dentists, doctors, lawyers, optometrists, osteopaths, podiatrists, psychologists, veterinarians	Minnesota Professional Corps. Act, Minn. Stat. 319A
Mississippi	All licensed professions	Mississippi Professional Corp. Law
Missouri	Accountants, architects, chiropodists, chiropractors, dentists, doctors, engineers, lawyers, optometrists, osteopaths, podiatrists, veterinarians	Title XXIII, Chap. 356 Revised Statutes of Missouri 1969, as amended

Min. No. of Shareholders	Title of Form to Be Filed	Address	Filing Fee
1	No forms available	Sec'y of State Corporations Division P. O. Box 44125 Baton Rouge, Louisiana	$25 min.
1	Articles of Incorporation	Sec'y of State Augusta, Maine 04333	$60 min.
1	Form No. 1 Form No. 25 (every year)	Dept. of Assessments and Taxation 301 West Preston St. Baltimore, Maryland 21201	$40 min.
1	Articles of Organization	Sec'y of the Commonwealth Corporation Division One Ashburton Place Boston, Massachusetts 02108	$125 min.
1	Articles of Incorporation Form C&S 101	Michigan Dept. of Commerce Corporation Division Box 30054 Lansing, Michigan 48909	$35 min.
1	Articles of Incorporation	Sec'y of State Corporation Division 180 State Office Bldg. St. Paul, Minnesota 55155	$75.50 min.
1	Articles of Incorporation	Sec'y of State P. O. Box 136 Jackson, Mississippi 39205	$25 min.
1	Articles of Incorporation Corp. Form #41	Sec'y of State Jefferson City, Missouri 65101	$53

State	Professions Covered by P. C. Act	Title and No. of P. C. Act
Montana	Accountants, architects, chiropodists, chiropractors, dentists, doctors, engineers, lawyers, nurses, optometrists, osteopaths, pharmacists, physical therapists, veterinarians	Professional Service Corp. Act, Chap. 21, Title 15, Revised Codes of Montana
Nebraska	All registered professions	Nebraska Professional Corp. Act, Chap. 21, Article 22
Nevada	All licensed professions	Professional Corps. and Associations Act
New Hampshire	Accountants, architects, chiropractors, dentists, doctors, engineers, nurses, optometrists, pharmacists, psychologists, veterinarians	Revised Statutes Annotated–Chap. 294-A, Professional Assns.
New Jersey	All licensed professions	Professional Service Corp. Act NJSA 14A:17-1 et seq.
New Mexico	All licensed professions	Professional Corp. Act Sections 51-22-1 to 51-22-13 NMSA 1953 Compilation
New York	All licensed professions	Business Corp. Law Article 15
North Carolina	Accountants, architects, chiropractors, dentists, doctors, engineers, landscape architects, lawyers, optometrists, osteopaths, podiatrists, psychologists, surveyors, veterinarians	Professional Corp. Act Chap. 55B
North Dakota	All licensed professions	Professional Corp. Act Chap. 10-13

Min. No. of Shareholders	Title of Form to Be Filed	Address	Filing Fee
1	Forms not prescribed or furnished by state	Sec'y of State Capitol Helena, Montana 59601	$70 min.
1	Articles of Incorporation	Sec'y of State Corporation Division #2304 State Capitol Bldg. Lincoln, Nebraska 68509	$20 min.
1	Articles of Incorporation	Sec'y of State Corporation Division Carson City, Nevada	$50 min.
1	Record of Organization	Sec'y of State Concord, New Hampshire	$60 min.
1	Certificate of Incorporation	New Jersey Department of State Commercial Recording Bureau Corporate Filing Section P.O. Box 1330 Trenton, New Jersey 08625	$60
1	Articles of Incorporation	State Corporation Commission Corporation & Franchise Tax Depts. P. O. Drawer 1269 Santa Fe, New Mexico 87501	$50 min.
1	Certificate of Incorporation	New York State Division of Corporations 162 Washington Avenue Albany, New York 12231	$60
1	Articles of Incorporation; Certification of Eligibility to Practice from licensing board	Sec'y of State Corporations Division 116 West Jones St. Raleigh, North Carolina 27603	$45 min.
1	Duplicate Originals of Articles of Incorporation	Sec'y of State Division of Corporations Bismarck, North Dakota 58505	$100

State	Professions Covered by P. C. Act	Title and No. of P. C. Act
Ohio	All licensed professions	Chap. 1785, Ohio Revised Code
Oklahoma	Accountants, architects, chiropodists, chiropractors, dentists, doctors, nurses, optometrists, osteopaths, physical therapists, podiatrists, psychologists, veterinarians	Professional Corp. Act Title 18
Oregon	All licensed professions	Chap. 58, Professional Corps.
Pennsylvania	Accountants, architects, auctioneers, chiropractors, dentists, doctors, engineers, funeral directors, landscape architects, lawyers, nurses, optometrists, osteopaths, pharmacists, podiatrists, psychologists, veterinarians	Pennsylvania Corp. Law—Act 160 of 1970
Rhode Island	Accountants, architects, chiropodists, chiropractors, dentists, doctors, engineers, nurses, optometrists, veterinarians	Title 7, Chap. 5.1 Professional Service Corps.
South Carolina	All licensed professions	South Carolina Professional Association Act
South Dakota	Accountants, chiropractors, dentists, doctors, lawyers, optometrists, veterinarians	SDCL Chapter 47-11 through 47-138-18
Tennessee	All licensed professions	Title 48, Chap. 20, Tennessee Code Annotated (Tennessee Professional Corp. Act)

Min. No. of Share- holders	Title of Form to Be Filed	Address	Filing Fee
1	Articles of Incorporation	Sec'y of State Division of Corporations 30 East Broad St. Columbus, Ohio 43215	$75
1	Duplicate Originals of Articles of Incorporation	Sec'y of State Rm. 101 Oklahoma State Capitol Bldg. Oklahoma City, Oklahoma 73105	$11 min.
1	Duplicate Originals of Professional Corp. Articles of Incorporation 11-P	Corporation Commissioner Commerce Bldg. Salem, Oregon 97310	$20 min.
1	Articles of Incorporation—Domestic Professional Corp.	Commonwealth of Pennsylvania Corporation Bureau Harrisburg, Pennsylvania	$75 min.
1	Duplicate Originals of Articles of Incorporation	Sec'y of State Providence, Rhode Island	$110
1	Articles of Association	Register of Mesne Conveyance Richland County Court House Columbia, South Carolina 29202	sliding scale
1	Articles of Incorporation	Sec'y of State State Capitol Pierre, South Dakota 57501	$40 min.
1	Corporation Charter	Sec'y of State Corporation Division Nashville, Tennessee 37219	$10 min.

State	Professions Covered by P. C. Act	Title and No. of P. C. Act
Texas	Accountants, dentists, doctors, nurses, optometrists, osteopaths, podiatrists, psychologists, surveyors, veterinarians	Texas Professional Corp. Act
Utah	All licensed professions	Title 16, Chap. 11, Professional Corp. Act
Vermont	Architects, doctors, lawyers	Title 11
Virginia	All licensed professions	Chap. 7, Professional Corps.
Washington	All licensed professions	RCW 18.100
West Virginia	All licensed professions	Under general corporation laws
Wisconsin	All licensed professions	Service Corp. Law, Wisconsin Statute 180.99
Wyoming	Not specifically covered by statute	Sections 17-49.1 and 17.49-2 Wyoming Statutes 1957

Min. No. of Shareholders	Title of Form to Be Filed	Address	Filing Fee
1	Articles of Incorporation	Sec'y of State Corporation Division Sam Houston State Office Bldg. Austin, Texas 78711	$100
1	Application for a Certificate of Authority; Articles of Incorporation	Room 203 State Capitol Bldg. Salt Lake City, Utah 84114	$50 min.
2	DCI Articles of Association with proof of profession attached	Sec'y of State Montpelier, Vermont 05602	$20 min.
1	Articles of Incorporation	State Corporation Commissioner Box 1197 Richmond, Virginia 23209	$25 min.
1	Forms not supplied	Corporations Division Sec'y of State Legislative Bldg. Olympia, Washington 98501	$100 min.
1	Form 101, Articles of Incorporation	Sec'y of State Corporation Division Charleston, West Virginia 25305	$20 min.
1	Articles of Incorporation, Form 2	Sec'y of State Corporation Division State Capitol Bldg. Madison, Wisconsin 53702	$55 min.
No provision for minimum	No forms are furnished	Sec'y of State Division of Corporations Cheyenne, Wyoming	$27.50 min.*

* Bill pending in legislature to increase fees.

State	Title and No. of General Business Corp. Act	Min. No. of Shareholders	Title of Form to Be Filed	Address	Filing Fee
Alabama	Title 10, 1958 Re-compiled Code	1	Charter	Judge of Probate of County	N/A
Alaska	Alaska Statute 10.05	1	Duplicate Originals of Articles of Incorporation	Dept. of Commerce and Economic Development Pouch D Juneau, Alaska 99811	$30
Arizona	Arizona Revised Statutes 10-050—10-149	1	Articles of Incorporation	Sec'y of State 2222 West Encanto Blvd. Phoenix, Arizona 85009	$50
Arkansas	Act 576 of 1965	1	Articles of Incorporation	Sec'y of State Corporation Dept. State Capitol Bldg. Little Rock, Arkansas 72201	$15 min.
California	Title 1, Division 1, Calif. Corps. Code	1	Articles of Incorporation	Sec'y of State 111 Capitol Mall Sacramento, California 95814	$265
Colorado	Title 7, Volume 3	Not given	Articles of Incorporation	Sec'y of State 1575 Sherman Denver, Colorado 80203	$24.75 min.

State	Title and No. of General Business Corp. Act	Min. No. of Shareholders	Title of Form to Be Filed	Address	Filing Fee
Connecticut	Stock Corporation Act Chap. 599	1	Certificate of Incorporation	Sec'y of State P. O. Box 846 30 Trinity St. Hartford, Connecticut 06115	$91 min.
Delaware	Title 8, General Corp. Law	1	Certificate of Incorporation	*	N/A
Florida	General Corp. Act Chap. 607	1	Articles of Incorporation	Charter Section Sec'y of State Tallahassee, Florida 32304	$63
Georgia	Georgia Title 22—Corporations	1	Articles of Incorporation	Sec'y of State 225 Peachtree St., N. E. Atlanta, Georgia 30303	$93
Hawaii	Chap. 416, Hawaii Revised Statutes	1	Articles of Incorporation and Affidavits of Officers	Dept. of Regulatory Agencies 1010 Richards Street Honolulu, Hawaii 96813	$50 min.
Idaho	Title 30, Chap. 1	1	None	Division of Corporations Boise, Idaho	$20 min.
Illinois	Business Corp. Act	1	Articles of Incorporation	Sec'y of State Corporation Division Springfield, Illinois	$75 filing fee $25 min. initial franchise

N/A—not available
* Corporation must have registered office with registered agent in state. Certificate must be filed through registered agent.

State	Title and No. of General Business Corp. Act	Min. No. of Shareholders	Title of Form to Be Filed	Address	Filing Fee
Indiana	Indiana General Corp. Act IC 23	1	Articles of Incorporation	Corporations Division #155 State House Indianapolis, Indiana 46204	$36 min.
Iowa	Iowa Business Corp. Act Chap. 496A	1	Articles of Incorporation	Sec'y of State Corporation Division Des Moines, Iowa 50319	$20 min.
Kansas	Kansas General Corp. Code Chap. 17	1	Articles of Incorporation	Sec'y of State Corporation Division Topeka, Kansas 66612	$50
Kentucky	Kentucky Business Corp. Act, Kentucky Revised Statutes Chap. 271A	1	No standard form for public use	Sec'y of State #150 Capitol Bldg. Frankfort, Kentucky 40601	$25 min.

State	Title and No. of General Business Corp. Act	Min. No. of Shareholders	Title of Form to Be Filed	Address	Filing Fee
Louisiana	Louisiana Revised Statutes 12:1, 2, 3	1	No standard form	Sec'y of State Corporations Division P. O. Box 44125 Baton Rouge, Louisiana 70804	$25 min.
Maine	Maine Business Corp. Act Title 13-A	1	Articles of Incorporation	Sec'y of State Augusta, Maine 04333	$60 min.
Maryland	Corps. and Assns. Article of Annotated Code of Maryland	1	Form 1	Dept. of Assessments and Taxation 301 West Preston St. Baltimore, Maryland 21201	$40 min.
Massachusetts	Business Corps. Chap. 156B	1	Articles of Organization	Sec'y of the Commonwealth Corporation Division One Ashburton Place Boston, Massachusetts 02108	$125 min.

State	Title and No. of General Business Corp. Act	Min. No. of Shareholders	Title of Form to Be Filed	Address	Filing Fee
Michigan	Act 284, P. A. of 1972, as amended	1	Articles of Incorporation Form C&S 101	Michigan Dept. of Commerce Corporation Division Box 30054 Lansing, Michigan 48909	$35 min.
Minnesota	Minn. Stat. 301	1	Articles of Incorporation	Sec'y of State Corporation Division 180 State Office Bldg. St. Paul, Minnesota 55155	$75.50 min.
Mississippi	Mississippi Business Corp. Law	2	Articles of Incorporation	Sec'y of State P. O. Box 136 Jackson, Mississippi 39205	$25 min.
Missouri	Title XXIII, Chap. 351 Revised Statutes of Missouri 1969, as amended	1	Articles of Incorporation Corp. Form #41	Sec'y of State Jefferson City, Missouri 65101	$53
Montana	Montana Business Corp. Act, Chap. 22, Title 15, Revised Code of Montana	1	Not prescribed or furnished by state	Sec'y of State Capitol Helena, Montana 59601	$70 min.

State	Title and No. of General Business Corp. Act	Min. No. of Shareholders	Title of Form to Be Filed	Address	Filing Fee
Nebraska	Nebraska Business Corp. Act, Chap. 21, Article 20	1	Articles of Incorporation	Sec'y of State Corporation Division #2304 State Capitol Bldg. Lincoln, Nebraska 68509	$20 min.
Nevada	Private Corps. Chap. 78	3	Articles of Incorporation	Sec'y of State Corporation Division Carson City, Nevada	$50 min.
New Hampshire	Revised Statutes Annotated (1955) Chap. 294, Business Corps.	1	Record of Organization	Sec'y of State Concord, New Hampshire	$60 min.
New Jersey	New Jersey Business Corp. Act NJSA 14:A 1-1 et seq.		Certificate of Incorporation	New Jersey Department of State Commercial Recording Bureau Corporate Filing Section P.O. Box 1330 Trenton, New Jersey 08625	$60
New Mexico	Business Corp. Act Sections 51-24-1— 51-31-11, NMSA 1953 Compilation	1	Articles of Incorporation	State Corporation Commission Corporation and Franchise Tax Depts. P. O. Drawer 1269 Santa Fe, New Mexico 87501	$50 min.
New York	Business Corp. Law	1	Certificate of Incorporation	New York State Division of Corporations 162 Washington Avenue Albany, New York 12231	$60

State	Title and No. of General Business Corp. Act	Min. No. of Shareholders	Title of Form to Be Filed	Address	Filing Fee
North Carolina	Business Corp. Act Chap. 55	1	Articles of Incorporation	Sec'y of State Corporations Division 116 West Jones Street Raleigh, North Carolina 27603	$45 min.
North Dakota	North Dakota Business Act	3	Duplicate Originals of Articles of Incorporation	Sec'y of State Division of Corporations Bismarck, North Dakota 58505	$100
Ohio	Chap. 1701, Ohio Revised Code	1	Articles of Incorporation	Sec'y of State Division of Corporations 30 East Broad Street Columbus, Ohio 43215	$75
Oklahoma	General Business Corp. Act Title 18	3	Duplicate Originals of Articles of Incorporation	Sec'y of State Rm. 101 Oklahoma State Capitol Bldg. Oklahoma City, Oklahoma 73105	$11 min.
Oregon	Chap. 57, Private Corporations	1	Duplicate Originals of Articles of Incorporation 11-B	Corporation Commissioner Commerce Bldg. Salem, Oregon 97310	$20 min.

State	Title and No. of General Business Corp. Act	Min. No. of Shareholders	Title of Form to Be Filed	Address	Filing Fee
Pennsylvania	P. L. 364	1	Articles of Incorporation—Domestic Business Corp.; Registry Statement (triplicate)	Commonwealth of Pennsylvania Corporation Bureau Harrisburg, Pennsylvania	$75 min.
Rhode Island	Title 7, Corporations, Associations and Partnerships	1	Duplicate Originals of Articles of Incorporation	Sec'y of State Providence, Rhode Island	$110
South Carolina	Chap. 1 of 1962 Code—Vol. 3	1	Articles of Incorporation	Sec'y of State Box 11350 Columbia, South Carolina 29201	$45 min.
South Dakota	SDCL 47-1—47-31	1	Articles of Incorporation	Sec'y of State State Capitol Pierre, South Dakota 57501	$40 min.
Tennessee	Title 48, Tennessee Code Annotated (Tennessee General Corp. Act)	1	Corporation Charter	Sec'y of State Corporate Division Nashville, Tennessee 37219	$10 min.

State	Title and No. of General Business Corp. Act	Min. No. of Shareholders	Title of Form to Be Filed	Address	Filing Fee
Texas	Texas Business Corp. Act	1	Articles of Incorporation	Sec'y of State Corporation Division Sam Houston State Office Bldg. Austin, Texas 78711	$100
Utah	Title 16, Chap. 10	1	Application for Certificate of Authority; Articles of Incorporation	Room 203 State Capitol Bldg. Salt Lake City, Utah 84114	$50 min.
Vermont	Title 11	1	DCI—Articles of Association	Sec'y of State Montpelier, Vermont 05602	$20 min.
Virginia	Virginia Stock Corp. Act	1	Articles of Incorporation	State Corporation Commission Box 1197 Richmond, Virginia 23209	$25 min.
Washington	RCW 23A	1	Forms not supplied	Corporations Division Sec'y of State Legislative Bldg. Olympia, Washington 98501	$100 min.

State	Title and No. of General Business Corp. Act	Min. No. of Shareholders	Title of Form to Be Filed	Address	Filing Fee
West Virginia	Chap. 31 Article 1	1	Articles of Incorpo-ration	Sec'y of State Corporation Division Charleston, West Virginia 25305	$20 min.
Wisconsin	Wisconsin Busi-ness Corp. Law, Chap. 180	1	Articles of Incorpo-ration, Form 2	Sec'y of State Corporation Division State Capitol Bldg. Madison, Wisconsin 53702	$55 min.
Wyoming	Section 17-36.1— Section 17-36.128 Wyoming Stat-utes 1957	No provision for mini-mum	No forms are fur-nished	Sec'y of State Division of Corporations Cheyenne, Wyoming	$27.50 min.*

* Bill pending in legislature to increase fees.

APPENDIX C:

Sample Minutes and Bylaws for a Small Corporation

(FOR USE IF THERE IS ONE INCORPORATOR)

MINUTES OF ORGANIZATION MEETING OF
(NAME OF CORPORATION)

The undersigned, being the sole incorporator of this corporation, held an organization meeting at the date and place set forth below, at which meeting the following action was taken:

It was resolved that a copy of the Certificate of Incorporation together with the receipt issued by the Department of State showing payment of the statutory organization tax and the date and payment of the fee for filing the original Certificate of Incorporation be appended to these minutes.

Bylaws regulating the conduct of the business and affairs of the corporation, as prepared by _____ _____, counsel for the corporation, were adopted and ordered appended hereto.

The persons whose names appear below were named as directors.

The board of directors was authorized to issue all of the unsubscribed shares of the corporation at such time and in such amounts as determined by the board and to accept in payment money or other property, tangible or intangible, actually received or labor or services actually performed for the corporation or for its benefit or in its formation.

The principal office of the corporation was fixed at

Dated at
this   day of   19   _____
                                                            Sole Incorporator

The undersigned accept their nomination as directors:

_____   _____
        Type director's name   Signature

_____   _____

The following are appended to the minutes of this meeting:

> Copy of Certificate of Incorporation, filed on
> Receipt of Department of State
> Bylaws

(FOR USE IF THERE IS MORE THAN ONE INCORPORATOR)

MINUTES OF ORGANIZATION MEETING OF
(NAME OF CORPORATION)

The organization meeting of the incorporators was held at
on the   day of   19   at   o'clock   M.
The following were present:

being a quorum and all of the incorporators.

One of the incorporators called the meeting to order. Upon motion duly made, seconded, and carried, _____ was duly elected
chairman of the meeting and _____ duly elected secretary thereof.
They accepted their respective offices and proceeded with the dis-
charge of their duties.

A written Waiver of Notice of this meeting signed by all the incorporators was submitted, read by the secretary, and ordered appended to these minutes.

The secretary then presented and read to the meeting a copy of
the Certificate of Incorporation of the corporation and reported that
on the   day of   , 19   , the original thereof was duly filed
by the Department of State.

Upon motion duly made, seconded, and carried, said report was
adopted and the secretary was directed to append to these minutes a
copy of the Certificate of Incorporation, together with the original
receipt issued by the Department of State, showing payment of the
statutory organization tax, the filing fee, and the date of filing of the
certificate.

The chairman stated that the election of directors was then in
order.

The following were nominated as directors:

Upon motion duly made, seconded, and carried, it was unanimously

RESOLVED, that each of the abovenamed nominees be and hereby is elected a director of the corporation.

Upon motion duly made, seconded, and carried, and by the affirmative vote of all present, it was

RESOLVED, that the board of directors be and it is hereby authorized to issue all of the unsubscribed shares of the corporation at such time and in such amounts as determined by the board, and to accept in payment money or other property, tangible or intangible, actually received or labor or other services actually performed for the corporation or for its benefit or in its formation.

The chairman presented and read, article by article, the proposed bylaws for the conduct and regulation of the business and affairs of the corporation as prepared by _____ _____ , counsel for the corporation.

Upon motion duly made, seconded, and carried, they were adopted and in all respects, ratified, confirmed and approved, as and for the bylaws of this corporation.

The secretary was directed to cause them to be inserted in the minute book immediately following the receipt of the Department of State.

Upon motion duly made, seconded, and carried, the principal office of the corporation was fixed at_____ , County of _____ , State of New York.

Upon motion duly made, seconded, and carried, and by the affirmative vote of all present, it was

RESOLVED, that the signing of these minutes shall constitute full ratification thereof and Waiver of Notice of the Meeting by the signatories.

There being no further business before the meeting, the same was, on motion, duly adjourned.

Dated this   day of   , 19 .

_____
Secretary of meeting

_____
_____
Chairman of meeting
_____
_____
_____

The following are appended to the minutes of this meeting:

Waiver of Notice of organization meeting
Copy of Certificate of Incorporation, filed on
Receipt of Department of State
Bylaws

WAIVER OF NOTICE OF ORGANIZATION MEETING
OF
(NAME OF CORPORATION)

We, the undersigned, being all the incorporators named in the Certificate of Incorporation of the above corporation, hereby agree and consent that the organization meeting thereof be held on the date and at the time and place stated below and hereby waive all notice of such meeting and of any adjournment thereof.

Place of meeting:
Date of meeting:
Time of meeting:

_____
Incorporator

_____
Incorporator

_____
Incorporator

Dated:

BYLAWS
OF
(NAME OF CORPORATION)

ARTICLE I — Offices

The principal office of the corporation shall be in the   of
         , County of   , State of New York. The corporation may
also have offices at such other places within or without the State of
New York as the board may from time to time determine or the business of the corporation may require.

ARTICLE II — Shareholders

1. *Place of Meetings.* Meetings of shareholders shall be held at
the principal office of the corporation or at such place within or
without the State of New York as the board shall authorize.

2. *Annual Meeting.* The annual meeting of the shareholders shall
be held on the   day of   at   M. in each year if not a
legal holiday, and, if a legal holiday, then on the next business day
following at the same hour, when the shareholders shall elect a
board and transact such other business as may properly come before
the meeting.

3. *Special Meetings.* Special meetings of the shareholders may be
called by the board or by the president and shall be called by the
president or the secretary at the request in writing of a majority of
the board or at the request in writing by shareholders owning a majority in amount of the shares issued and outstanding. Such request
shall state the purpose or purposes of the proposed meeting. Business transacted at a special meeting shall be confined to the purposes stated in the notice.

4. *Fixing Record Date.* For the purpose of determining the shareholders entitled to notice of or to vote at any meeting of shareholders or any adjournment thereof, or to express consent to or dissent from any proposal without a meeting, or for the purpose of

determining shareholders entitled to receive payment of any dividend or the allotment of any rights, or for the purpose of any other action, the board shall fix, in advance, a date as the record date for any such determination of shareholders. Such date shall not be more than fifty nor less than ten days before the date of such meeting, nor more than fifty days prior to any other action. If no record date is fixed, it shall be determined in accordance with the provisions of law.

5. *Notice of Meetings of Shareholders.* Written notice of each meeting of shareholders shall state the purpose or purposes for which the meeting is called, the place, date, and hour of the meeting, and unless it is the annual meeting, shall indicate that it is being issued by or at the direction of the person or persons calling the meeting. Notice shall be given either personally or by mail to each shareholder entitled to vote at such meeting, not less than ten nor more than fifty days before the date of the meeting. If action is proposed to be taken that might entitle shareholders to payment for their shares, the notice shall include a statement of that purpose and to that effect. If mailed, the notice is given when deposited in the United States mail, with postage thereon prepaid, directed to the shareholder at his address as it appears on the record of shareholders, or, if he shall have filed with the secretary a written request that notices to him be mailed to some other address, then directed to him at such other address.

6. *Waivers.* Notice of meeting need not be given to any shareholder who signs a waiver of notice, in person or by proxy, whether before or after the meeting. The attendance of any shareholder at a meeting, in person or by proxy, without protesting prior to the conclusion of the meeting the lack of notice of such meeting, shall constitute a waiver of notice by him.

7. *Quorum of Shareholders.* Unless the Certificate of Incorporation provides otherwise, the holders of (a majority) (your own determination of a quorum, expressed either as a fraction or a percentage) of the shares entitled to vote thereat shall constitute a quorum at a meeting of shareholders for the transaction of any business, provided that when a specified item of business is required to be

voted on by a class or classes, the holders of (a majority) (your own determination of a quorum, expressed either as a fraction or a percentage) of the shares of such class or classes shall constitute a quorum for the transaction of such specified item of business.

When a quorum is once present to organize a meeting, it is not broken by the subsequent withdrawal of any shareholders.

The shareholders present may adjourn the meeting despite the absence of a quorum.

8. *Proxies.* Every shareholder entitled to vote at a meeting of shareholders or to express consent or dissent without a meeting may authorize another person or persons to act for him by proxy.

Every proxy must be signed by the shareholder or his attorney-in-fact. No proxy shall be valid after expiration of eleven months from the date thereof unless otherwise provided in the proxy. Every proxy shall be revocable at the pleasure of the shareholder executing it, except as otherwise provided by law.

9. *Qualification of Voters.* Every shareholder of record shall be entitled at every meeting of shareholders to one vote for every share standing in his name on the record of shareholders, unless otherwise provided in the Certificate of Incorporation.

10. *Vote of Shareholders.* Except as otherwise required by statute or by the Certificate of Incorporation:

(Create your own election requirements, or use the following:)

(a) directors shall be elected by a plurality of the votes cast at a meeting of shareholders by the holders of shares entitled to vote in the election;

(b) all other corporate action shall be authorized by a majority of the votes cast.

11. *Written Consent of Shareholders.* Any action that may be taken by vote may be taken without a meeting on written consent, setting forth the action so taken, signed by the holders of all the outstanding shares entitled to vote thereon or signed by such lesser number of holders as may be provided for in the Certificate of Incorporation.

ARTICLE III — Directors

1. *Board of Directors.* Subject to any provision in the Certificate of Incorporation, the business of the corporation shall be managed by its board of directors, each of whom shall be at least 18 years of age and (choose the number) be shareholders.

2. *Number of Directors.* The number of directors shall be ———. When all of the shares are owned by less than three shareholders, the number of directors may be less than three but not less than the number of shareholders.

3. *Election and Term of Directors.* At each annual meeting of shareholders, the shareholders shall elect directors to hold office until the next annual meeting. Each director shall hold office until the expiration of the term for which he is elected and until his successor has been elected and qualified, or until his prior resignation or removal.

4. *Newly Created Directorships and Vacancies.* Newly created directorships resulting from an increase in the number of directors and vacancies occurring in the board for any reason except the removal of directors without cause may be filled by a vote of a majority of the directors then in office, although less than a quorum exists, unless otherwise provided in the Certificate of Incorporation. Vacancies occurring by reason of the removal of directors without cause shall be filled by vote of the shareholders unless otherwise provided in the Certificate of Incorporation. A director elected to fill a vacancy caused by resignation, death, or removal shall be elected to hold office for the unexpired term of his predecessor.

5. *Removal of Directors.* Any or all of the directors may be removed for cause by vote of the shareholders or by action of the board. Directors may be removed without cause only by vote of the shareholders.

6. *Resignation.* A director may resign at any time by giving written notice to the board, the president, or the secretary of the corporation. Unless otherwise specified in the notice, the resignation shall take effect upon receipt thereof by the board or such officer,

and the acceptance of the resignation shall not be necessary to make it effective.

7. *Quorum of Directors.* Unless otherwise provided in the Certificate of Incorporation, (a majority) (your own determination of a quorum, expressed either as a fraction or a percentage) of the entire board shall constitute a quorum for the transaction of business or of any specified item of business.

8. *Action of the Board.* Unless otherwise required by law, the vote of (a majority) (your own determination of a quorum, expressed either as a fraction or a percentage) of directors present at the time of the vote, if a quorum is present at such time, shall be the act of the board. Each director present shall have one vote regardless of the number of shares, if any, which he may hold.

9. *Place and Time of Board Meetings.* The board may hold its meetings at the office of the corporation or at such other places, either within or without the State of New York, as it may from time to time determine.

10. *Regular Annual Meeting.* A regular annual meeting of the board shall be held immediately following the annual meeting of shareholders at the place of such annual meeting of shareholders.

11. *Notice of Meetings of the Board, Adjournment.*

(a) Regular meetings of the board may be held without notice at such time and place as it shall from time to time determine. Special meetings of the board shall be held upon notice to the directors and may be called by the president upon three days' notice to each director either personally or by mail or by wire; special meetings shall be called by the president or by the secretary in a like manner on written request of two directors. Notice of a meeting need not be given to any director who submits a Waiver of Notice whether before or after the meeting or who attends the meeting without protesting prior thereto or at its commencement, the lack of notice to him.

(b) A majority of the directors present, whether or not a quorum is present, may adjourn any meeting to another time and place. Notice of the adjournment shall be given all directors who were absent at the time of the adjournment and, unless such time and place are announced at the meeting, to the other directors.

12. *Chairman.* The president, or, in his absence, a chairman chosen by the board, shall preside at all meetings of the board.

13. *Executive and Other Committees.* By resolution adopted by a majority of the entire board, the board may designate from among its members an executive committee and other committees, each consisting of three or more directors. Each such committee shall serve at the pleasure of the board.

14. *Compensation.* No compensation, as such, shall be paid to directors for their services, but by resolution of the board, a fixed sum and expenses for actual attendance at each regular or special meeting of the board may be authorized. Nothing herein contained shall be construed to preclude any director from serving the corporation in any other capacity and receiving compensation therefor.

ARTICLE IV — Officers

1. *Offices, Election, Term.*

(a) Unless otherwise provided for in the Certificate of Incorporation, the board may elect or appoint a president, one or more vice-presidents, a secretary and a treasurer, and such other officers as it may determine, who shall have such duties, powers, and functions as hereinafter provided.

(b) All officers shall be elected or appointed to hold office until the meeting of the board following the annual meeting of shareholders.

(c) Each officer shall hold office for the term for which he is elected or appointed and until his successor has been elected or appointed and qualified.

2. *Removal, Resignation, Salary, Etc.*

(a) Any officer elected or appointed by the board may be removed by the board with or without cause.

(b) In the event of the death, resignation, or removal of an officer, the board in its discretion may elect or appoint a successor to fill the unexpired term.

(c) Unless there is only one shareholder, any two or more offices may be held by the same person, except the offices of president and secretary. If there is only one shareholder, all offices may be held by the same person.

(d) The salaries of all officers shall be fixed by the board.

(e) The directors may require any officer to give security for the faithful performance of his duties.

3. *President.* The president shall be the chief executive officer of the corporation; he shall preside at all meetings of the shareholders and of the board; he shall have the management of the business of the corporation and shall see that all orders and resolutions of the board are effected.

4. *Vice-presidents.* During the absence or disability of the president, the vice-president, or, if there are more than one, the executive vice-president, shall have all the powers and functions of the president. Each vice-president shall perform such other duties as the board shall prescribe.

5. *Secretary.* The secretary shall:

(a) attend all meetings of the board and of the shareholders;

(b) record all votes and minutes of all proceedings in a book to be kept for that purpose;

(c) give or cause to be given notice of all meetings of shareholders and of special meetings of the board;

(d) keep in safe custody the seal of the corporation and affix it to any instrument when authorized by the board;

(e) when required, prepare or cause to be prepared and available at each meeting of shareholders a certified list in alphabetical order of the names of shareholders entitled to vote thereat, indicating the number of shares of each respective class held by each;

(f) keep all the documents and records of the corporation as required by law or otherwise in a proper and safe manner;

(g) perform such other duties as may be prescribed by the board.

6. *Assistant Secretaries.* During the absence or disability of the secretary, the assistant secretary, or, if there are more than one, the one so designated by the secretary or by the board, shall have all the powers and functions of the secretary.

7. *Treasurer.* The treasurer shall:

(a) have the custody of the corporate funds and securities;

(b) keep full and accurate accounts of receipts and disbursements in the corporate books;

(c) deposit all money and other valuables in the name and to the credit of the corporation in such depositories as may be designated by the board;

(d) disburse the funds of the corporation as may be ordered or authorized by the board and preserve proper vouchers for such disbursements;

(e) render to the president and board at the regular meetings of the board, or whenever they require it, an account of all his transactions as treasurer and of the financial condition of the corporation;

(f) render a full financial report at the annual meeting of the shareholders if so requested;

(g) be furnished by all corporate officers and agents, at his request, with such reports and statements as he may require as to all financial transactions of the corporation;

(h) perform such other duties as are given to him by these bylaws or as from time to time are assigned to him by the board or the president.

8. *Assistant Treasurer.* During the absence or disability of the treasurer, the assistant treasurer, or, if there are more than one, the one so designated by the secretary or by the board, shall have all the powers and functions of the treasurer.

9. *Sureties and Bonds.* In case the board shall so require, any officer or agent of the corporation shall execute to the corporation a bond in such sum and with such surety or sureties as the board may direct, conditioned upon the faithful performance of his duties to the corporation and including responsibility for negligence and for the accounting for all property, funds, or securities of the corporation which may come into his hands.

ARTICLE V — Certificates for Shares

1. *Certificates.* The shares of the corporation shall be represented by certificates. They shall be numbered and entered in the books of the corporation as they are issued. They shall exhibit the holder's

name and the number of shares and shall be signed by the president or a vice-president and the treasurer or the secretary and shall bear the corporate seal.

2. *Lost or Destroyed Certificates.* The board may direct a new certificate or certificates to be issued in place of any certificate or certificates theretofore issued by the corporation, alleged to have been lost or destroyed, upon the making of an affidavit of that fact by the person claiming the certificate to be lost or destroyed. When authorizing such issue of a new certificate or certificates, the board may, in its discretion and as a condition precedent to the issuance thereof, require the owner of such lost or destroyed certificate or certificates, or his legal representative, to advertise the same in such manner as it shall require and/or give the corporation a bond in such sum and with such surety or sureties as it may direct as indemnity against any claim that may be made against the corporation with respect to the certificate alleged to have been lost or destroyed.

3. *Transfers of Shares.*

(a) Upon surrender to the corporation or the transfer agent of the corporation of a certificate for shares duly endorsed or accompanied by proper evidence of succession, assignment, or authority to transfer, it shall be the duty of the corporation to issue a new certificate to the person entitled thereto, and cancel the old certificate; every such transfer shall be entered in the transfer book of the corporation which shall be kept at its principal office. No transfer shall be made within ten days next preceding the annual meeting of shareholders.

(b) The corporation shall be entitled to treat the holder of record of any share as the holder in fact thereof and, accordingly, shall not be bound to recognize any equitable or other claim to or interest in such share on the part of any other person whether or not it shall have express or other notice thereof, except as expressly provided by the laws of the State of New York.

4. *Closing Transfer Books.* The board shall have the power to close the share transfer books of the corporation for a period of not more than ten days during the thirty-day period immediately preceding (1) any shareholders' meeting, or (2) any date upon which share-

holders shall be called upon to or have a right to take action without a meeting, or (3) any date fixed for the payment of a dividend or any other form of distribution, and only those shareholders of record at the time the transfer books are closed, shall be recognized as such for the purpose of (1) receiving notice of or voting at such meeting, or (2) allowing them to take appropriate action, or (3) entitling them to receive any dividend or other form of distribution.

ARTICLE VI — Dividends

Subject to the provisions of the Certificate of Incorporation and to applicable law, dividends on the outstanding shares of the corporation may be declared in such amounts and at such time or times as the board may determine. Before payment of any dividend, there may be set aside out of the net profits of the corporation available for dividends such sum or sums as the board from time to time in its absolute discretion deems proper as a reserve fund to meet contingencies, or for equalizing dividends, or for repairing or maintaining any property of the corporation, or for such other purpose as the board shall think conducive to the interests of the corporation, and the board may modify or abolish any such reserve.

ARTICLE VII — Corporate Seal

The seal of the corporation shall be circular in form and bear the name of the corporation, the year of its organization, and the words "Corporate Seal, New York." The seal may be used by causing it to be impressed directly on the instrument or writing to be sealed, or upon adhesive substance affixed thereto. The seal on the certificates for shares or on any corporate obligation for the payment of money may be a facsimile, engraved or printed.

ARTICLE VIII — Execution of Instruments

All corporate instruments and documents shall be signed or countersigned, executed, verified, or acknowledged by such officer or officers or other person or persons as the board may from time to time designate.

ARTICLE IX — Fiscal Year

This fiscal year shall begin the first day of (month) in each year.

ARTICLE X — References to Certificate of Incorporation

References to the Certificate of Incorporation in these bylaws shall include all amendments thereto or changes thereof unless specifically excepted.

ARTICLE XI — Bylaw Changes
Amendment, Repeal, Adoption, Election of Directors

(a) Except as otherwise provided in the Certificate of Incorporation, the bylaws may be amended, repealed, or adopted by vote of the holders of the shares at the time entitled to vote in the election of any directors. Bylaws may also be amended, repealed, or adopted by the board, but any bylaw adopted by the board may be amended by the shareholders entitled to vote thereon as hereinabove provided.

(b) If any bylaw regulating an impending election of directors is adopted, amended, or repealed by the board, there shall be set forth in the notice of the next meeting of shareholders for the election of directors the bylaw so adopted, amended, or repealed, together with a concise statement of the changes made.

MINUTES OF FIRST MEETING OF BOARD OF DIRECTORS
OF
(NAME OF CORPORATION)

The first meeting of the board was held at
on the   day of   , 19   at   o'clock   M.
The following were present:

being a quorum and all of the directors of the corporation.

_____ was nominated and elected temporary chairman and acted as such until relieved by the president.

_____ was nominated and elected temporary secretary, and acted as such until relieved by the permanent secretary.

The secretary then presented and read to the meeting a Waiver of Notice of Meeting, subscribed by all the directors of the corporation, and it was ordered that it be appended to the minutes of this meeting.

The following were duly nominated and, a vote having been taken, were unanimously elected officers of the corporation to serve for one year and until their successors are elected and qualified:

President:

Vice-President:

Secretary:

Treasurer:

The president and secretary thereupon assumed their respective offices in place and stead of the temporary chairman and the temporary secretary.

Upon motion duly made, seconded, and carried, it was

RESOLVED, that the seal now presented at this meeting, an impression of which is directed to be made in the margin of the minute book, be and the same is hereby adopted as .the seal of this corporation, and further

RESOLVED, that the president and treasurer be and they hereby are authorized to issue certificates for shares in the form as submitted to this meeting, and further

RESOLVED, that the share and transfer book now presented at this meeting be and the same hereby is adopted as the share and transfer book of the corporation. Upon motion duly made, seconded, and carried, it was

RESOLVED, that the treasurer be and hereby is authorized to open a bank account in behalf of the corporation with (name of bank) located at (address) and a resolution for that purpose on the printed form of said bank was adopted and was ordered appended to the minutes of this meeting.

Upon motion duly made, seconded, and carried, it was

RESOLVED, that the corporation proceed to carry on the business for which it was incorporated.

(The following is the appropriate form to be included here if a proposal or offer for the sale, transfer, or exchange of property has been made to the corporation:)

The secretary then presented to the meeting a written proposal from _____ _____ to the corporation.

Upon motion duly made, seconded, and carried, the said proposal was ordered filed with the secretary, and he was requested to spread the same at length upon the minutes, said proposal being as follows:

(Insert proposal here.)

The proposal was taken up for consideration, and, on motion, the following resolution was unanimously adopted:

WHEREAS, a written proposal has been made to this corporation in the form as set forth above in these minutes, and

WHEREAS, in the judgment of this board the assets proposed to be transferred to the corporation are reasonably worth the amount of the consideration demanded therefor, and that it is in the best interests of this corporation to accept the said offer as set forth in said proposal,

NOW, THEREFORE, IT IS RESOLVED, that said offer, as set forth in said proposal, be and the same hereby is approved and accepted, and that in accordance with the terms thereof, this corporation shall, as full payment for said property, issue to said offeror(s) or nominee(s) (number of shares) fully paid and nonassessable shares of this corporation, and it is

FURTHER RESOLVED, that upon the delivery to this corporation of said assets and the execution and delivery of such proper instruments as may be necessary to transfer and convey the same to this corporation, the officers of this corporation are authorized and directed to execute and deliver the certificate or certificates for such shares as are required to be issued and delivered on acceptance of said offer in accordance with the foregoing.

The chairman presented to the meeting a form of certificate required under Tax Law Section 275A to be filed in the office of the tax commission.

Upon motion duly made, seconded, and carried, it was

RESOLVED, that the proper officers of this corporation are hereby authorized and directed to execute and file such certificate forthwith. On motion duly made, seconded, and carried, it was

RESOLVED, that all of the acts taken and decisions made at the organization meeting be and they hereby are ratified, and it was

FURTHER RESOLVED, that the signing of these minutes shall constitute full ratification thereof and Waiver of Notice of the Meeting by the signatories.

There being no further business before the meeting, on motion duly made, seconded, and carried, the meeting was adjourned. Dated this   day of   , 19   .

_____

_____   Secretary

_____   _____

_____   Chairman

A true copy of each of the following documents referred to in the foregoing minutes is appended hereto.
Waiver of Notice of Meeting
Specimen certificate for shares
Resolution designating depository of funds

WAIVER OF NOTICE OF FIRST MEETING OF BOARD
OF
(NAME OF CORPORATION)

We, the undersigned, being all the directors of the above corporation, hereby agree and consent that the first meeting of the board be held on the date and at the time and place stated below for the purpose of electing officers and the transaction thereat of all such other business as may lawfully come before said meeting and hereby waive all notice of the meeting and of any adjournment thereof.

Place of meeting:
Date of meeting:
Time of meeting:

————————————————
Director

————————————————
Director

————————————————
Director

Dated:

MINUTES OF FIRST MEETING OF SHAREHOLDERS
OF
(NAME OF CORPORATION)

The first meeting of the shareholders was held at
on the   day of   , 19   at   o'clock   M.

The meeting was duly called to order by the president, who stated the object of the meeting.

The secretary then read the roll of the shareholders as they appear in the share record book of the corporation and reported that a quorum of the shareholders was present.

The secretary then read a Waiver of Notice of Meeting signed by all the shareholders and on motion duly made, seconded, and carried, it was ordered that the said waiver be appended to the minutes of this meeting.

The president then asked the secretary to read the minutes of the organization meeting and the minutes of the first meeting of the board.

On motion duly made, seconded, and unanimously carried, the following resolution was adopted:

WHEREAS, the minutes of the organization meeting and the minutes of the first meeting of the board have been read to this meeting, and

WHEREAS, at the organization meeting the bylaws of the corporation were adopted, it is

RESOLVED, that this meeting hereby approves, ratifies, and adopts the said bylaws as the bylaws of the corporation, and it is

FURTHER RESOLVED, that all of the acts taken and the decisions made at the organization meeting and at the first meeting of the board hereby are approved and ratified, and it is

FURTHER RESOLVED, that the signing of these minutes shall constitute full ratification thereof and Waiver of Notice of the Meeting by the signatories.

There being no further business, the meeting was adjourned.
Dated this   day of   , 19 .

_____
                                        Secretary
_____
_____
_____

The following is appended hereto:
Waiver of Notice of Meeting

WAIVER OF NOTICE OF FIRST MEETING OF SHAREHOLDERS
OF
(NAME OF CORPORATION)

We, the undersigned, being all of the shareholders of the above corporation, hereby agree and consent that the first meeting of the shareholders be held on the date and at the time and place stated below for the purpose of electing officers and the transaction thereat of all such other business as may lawfully come before said meeting and hereby waive all notice of the meeting and of any adjournment thereof.

Place of meeting:
Date of meeting:
Time of meeting:

                 _____
                 _____
                 _____

Dated:

INDEX

American Property Investors, 132
amortization, as tax preference item, 13
annuities, 34, 118–22, 123
  convertible bonds as alternative to, 122–23
  costs of, 118, 119, 123
  differences in, 119, 120
  "inside buildup" in, 118, 122
  "investment," 122
  payout treatment, 120–22
  risks of, 122, 123
  variable, 122
  withdrawal penalties, 119
  withdrawals from, 119–20
Apache Corp. (drilling program), 173, 174–75
Asset Depreciation Range (ADR) guidelines, 198
at risk. See Recourse notes/nonrecourse notes

Black Watch Farms/Berman Leasing, 227

books, 29–30, 33, 193–94
  nonrecourse prohibition, 193, 194

cable television systems, 194–95
Can-Am (drilling program), 173, 175
capital gains, capital gains taxes, 13, 29, 31, 32, 110, 114, 117, 122, 161, 170, 171, 174, 176, 177
Caplin, Mortimer M., 170
cash flow:
  in oil and gas, 172, 173
  in real estate, 33, 129, 132, 164–65
cat breeding, 227
cattle breeding, 33, 225–27
cattle feeding, 33, 166, 224–25
Century Properties Fund, 132
charitable gifts, 135–38
  appraisal problems, 137–38
  art as, 135–36, 137–38
  gemstones as, 135, 136–37
  IRS on, 136–37, 138

charitable gifts (*cont.*)
  limitations on, 138
  real estate as, 138
  stamps and coins as, 136
Clifford, George B., Jr., 126
Clifford trusts, 125–28
  advantages of, 126–27
  in equipment leasing, 127–28
  oil and gas programs in, 178
  tax savings using, 126–28, 178
coal, 29–30, 178–79
convertible bonds, 122–23
Corporate Property Associates, 132
current yield, 109, 110

deferred annuities. *See* Annuities
depletion:
  as tax preference item, 13, 30, 172
  See also Oil and gas
depreciation, 5, 6–9
  accelerated, 6–8, 9, 13, 130–31, 160, 163, 164, 167, 198, 200, 226
  bonus, 226
  double declining balance (accelerated), 6–8, 9
  in equipment leasing, 13, 198, 200
  in movies, 189, 190
  in real estate, 13, 129, 130–31, 160, 163, 164, 167
  straight-line, 6, 9, 167
  sum of the digits, 6, 8–9
  as tax preference item, 13
dog breeding, 227

Employees' Stock Ownership Plan (ESOP), 139, 148
equipment leasing, 197–204
  accelerated depreciation in, 13, 198, 200
  capital gains in, 203–04
  Clifford trust in, 127–28
  as deferral tax shelter, 33, 197, 200, 202
  illiquidity of, 200
  investment interest in, 202–03
  leverage in, 12, 197–98
  nonrecourse prohibition, 11
  recourse in, 203
  risk in, 203
  tax preference item in, 13, 202
  unearned income in, 200
Esquire, 225

farming, 33, 223–27
  acreage prices, 223–24
  cattle breeding, 33, 225–27
  cattle feeding, 33, 166, 224–25
  horse breeding, 227
  horse racing, 227
  nonrecourse prohibition, 11
  orchards, 224
finder's fees, 26, 28, 162, 192, 194, 195

gas. *See* Oil and gas

Hereford cows, as tax shelter, 225–26
historic preservation, 205–22
  advantages of, 220
  depreciation and amortization in, 218–19
  reading list, 221–22
  rehabilitation standards for, 207–18
  "sweat equity" in, 219–20
  See also Real estate
Home-Stake Production Company swindle, 169–70
horse breeding, 227
horse racing, 227
Housing and Urban Development Act of 1968, 163

Hutton, E. F., 132
    tax-shelter review procedure,
        25–27

income taxes:
    on capital gains, 13, 29, 31, 32,
        114, 117
    city, 4, 111–13
    on earned income, 29, 30
    federal, 4, 111–12
    on ordinary (unearned) in-
        come, 30, 138, 172, 173
    on salaries (earned income),
        29, 30
    sample returns, 53–101
    state, 4, 111–13
    on tax preference items,
        12–13, 30, 172, 173
    on unearned (ordinary) in-
        come, 30, 138, 172, 173
incorporation, as tax shelter,
        139–51
    disability insurance benefits,
        139, 140–41
    life insurance benefits, 139–40
    medical benefits, 139, 141–47
    minutes and bylaws for, 151,
        264–88
    retirement benefits, 139, 148
    state requirements for, 151,
        241–63
    tax-free dividend income, 139,
        148–51
intangible drilling costs (IDCs):
    as tax preference item, 12, 13,
        30
    See also Oil and gas
Internal Revenue Service:
    on advance expenditures, 179
    on annuity withdrawals,
        119–20
    on charitable gifts, 135,
        136–37, 138
    on Clifford trusts, 126, 127

on corporate benefits, 141–42
on historical preservation, 205,
    206, 220
on hobbies vs. tax shelters,
    226–27
on individual investments, 190
on inflated values in tax shel-
    ters, 31, 161, 162, 188,
    194
on investment annuities, 122
on municipal bond funds,
    114–15
on personal holding com-
    panies, 151
on preference items, 12
on tax-shelter audits, 14, 29,
    229–40
inter vivos trusts. See Clifford
    trusts
investment interest, 202–03, 226
investment tax credit, 188–89

joint ventures, joint venturers,
    13, 179

Keogh Plan, 139, 148

Lerner v. Commissioner, 127–28
leverage, 11–12
    in equipment leasing, 197–98
    in private placements, 13
    in real estate, 11–12, 31–32,
        159–60, 161, 164
life insurance, 117–22, 123
    straight life, 117–18
    tax-exempt feature of, 117,
        118
    See also Annuities
lifting charges, 172
living trusts. See Clifford trusts

McClintick, David, Stealing from
    the Rich: The Home-Stake
    Oil Swindle, 169 n

McCormick (drilling program), 173, 174
McQuown, Judith H., *Inc. Yourself: How to Profit by Setting Up Your Own Corporation,* 151
Moody's Investor Service, 108–9
movies, 29–30, 33, 187–92
   investment tax credits for, 188–89, 190
   nonrecourse prohibition, 11, 187, 189–90
   prospectus examination in, 191
   pyramiding in, 189
   risks of, 191
municipal bond(s), 34, 105–15, 155–58
   analysis of, 107
   buying and selling of, 113–14
   call dates of, 107
   capital gains on, 110, 114
   current yield on, 109, 110, 114
   default in, 106, 155, 157, 158
   at discount, 114
   "double-barreled," 106
   full faith and credit in, 105–6
   general obligation, 105–6, 108
   industrial development, 106–7, 156, 157
   insured, 108
   maturities of, 107
   moral obligation, 108
   pollution control, 106
   at premium, 114
   ratings of, 106, 107–9, 111, 157
   revenue, 105, 106
   risks in, 105, 155–58
   sample tax returns using, 54–55, 68–75, 97–101
   sinking funds for, 107
   as speculations, 155–58
   tax-equivalent yields on, 110–11

   unrated, 158
   yield to maturity on, 109–10
   yields on, 109–11
municipal bond funds, 114–15
   local vs. national, 115
   managed vs. nonmanaged, 115

National Park Service, 206, 207
National Register of Historic Places, 206
nonrecourse notes. *See* Recourse notes/nonrecourse notes

oil and gas, 25–27, 33, 169–78
   advantages of, 170
   assessments in, 175–76
   capital gains treatment of, 170, 174, 176, 177
   in Clifford trusts, 178
   depletion in, 13, 30, 172, 173, 178
   development programs, 30, 171, 173–74, 175, 177
   discounting in, 176–78
   exploratory programs, 170–71, 172–73, 174, 175
   as gifts, 176, 178
   high-bracket nature of, 22
   intangible drilling costs in, 12, 13, 30, 171–72
   lifting charges in, 172
   liquidation values of, 170, 176–77
   liquidity of, 170, 176
   nonrecourse prohibition, 11
   performance of, 174–75
   portfolio strategies, 166, 173–74
   prospectus examination in, 41–50
   risk gradients in, 174
   sample tax returns using, 54, 55, 76–89

tax preference items in, 13, 30,
   172
used units in, 177–78
write-offs on, 170, 171–72, 178
orchards, 224

partnerships, 13–14
   See also Tax shelters
private placements, 13, 163, 167,
   194, 223, 225–26
   See also Public offerings
professional corporations. *See*
   Incorporation
prospectuses, 27
   analysis and examination of,
      35–51, 191
public offerings, 13, 35
   See also Private placements

real estate:
   accelerated depreciation on,
      13, 130–31, 160, 163, 167,
      218–19
   "bailouts," 162
   benefits of, 129–30, 160–61
   cash flow in, 33, 129, 132, 160,
      164–65
   as charitable gift, 138
   conservative, 129–34
   conventional, 33, 159–61, 164,
      166
   "deep," 33, 163
   demolition disincentives,
      206–07
   depreciation in, 13, 129,
      130–31, 161
   distressed property, 161–62
   as equity builder, 33, 160–61
   with fee-simple ownership,
      133–34
   government-subsidized, 32, 33,
      162–66
   high-risk, 159–67
   historic preservation, 205–22

income-oriented, 34
leverage in, 11–12, 31–32,
   159–60, 161, 164
net-lease, 33
nonrecourse advantages of, 10,
   160
portfolio strategies, 166
prospectus examination in,
   36–41, 50
pyramiding of, 165–66
"rehab," 166–67
rehabilitation standards for
   historic preservation,
   207–18
for retirees, 133, 134
risks of, 161–62, 165
sample tax returns using, 53,
   54, 55, 56–67, 90–96
tax preference items in, 13
triple-net-lease, 131–33
urban reclamation, 205–22
Real Estate Associates Limited,
   163
recapture, 9, 31
records, 29–30, 33, 193–94
   nonrecourse prohibition, 193,
      194
recourse notes/nonrecourse
   notes, 9–11, 32, 189–90, 193
   structuring of, 10–11
retirees:
   real estate tax shelters for, 133,
      134
   sample tax returns using tax
      shelters, 54–55, 97–101
   tax shelters necessary for, 4
   See also Municipal bonds
Revenue Act of 1978, 30
   on advance expenditures,
      178–79
   on capital gains tax, 13, 29,
      114
   on nonrecourse notes, 10, 193

Revenue Act of 1978 (*cont.*)
on tax preference items,
12–13, 30
reversionary trusts. *See* Clifford
trusts

Securities and Exchange Commission, 13, 35, 50
Standard & Poor's Corporation:
bond ratings, 108–9
stock ratings, 148, 149
Subchapter S corporations, 13,
190

tax-equivalent yields, 110–11,
118
tax preference items:
accelerated depreciation, 13,
30
amortization, 13
depletion, 13, 30
intangible drilling costs, 12,
13, 30
Tax Reform Act of 1976, 9–10,
177, 178, 187, 189, 190, 193,
206
tax shelters and tax-sheltered
investments:
accountant's examination of,
24–25, 27–28, 51
audits of, 14, 29, 229–40
benefits of, 4
"deep," 33, 163
deferrals, 32–33, 197, 200, 202
defined, 3, 28, 225
as equity builders, 33, 160–61
finder's and promoter's fees in,
26, 28, 162, 192, 194, 195
first-year and subsequent payments in, 10–11
function of, 32–35

general partner in, 14, 28
government's role in, 22, 25,
28, 205, 206, 220
lawyer's examination of, 27,
51
liability in, 14
limited partner in, 14
liquidity of, 22, 24
for middle class, 5, 28
ordinary (unearned) income
in, 30
partnership aspect of, 13–14
portfolio strategies, 166,
224–25
professional advice in, 27–28,
29–32, 36, 51
prospectus examination in, 27,
35–51, 191
pyramiding in, 166, 189
for retirees, 4, 54–55, 97–101,
105–15, 133, 134
risks in, 21–22, 24–25, 28–29,
35–51, 105
sample tax returns using,
53–101
tax brackets as factors in, 22
for two-income family, 4
See also Income taxes; individual tax shelters
theatrical investing, 181–85
Tobias, Andrew, 225

U.S. Housing Act of 1937, 163

Wall Street Journal, 3
write-offs. *See* Depreciation; Recourse notes/nonrecourse
notes; individual tax shelters

yield to maturity, 109–10